contents

D0508796

brain child

LIST OF MIND MAPS

Dedication

Brain Child is dedicated to all future Brain Children and parents, and to the memory of my dear-departed friend Ian Dawson-Shepherd, founder of the Spastics Society and founder of the Little Foundation, devoted to providing information to parents on the nurturing and environment of the embryo in the womb. Ian was a Warrior of the Mind who fought every adversity for the right of the baby's brain to develop in an atmosphere of support and love. May *Brain Child* help to immortalize both his memory and his fight for and support of us all.

The book is also dedicated to HSH Princess Isobelle von und zu Liechtenstein, who has supported me morally, spiritually and practically in fighting for the rights of all parents and children to learn about the miracles they are, and to O.J.Bush, in his three-year-old manifestation, for teaching two black belts (his father, John, and me) advanced gamesmanship and John Bush, his father, for having him, and finally to the team of young and grown-up children who helped me bring *Brain Child* to life.

Because Brain Boys and Brain Girls are equally incredible and inspiring, the author has chosen to alternate between the use of he/she, his/her etc. on a chapter-by-chapter basis.

foreword

Dear Reader,

A car (which is far simpler than one of your baby's fingers) comes with a 100-page manual.

A one-megabyte computer (which is less intelligent than just one of your baby's million million brain cells) comes with a *thousand-page operations manual*.

Contemplating these and many other similar facts thrown up by modern brain research over the last 10 years, an idea sprang to mind: why not write a book on bringing up a baby *from the baby's point of view?*

Brain Child is that book. Let me therefore momentarily hand you over to the subject and object of the book: the baby of the future.

Hello Mum! Hello Dad!

Brain Child is my book for you, written from my perspective – your future baby-to-be.

Brain Child is a utopian book, written to describe everything I would ideally like in my upbringing to help me to develop the full potential of my mind, body and spirit, in a way that makes life easier and happier for all of us.

I am sure you will have heard that I, your baby, will own the most astonishingly complex yet compact piece of equipment ever developed by nature or humankind: my baby brain – a truly magical gift for both you and me. I will similarly own an astonishingly complex body with its extraordinary super-natural senses.

My book for you explains why each baby's brain is such a magical gift, and what an important part you, my dear parents, have played and will continue to play in its development.

Most books on bringing up babies have focussed on feeding the mouth. My book for you and me focuses on feeding the brain.

At my birth, that brain will already contain its full complement of brain cells: one million million (1,000,000,000,000). **Please**, *help me feed them well!*

With love from
YOUR BRAIN CHILD

I have recently completed filming a documentary series with the BBC entitled *In Search of Genius*. This has been an enthralling and exciting investigation into what happens if you take children who have been dismissed as failures, both at school and by society, and nurture them in a way that allows them to express their genius. The results confirmed that **nurture** is the primary factor in developing (or not) a child's latent potentials.

The children in the programme transformed their traditional intelligences, their social aptitudes, their ability to work in teams, their personal happiness and their self-confidence.

Indeed, scientific research has recently confirmed that when used to their full potential, every child's body and mind have the power to transform the physical universe.

There is no question in my mind that given the right stimulation and the correct nurturing environment, every child can manifest his or her genius.

And, most importantly, grow up to be a fulfilled and happy human being.

introduction

THE STRUCTURE OF BRAIN CHILD

Brain Child is organized into six main parts:

PART I   THE BRAIN
PART II   UNIQUENESS
PART III   BRAIN PRINCIPLES
PART IV   DEVELOPMENT AND ENVIRONMENT
PART V   THE SENSES
PART VI   LEARNING

PART I THE BRAIN

This part devotes itself to that 'fabulous instrument', the human brain, providing state-of-the-art information on the brain cell and its functions, the mysterious and explosive development of the brain, the left and right brain functions and their relevance to the development of the baby, the multiple intelligences, the critical intellectual skills of memory, creativity and Mind Mapping, and the importance to the baby's brain and body of her flowering emotional intelligence, her fantasy friends, her prime brain foods and love.

PART II UNIQUENESS

Uniqueness addresses in depth the perplexed question of why are any two children two 'peas from the same pod', so astonishingly different.

PART III BRAIN PRINCIPLES

This part introduces the seven main brain principles that govern your baby's life. These principles will dissolve many of the 'problems' that numerous parents experience when bringing up their children, and give powerful guidelines for maximizing the growth of your Brain Child's potential.

PART IV DEVELOPMENT AND ENVIRONMENT

This part addresses the major areas of current debate about the child, her development and her behaviours, and provides a detailed guide to the average developmental stages of the brain and its talents, the body and the emotions.

Brain Child comes down firmly on the side of Nurture in the Nature–Nurture debate. *Brain Child*'s thesis is that the parents, friends, the surrounding environment and the school are the prime factors in the architecture of the child's intellectual, physical and emotional being, and that with the appropriate knowledge the parents, especially, can help direct their child to paradise.

PART V THE SENSES

The senses are the baby's infinitely capable extensions into, and sensors of, the known Universe.

This part introduces the astonishing 'homunculus' – the 'brain's eye view' of what is really important, and from this standpoint discusses each of the senses, their capacity, their development and their freedom!

PART VI LEARNING

This part is an in-depth investigation of those major areas which, surveys show, parents consider most important for their baby's development and about which they have the least knowledge. These include the following:

Curiosity
Concentration
Logic
Art
Music
Mathematics
Reading
Baby Talk
Hot Housing
Mind Sports
Information Technology
Dance
Sensuality and Sexuality
Learning Difficulties
Pets
Discipline – Physical and Mental
Schools

For a visual overview of *Brain Child*, turn to the first Mind Map in the section in the middle of this book. Its brain-friendly layout will help you navigate your way through all six sections of the book. Keep referring back to it to remind yourself how your little cygnet is going to grow up into a beautiful swan!

THINGS FOR YOU TO DO

Each of *Brain Child*'s chapters contains Things For You To Do. This is a smorgasbord from which to choose activities you find most relevant or interesting. Things For You To Do also includes cross-references to other chapters that are of particular relevance, and at the back of the book (see page 321) you will find a recommended reading list for each chapter that by the end of the book, could eventually form a complete Brain Child library. Were you to read and Mind Map them all, you would have the equivalent of a PhD (a Doctorate) in Babydom! (It is both amusing and disturbing to note that for a motorcycle, a car and a gun you need to have hours of training and a licence to prove that you are competent. To 'own' a baby, the most astounding responsibility and privilege imaginable, no preparation, knowledge, training or commitment is required.)

Brain Child is written to provide the opportunity for every parent-to-be and parent in the world to access this vital knowledge.

Brain Child also has a number of other missions:

To put into practice the lessons we all learn, and unfortunately tend to discard, coming from children themselves.

To let parents, by their total submersion in the Universe of the child's brain, become child-like again!

To extend the arguments from the baby/child stage through to the teenage years.

To emphasize the resilience of the baby and the human brain, and to provide the comforting message that almost no matter how badly a baby's brain has been abused, it is magnificently resilient, and can overcome almost all difficulties and disadvantages.

To provide a statistical demonstration and proof that your baby's capacities are potentially infinite.

To provide a beacon of hope at the beginning of the twenty-first century, named by The Brain Trust Charity 'The Century of the Brain'; also to inspire minds at the beginning of the third millennium, named the 'Millennium of the Mind'.

To help all parents realize that they are also natural-born geniuses who still possess the latent potential of the baby. To help and encourage them in her development.

Perhaps the most important aim of Brain Child is to help parents maximize their child's all-round development by looking at everything from her point of view, and consider such questions as:

- What should be my child's very first experiences?
- What sort of environment will stimulate my child's senses and her awareness of them?
- How can I help my child to understand the power of her brain and encourage her to use it to its full potential?
- How can my child learn to use her memory to its full capacity?
- How can I help and guide my child through the key stages of mental, physical and emotional development?
- Which are the most important foods to help my child's brain and body develop?
- How can I encourage my child to appreciate her uniqueness and grow up to be a 'swan'; a happy, confident, well-rounded person?

In the first chapter you will start this magical journey, and be introduced to your baby's, and your own, ultimately super bio-computer chip: the brain cell and its myriad Merlin-like powers ...

part one

the brain

brain cell

'It is a fabulous instrument, the brain.'
Dr Glenn Doman

———————————————— ☆ ————————————————

The essential unit, the 'bio-computer chip' of your baby's brain is the brain cell. At birth your baby's brain already contains its full complement of one million million (1,000,000,000,000) brain cells, or neurons. To get an idea of how gigantic this number is, compare it to the current population of Planet Earth at the turn of the twenty-first century: a mere six million million (6,000,000,000). Therefore, inside your baby's head there are 166 times as many brain cells as there are human beings currently living on our planet!

———————————————— ☆ ————————————————

Your baby's 1 million million brain cells are so tiny that you could fit 100 onto a single pinhead. If you lined them all up, they would reach to the moon and back.

Each one of your baby's brain cells has *hundreds* and *thousands* of branches or tentacles, much like a microcosmic super-octopus. Each one of these hundreds and thousands of branches or tentacles contains *thousands* of 'mushrooms', or dendritic spines. It is these that are the connecting points between the brain cells. Each of the hundreds of thousands of mushrooms or dendritic spines contains thousands of packets of chemicals. It is these that are the messengers between the brain cells, carrying all the information in *every* thought, *every* learning experience, and *every* memory that your baby has and will ever have.

When your baby thinks, an electromagnetic impulse travels down a brain cell's branch, triggers the chemicals in one of the mushrooms, and these then rush across a little gap (the synaptic gap) to trigger chemicals in another dendritic spine. This, in turn, triggers another electromagnetic response in the adjoining brain cell, the process continuing on a track or pathway much like a complex trail or path in a gigantic forest. The rush of chemicals from one dendritic spine to another, when seen with a superb electron-microscope, would resemble the Niagara Falls.

brain child

What I have described above is only one thought, one fraction of one fraction of one fraction of one fraction of one fraction of *one* of your baby's perceptions, ideas, thoughts and memories.

─────────────────────────── ☆ ───────────────────────────

The possible number of 'thought tracks' (learned information, habits or memories) that are possible for your baby was worked out in the 1960s to be the number one followed by one hundred noughts (100000000000000000000000000000000000000000000000000000 000000000000000000000000000000000000000000). This number is a greater number than the sum of all the myriad stars in the known Universe!

─────────────────────────── ☆ ───────────────────────────
─────────────────────────── ☆ ───────────────────────────

That number calculated in the 1960s was wrong! In the early 1970s it was re-calculated, and became the new number: one followed by eight hundred noughts!

(100000000000000000000000000000000000000000000000000000000 0000000000000000000000000000000000000000000000000000000000 0000000000000000000000000000000000000000000000000000000000 0000000000000000000000000000000000000000000000000000000000 0000000000000000000000000000000000000000000000000000000000 0000000000000000000000000000000000000000000000000000000000 0000000000000000000000000000000000000000000000000000000000 0000000000000000000000000000000000000000000000000000000000 0000000000000000000000000000000000000000000000000000000000 0000000000000000000000000000000000000000000000000000000000 0000000000000000000000000000000000000000000000000000000000 0000000000000000000000000000000000000000000000000000000000 0000000000000000000000000000000000000000000000000000000000 0000000000000000000000000000000000000000000000000000000000)

─────────────────────────── ☆ ───────────────────────────

This number is approximately equal to the number of atoms in our known Universe!

This gigantic number also turned out to be wrong!

Just before his death in 1974, Petr Anokhin, the famous Russian brain scientist and main student of Pavlov, recalculated the number. He said, in his final public statement, that all previous numbers were wrong, and that concerning the pattern-making ability of the baby's brain, or degrees of freedom for thought throughout the brain, the actual number was:

'..... so great that writing it would take a line of figures, in normal manuscript characters, more than 10.5 million kilometres in length! With such a number of possibilities, the human brain is a keyboard on which hundreds of million millions of different melodies – acts of behaviour or intelligence – can be played. No one yet exists or has existed who has even approached using the full brain. We accept no limitations on the power of the human brain – it is limitless.'

The Power Of The Individual Brain Cell

To help you realize why Anokhin would make such a massive claim for your baby's potential, consider for a moment what the power of each one of its million million brain cells actually is. Consider the brain of a bee. All insects, fish and animals have exactly the same kind of brain cell as we do. It is just that they generally have fewer, and have a slightly different body chemistry. The function, structure and power of their brain cell is, however, identical.

The bee has less than one million brain cells!

Now consider what that tiny insect can do with such a small complement of brain bio-computer chips: list on a scrap of paper all of the bee's different capacities and skills, imagining as you do the amount of computing power required for each task.

Compare your thoughts with the following list of what a bee can do:

Fly	Navigate
Fight	Walk
See	Run
Hear	Remember
Smell	Play
Taste	Nurture
Touch	Reproduce
Build (the bee is an architect)	Work constructively and
Control temperature	co-operatively in a community
Count	
Protect	

If a bee can do this with less than one million brain cells, think of what your baby can do with a well-trained million million! ...

In addition to these astounding computational accomplishments, each brain cell contains the code for the perfect genetic cloning of your baby. In a very real sense, your baby's brain contains the potential to reproduce 166 planets-worth of babies identical to yours!

☆

Adding to this extraordinary Capacity Catalogue is the fact that each of your baby's brain cells contains one hundred thousand million million (100,000,000,000,000,000) working parts — the protein molecules that are the major energy and information structures in the brain.

☆

Is it any wonder that Sir Charles Sherrington, the renowned English neuro-scientist and father of modern neuro-physiology, compared your baby's brain to the Universe in the following poetic quote:

'The human brain is an enchanted loom where millions of flashing shuttles weave a dissolving pattern, always a meaningful pattern, though never an abiding one. It is as if the Milky Way entered upon some cosmic dance.'

A major leap in our understanding of the magnificence of the individual brain cell came in 1989, when the Max Planck Laboratory in Switzerland filmed for the first time in history a living brain cell. It was in a petri dish, and was filmed using an exceptionally powerful electron-microscope. It was, as all brain cells do, searching for connections, both physical and informational. What appeared under the microscope stunned and amazed everyone. The creature (for that was what it was) was an independently intelligent, astoundingly complex and extremely mobile being. It searched its microscopic Universe with utter thoroughness, leaving 'no atom of space unturned'. The protuberances with which it searched were like hundreds of baby hands, with fingers constantly reaching out, probing and exploring, searching for information and contact (this search for connectivity is reflected in the far more complex architecture of the brains of babies who have been stimulated). (See the Jeepers/Creepers case study, page 73.)

Many surveys have been done asking people to describe words and impressions that came to their mind upon seeing, for the first time, this living brain cell. The most common expressions were the following:

BRAIN CELL THOUGHTS
(which also perfectly describe your baby!)

ADVENTUROUS	INSPIRATIONAL
AMAZING	INTELLIGENT
AWESOME	MAGICAL
BEAUTIFUL	MIRACULOUS
COMPLEX	MYSTERIOUS
COSMIC	PERFECT
CURIOUS	PERSISTENT
DYNAMIC	POETRY
ENERGETIC	POWERFUL
EXTRAORDINARY	PRECIOUS
FANTASTIC	QUESTING
FASCINATING	RADIANT
GENIUS	UNIQUE
HOPEFUL	UNIVERSAL
IMMACULATE	VIBRANT
INCREDIBLE	WONDROUS
INFINITY	WOW!

These words are the unguarded, natural responses of intelligence viewing its own essence.

They accurately describe you.

They accurately describe us.

They accurately describe your baby ...

THINGS FOR YOU TO DO

Nourish your child's brain cells in every way conceivable. Just by starting to read this book, you are on the right track already. Carry on, and the remainder of Brain Child will supply you with many more suggestions.

Copy out (or enlarge and print out on your computer) the Brain Cell Thoughts listed previously and pin them up somewhere prominent in your home. Absorb them and 'etch' them into your own brain. Whenever you look at your baby, look at him through these vital windows of perception.

Make the Brain Cell Thoughts into beautiful illustrated word-images, and festoon your baby's room with them, so that both he and you will constantly be reflecting on his extraordinary qualities and potential. Take a collection of felt-tip pens and make a glorious colourful frieze, full of evocative and amusing embellishments.

As soon as your child can understand (which will be very early) tell him about the brain cell capacity of bees (see page 6). This story will bring your child into closer contact with nature and with living things in general, and will give him a life-long energy and self-confidence booster/reminder should he ever begin to doubt his extraordinary capabilities.

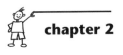

chapter 2

brain development

Your baby's brain is by far the most complex organ in her body, and although in adulthood her brain will comprise only two to four per cent of her full body weight, in the first weeks of foetal development it accounts for half the full size of her body.

For most of the organs in the body, the basic structural development is completed during a relatively short period while in the womb. All further growth in size is through simple cellular division as the individual grows.

The brain is different! Your baby's brain takes longer than any other organ to reach its full development and it has its full complement of brain cells long before birth. The 'size' in terms of number of brain cells therefore does not increase. The number of interconnections between the brain cells does increase. The amount by which it increases is determined by the way in which the brain is brought up and taught. Your privilege as a parent is to help your child develop thinking and learning habits that will help to create a physical brain that is beautifully intricate both physically and mentally. This *structural* development should continue throughout life, as stimulated nerve cells become more and more intricately interconnected as a result of appropriate upbringing (see Brain Foods, page 71).

Brain Spurt One

During the first five weeks after conception the embryo is 'sorting out' top from bottom. By five weeks the top of the embryo has formed into a prototypical brain, and has curved over into the familiar 'question-mark' embryonic shape. Shortly after this, at eight weeks, the first of two major brain spurts begins. 'Brain spurt' refers to those periods in which there is a very rapid brain development. The first brain spurt starts from week eight and continues for five more weeks, through to the fourteenth week after conception.

The first brain spurt involves the production and manufacture of a million million cells called neuroblasts, which are the basic 'pupae' of the brain cells. From these the 'butterflies' of the brain cells (neurons) develop. Thus the number of neuroblasts formed at this stage determine your baby's final number of brain cells (this will be in the order of a million million (1,000,000,000,000)). From week 14 to week 26, the neuroblasts transform themselves into the brain cells. This stage is followed by the second massive and prolonged brain spurt.

Brain Spurt Two

The number of brain cells in your baby's brain is a significant factor in the development of her intelligence (a baby with one brain cell would be sorely challenged!). More important, however, is the degree of interconnection *between* the brain cells.

The all-important 'wiring up' of your baby's brain cells occurs in a major way during the second major brain spurt. This starts approximately 10 weeks after your baby's birth and continues its riotous profusion for *at least* two years afterwards. During this dendritically fecund period, much of your child's fundamental learning takes place.

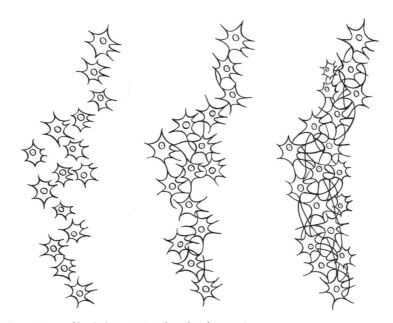

The three stages of brain interconnection development

During the second brain spurt each one of your baby's million million neurons starts sending out a vast number of delicate, fine fibres ('feelers') in all directions, looking for and making connections with thousands to tens of thousands of the surrounding brain cells. Sometimes some of these connections even occur between brain cells on opposite sides of your baby's brain!

During this vitally important period, the individual neurons grow larger and more 'muscular' and the cerebral cortex, the 'thinking cap' that sits at the top of the brain, becomes much thicker and more resilient.

As the million million brain cells are making their even greater number of a million million connections, the tentacles they are sending out are being coated with an insulating material called *myalin*. This myalin sheath speeds the conduction of the baby brain's impulses along the branches of the brain cells.

It is this massive increase in connectivity throughout the brain that results in its phenomenally rapid growth. When she is born your baby's brain will weigh approximately one third of a kilogram (25 per cent of its adult weight). At this time the weight of the brain is increasing at an astonishing *one milligram a minute*!

AGE	% OF THE BRAIN'S ADULT WEIGHT
6 months	50
2½ years	75
5 years	90

At this stage a major part of your child's basic 'cortical architecture' will have been constructed. It is important to realize that it is the number of interconnections and neither the size of the brain nor the number of brain cells that determines your child's intelligence. *It is the number of physical interconnections.* The *number* of these interconnections is determined in large part by the excellence of the Brain Foods (see page 71) with which they are nurtured. The parent thus has a major role to play in overseeing the nurturing and growth of this 'Hanging Gardens of Babylon' of the brain!

THINGS FOR YOU TO DO

Make sure that both the internal and external environments of the developing embryo are optimal for its development. You can do this by taking good care of yourself during pregnancy, and during the weeks before conception. Eat a good healthy diet, avoid alcohol and smoking, get plenty of sleep and try to avoid stress.

brain child

Check that your diet is good enough to nourish you and your baby's developing brain.

Encourage and stimulate multi-sensory and intellectual development in order to guarantee greater connectivity and therefore development in your baby's brain. You can do this by creating a stimulating environment for yourself and for your family. This involves, for example, creating a home that is rich in different colours and textures, where music is a constant feature, where people talk to one another, where play for all ages happens around the clock and where there is laughter on a daily basis. If you are doing this for yourself and the rest of your family, your baby will automatically inherit it.

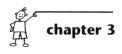

chapter 3

left and right brain

☆

In the second half of the twentieth century a remarkable scientist with exceptional curiosity, by the name of Roger Sperry, performed research that was to: win him the Nobel Prize; change the way in which the world thinks about the brain; and transform the image you have of your baby's brain.

☆

Professor Sperry's research was to measure the different functions of the brain's two cerebral hemispheres (yes, your baby has *two* upper brains!) To perform his experiment, he placed caps on his students' heads, from which protruded electric wires that could measure the different brainwaves their brains gave off as they performed different mental activities. These activities included, for example: listening to music; doing mathematical calculations; reading poetry; reading text; looking at pictures; daydreaming; talking; logical thinking; and creative thinking, etc. The results were enthralling.

Professor Sperry found that the brain tended to divide the activities into two distinct categories, one group of activities was handled by the left hemisphere, and the other group was handled by the right. While one hemisphere was 'active' the other tended to 'rest'. In general the left hemisphere became active when the brain had to deal with logic, lists, lines, words, numbers and analysis. The right hemisphere became active when the brain had to deal with rhythm, colour, image (imagination), daydreaming and 'seeing the whole picture'.

What was additionally significant about this research was that Sperry found that every brain had the full range of abilities potentially available, and that some brains had simply developed certain abilities more than others.

Your baby has the full range of these potentials.

Adding further to the significance of this research was the subsequent research by Professor Robert Ornstein, Doctor Robert Bloch, myself and others which showed that developing both sets of activities in harmony led to a synergetic multiplying of the basic capacities (see Synergy, page 99).

This natural development of the synergetic brain (commonly called 'Whole Brain Development/Thinking'), is confirmed by study of the Great Geniuses. Albert Einstein combined logical, numerical and analytical capacity with his phenomenal ability to imagine and daydream, to give us the synergetic fruit of his thinking: the theory of the shape and structure of our relativistic Universe (it was he who said: 'I believe in intuition and inspiration … At times I feel certain that I am right while not knowing the reason … Imagination is more important than knowledge. For knowledge is limited, whereas imagination embraces the entire world, stimulating progress, giving birth to evolution.')

Similarly Leonardo da Vinci, the ultimate user of 'both sides' of the brain, said that in order to develop a good brain and exceptional thinking skills, you must 'study the art of science and the science of art'.

The great geniuses concluded that to realize full brain potential, you simply have to use all the cortical skills with which you have been blessed.

Modern education systems have tended to 'stream' even very young children into 'left' (the sciences and academia) or 'right' (the arts and trades). Critics point out that this is using only half their potential and is creating, literally, a world of half-wits!

The truth is far more disturbing.

To understand how all this applies to your baby's brain, let us use the metaphor of running. If we ask you to run a short distance with 'your full potential', i.e. using both arms and both legs, and we film your performance in order to examine your efficiency, you will probably do reasonably, or even very, well.

In the second half of the experiment we allow you to repeat the exercise. This time, however, we allow

The trials of using only half your brain

you to use only half your potential. To facilitate this we tie your right wrist to your right ankle and ask you to repeat your short run. With half of your potential available, will your performance be half as effective? Obviously not. Within a few attempts you will have fallen flat on your face. A performance hundreds of times less effective.

So it is with your baby's brain, although with the brain the distinction between 'half' and 'whole' is even more dramatic. If your child is allowed to use all of his mental skills in synergetic harmony, it will develop his capabilities not only hundreds but possibly thousands of times more effectively and successfully. Do not force him into 'one-legged' development and thinking.

THINGS FOR YOU TO DO

Make sure that your baby's mental development is 'whole-brained', by encouraging development of both the right and left hemispheres of the brain. For example, from an early age, get him interested in the fullest range of subjects and topics as possible. Don't let him be 'one-sided'. Encourage him to be practical as well as mentally adept and emphasize the value of being multi-talented in varied disciplines (for example it's great to be interested in and good at both art and physics). This is particularly important today, in a society that increasingly requires multi-facetted and creative people.

Provide an environment that stimulates activity and function of both the left and right hemispheres. For example, if your child wants to create his own fancy-dress outfit for a party, encourage him to sketch a suitable design, work out how much material he needs to buy, help him shop for suitable fabrics and materials and measure how much he needs. He can then work out the cost and make the purchase. You can then help him sew and decorate the outfit. A ten-year-old, with your assistance and encouragement, will enjoy using a simple sewing pattern and following the printed instructions. The results generate huge satisfaction and pride, and the child will be using both the left and right sides of his brain.

Encourage the development of your baby's ambidexterity (see Handedness, page 182) by noticing whether he favours one hand over the other and then getting him to play the game using the other, or doing things with both hands at the same time. This can apply to simple tasks such as picking up food and feeding himself, progressing to holding and manipulating a crayon. Later on, it is useful to be ambidextrous for specific tasks such as sewing, ironing, cooking, and manipulating tools of all kinds. Then if you are unlucky enough to break your 'writing' arm, you can use the other one! Make a special point of encouraging your child to reverse every left/right function, including the whole range of sporting activities, play and as many other activities as you can think of. This will generate all kinds of exciting, creative and amusing games.

Encourage your baby to draw with both hands

brain child

chapter 4

the multiple intelligences

☆

Closely linked with our discoveries of the left and right cortices of the brain was our realization, in the latter part of the twentieth century, that the human brain has more than one IQ; more than one intelligence. It has multiple intelligences.

☆

Your baby therefore comes into the world with an array of intelligences that are waiting to be developed.

It is useful here to use a musical analogy. Consider that your baby is about to learn to play the Piano Concerto of Life, and that his fingers are his multiple intelligences. It is obviously possible to play the piano with one finger only, or to use the 'hunt-and-peck', two-finger method, unfortunately used by so many. How much more functional, productive and aesthetically pleasing to play with all his fingers!

Your baby's multiple intelligences are as follows:

Verbal Intelligence
Numerical/Logical Intelligence
Engineering/Spatial Intelligence

Sensual Intelligence
Body/Kinaesthetic Intelligence
Creative Intelligence
Personal Intelligence
Social Intelligence
Spiritual Intelligence

Verbal Intelligence

This is a large part of the standard Intelligence Quotient (IQ) testing. It refers to your baby's ability to recognize the meanings of words, and, as time goes on, to repeat them in speech and written form, to understand more complex word structures including phrases, sentences, paragraphs and whole books, and to see increasingly complex forms of verbal relationships of the type: 'dog is to cat as puppy is to ...' This intelligence is not, as has been incorrectly assumed, static; it is very pliable and can be improved or lessened throughout both early and later life. It obviously includes the extent and range of vocabulary.

THINGS FOR YOU TO DO

 Make sure your baby is exposed to a large range of words in both aural and written form and that vocabulary development and playing with words are an ongoing and enjoyable part of the family culture. You can start when your baby is newborn, by talking and singing to him. Don't make the assumption that he cannot understand you just because he cannot speak yet. For him speech is communication with you and by

brain child

the time he is about two months of age, he will start to make voluntary sounds that will eventually be transformed into words. Later, at the toddler stage, you can include him in enjoyable family conversations, perhaps at mealtimes. In this way, he will not only add new words to his range but register the whole point of conversation. You, as a parent, will develop a special way of talking to your baby.

 Make sure that words are also regularly linked to images. Remember that verbal intelligence is the single intelligence most highly correlated with traditional success in school, university and the professions. A good way to start is to look at picture board books with your four-month-old, pointing at the pictures as you read or tell the story. This activity quickly becomes a welcome part of your day, turning into bedtime story sessions and then eventually transforming into private reading when the child is older. The pictures in books become less necessary as time goes on and the child creates the 'pictures' in his mind's eye.

Numerical/Logical Intelligence

This refers to the developing brain's ability to play with the alphabet of numbers, from the more simple levels of counting from one to the millions, into the middle ground of learning the basic functions of addition, subtraction, multiplication and division, into the more complex realms of higher mathematics, and including significantly for intelligence testing the ability to see multiple relationships between numbers of the type 'fill in the blank: 2, 4, 6, --, 10, 12, 14'. This intelligence, like verbal intelligence, can be changed significantly by training. It is obviously a major life skill, and can enhance the individual's performance and position in situations ranging from shopping, through higher education and into success in any of the professions.

THINGS FOR YOU TO DO

Make sure that your young child can count with ease, facility and enthusiasm before he enters school. This will add enormously to his confidence. You can do this in a fun way by making counting part of his daily play. For example, if you are walking along the road, you can count the trees, paving stones or lamp posts as you go along. If your child is not keen on walking (typical of many toddlers), this has the added advantage of encouraging him to do so.

As with words, include 'playing with numbers' in your family culture. When you are on a family outing you can split into two teams and see which team can count the most dogs, ladies wearing hats, babies in pushchairs, etc.

Make sure, as your Brain Child develops, that he learns how to do simple mental calculations (figuring it all out in his head without writing anything down) and that he is continually learning to estimate, in general terms, the answer to mathematical puzzles, problems and conundrums. Great mathematical geniuses, such as Trachtenburg and others, said that learning how to estimate was one of the first major steps that led them to realize that mathematics was much more fun, easy and accessible than many people had

Make guestimating a fun exercise when you are out and about

thought. It also helped them to become leaders in their field. You can help your child become numerically adept by encouraging him to work things out without writing anything down. The easiest time to do this is while you are out and about, encouraging him to make estimates rather than exact answers. For example, an older child might enjoy working out how tall a building is by guessing the size of one of the bricks and then multiplying this by a guestimate of the number of bricks it takes to reach the roof. Make this kind of activity a light-hearted challenge rather than a 'problem'.

Engineering/Spatial Intelligence

Engineering/spatial intelligence allows your baby to navigate the miraculous and intriguing world of the three dimensions. This intelligence can range from the observations of relationships in the microcosmic world, through to the more 'local spaces' of the painter, the sculptor, the architect, the surgeon or the mechanical engineer, through to the vast spaces such as those traversed by the sailor, the airline pilot or the astronomer. Most Mind Sports involve this intelligence to a major degree (see Mind Sports, page 278).

Like all other intelligences, engineering/spatial intelligence can be developed and enhanced. If it is, the full range of interests and professions mentioned above, including others such as geometry, cartography, meteorology and all forms of engineering, will be both more appealing to your child's developing brain and more likely to tempt the brain into further studies and activities.

THINGS FOR YOU TO DO

 Play Mind Sports with your child, especially those such as jigsaw puzzles, draughts, chess, and the Japanese/Chinese game of Go.

Whenever your child shows an interest in how things work, encourage him, where possible, to take things apart. If you have, for example, an old radio that you don't use any more, this would be a good thing to offer him. When that is done, you can then encourage him to put it all back together again! However, do make sure that your child can be trusted not to put any small parts in his mouth and swallow them.

 Acquire toys that encourage the development of engineering/spatial intelligence. These include: bricks; construction kits; toys that require manipulation in order to make them work; and multiple-assembly toys such as Lego. In addition, encourage him to mix up the types/sets of toys with each other. For example, a set of ordinary wooden bricks can be used to make a marvellous viaduct for the Brio train to go along. Rather than buying expensive toys, arrange swaps with other families or use toy libraries. Or if relatives ask about birthday wishes, take the opportunity to acquire what your child really needs. Alternatively, use objects and materials around the house to make toys with your child. A beautiful soft doll can be made by taking a square of plain fabric, stuffing the centre with cotton wool to make a head and securing the 'neck' with an elastic band, and sewing on wool for hair. Eyes and other features can be embroidered or stuck on using buttons and other bits and pieces. To make a cardboard dolls' house, collect four shoe boxes and stick them together to make four rooms. Paint the outside with emulsion and use scraps of wallpaper to paper the interiors. Use fabric scraps to make curtains and old matchboxes to create furniture. Carpets can be fashioned out of fabric scraps. Whatever you and your child make together, it is the act of creativity that is the important issue. If you, as a parent, exercise your own creativity, your child will become creative too. Together you will create a spiral of creativity.

At a very early stage, teach your child the directions of the compass (give him a beautiful one as a present) in conjunction with map reading. When you are out together, ask him to help find the way. This will make him feel 'useful' and purposeful as well as assisting his spatial intelligence.

When on journeys with your child, make up games in which you constantly give spatial references, including compass directions, distance from starting point and destination, and relationship to known landmarks. You could improvise a game of Hide and Seek or Sardines using compass references to find the hiders. In Hide and Seek the finder simply finds the one who is hiding, while in Sardines seekers squeeze up in the hiding place with the hider, hence the name. This will develop both your child's spatial intelligence and it will act as a major foundation to the development of all memory and thinking skills (see Memory, page 46). Show your child how to use a telescope and a microscope too.

Encourage the recycling habit in your child. Rather than buying new toys, visit your local charity shop and let your child give away his unwanted toys and buy some 'new' ones instead. He will be delighted to search for new and unexpected playthings and be helping a good cause with the things he donates and the money he spends.

Sensual Intelligence

This intelligence involves the five main senses of sight, hearing, smell, taste and touch. It can be usefully considered as not one, but *five, separate intelligences* and so separate chapters have been devoted to each sense in Part V – The Senses (see page 191).

Before you read on, it is worth noting that history's greatest creative minds and mnemonists (memorizers) all had highly developed sensory intelligences that they applied with both precision and abandon to their chosen areas of interest. They also tended to 'blend' their senses, seeing sounds as shapes and moods, 'tasting' colours and 'seeing' sounds. This skill is entitled '*synaesthesia*', meaning the ability to blend the senses. Your baby will do this naturally. Encourage it!

THINGS FOR YOU TO DO

Read Part V, The Senses, with the constant awareness that each of the senses is a distinct intelligence that can be developed.

Play synaesthesia games with your baby/child. One idea is to play different types of music, then give your child a set of coloured felt-tip pens and scrap paper and ask him to draw according to the way the music makes him feel. Admire the results and make a display of them on his bedroom wall. Contrasting music such as the opening bars of Beethoven's Fifth Symphony and 'Morning' from Grieg's Peer Gynt Suite are useful starting points. Explore all musical styles with your child. Try out Reggae, Soul, Hip Hop, Flamenco, Blues, Jazz, the various African forms and World Music, Rock and Roll and anything else that takes your, or your child's, fancy.

Constantly encourage both sensory exploration and expression. You can do this by letting your child compare different textures that exist in the home. Let him search for the softest-feeling thing in the house (the sheep-skin rug or your best pashmina), followed by the roughest (your nail brush or the pot-scourer), or perhaps when you are cooking, let him knead pastry, sift flour with his fingers, or wash lentils under running water. If you are sewing, let him stroke his cheek with different types of soft fabric so that he can feel the differences.

Body/Kinaesthetic Intelligence

This is a vitally important intelligence for your baby and growing child and involves the body's ability to relate, in a poised and balanced way, both to itself and to the world around it. This intelligence involves the ability to respond at various speeds, from exceptionally slow to exceptionally fast, to be constantly aware of the body's position in space in relation to all other objects in space, to be able to judge physical distances in relation to flying objects such as balls, and to do so in a condition of muscular strength, physical flexibility, and cardiovascular stamina.

Unfortunately, in the twentieth century we 'went down a wrong alley', and it was widely assumed that physical intelligence was associated with stupidity.

Happily we now know that the opposite is true, and that, as you might expect, and as the Romans realized, *mens sana in corpore sano* (healthy mind healthy body, healthy body healthy mind) is the rule that rules the roost.

To realize just how phenomenal this particular intelligence is, imagine taking the world's most powerful super-computer, placing it at one end of a soccer field, putting a ball in front of it, and programming it to dribble that ball through ten trained defenders dedicated to taking it away from you, and having succeeded in this task, placing it in the net behind a final defender whose sole object was to prevent you from doing so. By contrast, give the same task to a gifted though non-academically-minded football player and he can dazzle a crowd of thousands with this intelligence.

The development of your baby's physical intelligence goes hand-in-hand (body-in-brain!) with the commensurate development of all the other forms of intelligence. It is an intelligence to be both highly praised and prized.

THINGS FOR YOU TO DO

Make sure that your baby has ample opportunity, especially in his first five years, for complete freedom of movement, including the vital developmental stages of crawling. In some cultures crawling is not encouraged because it is associated with the animals. In Western cultures some parents find it inconvenient because the baby has to be watched constantly (kept away from dangers such as electric sockets and staircases) — hence the popularity of baby-walkers. However, you can get around this by keeping a playpen or fenced-off area, replete with tempting toys, to pop the child into whenever you have to leave the room briefly. If your baby has been used to lying on his back and is showing no inclination to crawl, lay him on his front when he's awake and see how quickly he gets the hang of it (see Persistence, page 115).

Play physical games with your baby/child on a daily basis (this has the added advantage of keeping you fitter as well!). When your child is old enough, gently swing him around by his arms or legs, run mini-races or hone your child's vital co-ordination skills by playing ball games. When the child is still little use a large soft, fluffy ball and then, as he gets older and more proficient, progress to smaller, firmer varieties.

brain child

Eradicate deep-seated prejudices from your mind. A person who is athletically adept is more likely to be mentally adept, rather than less.

Make physical health part of your family culture and something that is to be desired and developed. If you play a sport yourself, take your child along too, so that he gets the message that this is a good way to spend free time. He will soon see how enjoyable it is to be actively engaged in sport and also how congenial it is socially. For example, if you practise judo, take him along too and when he gets to an appropriate age see whether there is a junior section for him to join.

Creative Intelligence

Whereas traditional IQ (verbal and numerical intelligence) tends to focus on the more analytical and logical thought processes, creative intelligence refers to the more associative, radiant and explosive thought processes that lead the brain into new realms of thinking and expression.

Creative intelligence is at least as important as traditional IQ. It is not, as many have thought, a limited tankard from which you drink until it has run dry.

This intelligence is becoming particularly significant in the new change-orientated and information/thought-based twenty-first century, and as such special chapters have been devoted to it (see Creativity and Mind Mapping, pages 58 and 75).

Read the Creativity and Mind Mapping chapters (see pages 58 and 75) with the constant awareness that creativity is a vitally important intelligence that must be developed.

Encourage your child in the development of all creative skills, especially art, music and dance. However, there is no need to trail your young child round to endless after-school classes. If he wants to do classes, let him choose ones that he feels really enthusiastic about, not ones you think he 'ought' to be doing. (Make sure that you do not Hot House your child, see page 273.) There are plenty of creative activities that he can do at home. Just supply him with a stack of recycled computer paper, some paints and brushes or felt-tip pens. If you are worried about mess, put a plastic sheet on the floor, or in summer let him paint outside. When he is having a quiet moment, play some beautiful, relaxing piano music and when you put on some livelier sounds, get him to have a dance with you and his siblings, just for fun.

Personal Intelligence

Personal intelligence is being realized increasingly to be a major factor in the overall sum of multiple intelligences that one might call, rather than an Intelligence Quotient, a Brain Quotient (BQ).

This intelligence concerns individuals' deep and intricate personal relationships with themselves. This relationship can range from having 'the other' self as one's worst enemy and constantly chiding critic, to having one's 'other self' as one's best friend and life-long companion.

The development of personal intelligence is intricately connected to the four brain foods: oxygen; nutrition; love; and information (ONLI) (see also page 71). An increasing absence of these leads to self-doubt, self-denial and self-hatred. The increasing presence of the brain foods leads to self-confidence, self-fulfilment and self-love, a state of high personal intelligence.

Babies and children who have developed this particular intelligence will be 'in their skins' in a wide variety of situations, ranging from being and playing alone, to the full range of social activities.

As the child progresses, personal intelligence will increasingly become involved with self-knowledge, and can be assisted in its development by exposing the child to all the topics in this book, especially those areas concerning Mental Literacy – the understanding of the physical and behavioural alphabets of the child's brain including:

1. The multiple intelligences.
2. Physical literacy, involving an understanding, comprehensively, of the forms and methods of attaining multiple-physical fitnesses.
3. The nature of appropriate nutrition.
4. The required rhythms of rest and sleep on a short- and long-term basis.
5. Emotional intelligence and openness.

THINGS FOR YOU TO DO

Make sure your child 'only' gets ONLI — the four brain foods of Oxygen, Nutrition, Love and Information. With this multiple nutrition, the particular multiple intelligence of personal intelligence will be an automatic and meaningful occurrence.

From early days, encourage your child to be happy to be alone. This will be an important life resource for the future. A person who is content with his own company, who can rely on his own inner resources, is 'happy in his own skin' and he will lead a more fulfilled life. Help your young child to play on his own, to rely on his own imagination, while also teaching him to enjoy company when he has it. Playing alone improves your child's concentration, too. There is over-emphasis in society today on relying too much on others for one's own happiness, which has far-reaching negative implications in all areas of life.

Social Intelligence

Social intelligence has been described by Professor Howard Gardner of Harvard University, one of the major warriors in the global fight for the realization of the brain's multiple talents, as perhaps the most important of all. It is essential that this intelligence is developed on a continuing basis in your baby/child.

This intelligence involves the brain's innate capacity to 'get along with' all the other human and other brains around it, whether as individuals, small groups, large groups or as mass audiences.

It is an intelligence that can flower dramatically with age, and it incorporates all the other multiple intelligences. Absence of it can lead to loneliness and despair; an abundance of it can lead to unparalleled success.

A person with this intelligence highly developed delights in the multiplicity of human characters, and is sensitive to different personality types; is able to and loves to lead teams of different people to achieve given goals; negotiates for win-win situations in which both sides are satisfied and know that they have gained; listens with understanding and compassion; is

brain child

sought after for help; tends to be, in social gatherings, known for making others feel relaxed, at ease, and for making them laugh; is able to communicate his own point of view successfully without antagonizing others; and is seen by others both in a generally positive light and as a leader. Good leaders are also able to reverse roles and become the best followers.

It is an intelligence and competency *particularly* amenable to development and training.

THINGS FOR YOU TO DO

Make sure that the other multiple intelligences are developed in order that they may support and enhance this one.

Familiarize your child with the Brain Principles in Part Three, especially the multi-ordinate nature of the words and reality (see Radiant Thinking, page 123) in order that the child may fully understand the 'nature of the beast' with whom, throughout his life, he will necessarily be interacting. This can be done in a gradual and light-hearted way over a long period of time. Play games in which you and your child imagine what it is like to be a rich person, a poor person, a spider, a seagull, a healthy person, an unhealthy person, a world champion, etc. This will increasingly encourage your child (and yourself!) to be 'in other people's shoes', and thus to understand them better. At the same time, such games also vastly increase the child's Creative Intelligence, by teaching the all-important creative skills of multiple perspectives.

Make sure that your child's friends and circle of wider acquaintances include people of all ages, multiple nationalities, different professions, different personality types and both sexes. As Shakespeare said 'all the world's a stage ...' and it is vital for your child's developing mind to see as many and as varied players as possible.

Provide your child with the opportunity to perform, whether it be reading, talking, singing, dancing or mimicking in front of small and large groups of people. This provides a wonderful opportunity for the application of TEFCAS (see page 105) in the growing understanding of others, as well as leading to a notably enhanced self-confidence. Start up an informal theatre group for your child and his friends. Enlist the help of other parents to put on short plays, written by the children, including making simple scenery and costumes. Put on a performance and charge a small entrance fee in support of a charity chosen by the children (for example, Red Nose Day). You could also try recording, transcribing or illustrating the plays. Your child will become a Shakespeare-in-the-making!

Spiritual Intelligence

Spiritual intelligence is the comprehensive 'universal' intelligence described by the American psychologist A. A. Maslow as the ultimate goal in the hierarchy of needs. It is met once the more basic needs of food, shelter, education, productivity and security have been attained. People with an exceptionally high spiritual intelligence: feel that their lives have a sense of complete and positive purpose; are congruent in that they have a deep knowledge of themselves and do what they say they will do; against standard expectations have playful, irrepressible and bubbling senses of humour; feel a great connection to, and often 'feel at one' with the Universe; feel a passionate connection to and concern for other life forms, which generate a sense of awe, wonder, love and respect; are able to combine successfully humility with self-confidence; and are considered more mature and wise than average.

This intelligence is a 'mature' intelligence, with its development rooted in the early years and experience of the child's life. Despite this, many babies seem 'wise beyond their years' and are often described by those who know them as 'old souls'.

Never underestimate your baby!

THINGS FOR YOU TO DO

Help your child, with extreme delicacy (see Hot Housing, page 273), to establish a positive purpose in life and a large vision. Similarly help your child to appreciate the vast dimensions of the micro-cosmos and macro-cosmos, to appreciate the beauty and mystery of the natural world, and to develop a sense of wonder and awe. You can approach this gradually and casually in general conversations that crop up naturally. One simple idea to start with is 'Everything is connected to everything else'. When you talk about news items, for example, which tend to be negative, try to offer possible positive outcomes. Take your young child out on 'mystery walks', spending time just looking at things, without rushing. You might look at and discuss together any of the following things: leaves, trees, roadworks, cars, farm animals, clouds, puddles, etc. in as broad a way as possible. Retain a sense of wonder in your explorations.

Encourage the development and expression of multiple forms of humour. Make a habit of telling jokes, for example tell funny stories against yourself along the lines of: 'You'll never guess what happened to me when I went to the supermarket today … Engage in the concepts of irony or satire – two-year-olds are more than capable of understanding both (see OJ's story, page 260). As a family, try to have a good laugh about something every day. Everyone will feel the better for it. Laughter is an excellent exercise and has been found to strengthen the immune system while simultaneously reducing stress on all levels. Beware of teasing children excessively – even if it is only meant to be affectionate, it can have harmful and long-lasting consequences.

 Have pets in the home (see Pets, page 298)

 Acquire beautiful books on the Solar System and Universe. Such books will help a child realize the beauty and vastness of the Universe in which he has been born. Such books will help your child develop the ability to conceptualize on a grand scale, will put him in touch with the magnificence of nature, will literally 'open his mind' to greater things and will therefore help in the development of his feelings of wonder and awe in his Spiritual Intelligence.

chapter 5

the emotions

☆

The expression of emotions and the development of emotional intelligence, dismissed as totally irrelevant even as recently as the 1930s, are now known to be vital constituents of your baby's overall development. Emotional intelligence, like the other intelligences, is one that can be nurtured and developed.

☆

Indeed studies and experience suggest that the emotional health of the child starts in the womb, and is highly dependent upon the emotional state and intelligence of the parents, especially the mother.

Shortly after the Second World War, Thomas Verney and his team of researchers conducted some extremely delicate research on the emotional reactions and coping mechanisms of women who had been in the early stages of pregnancy when learning that their husbands had been killed in action. A second major prong to the study was the investigation of the emotional state of the children of these mothers.

The startling findings were that all the mothers-to-be had gone through virtually identical reactions when hearing of their husbands' deaths: devastation, despair and hopelessness.

The difference lay in their ability to cope with their grief: some of the women were able to start looking forward again in a relatively short space of time and found strength and purpose through their unborn children; others who were less able to overcome their loss sank deeper into depression, became more and more inactive, and were unable to think positively about the future.

Investigation of the emotional health of the children to whom they eventually gave birth, revealed highly significant correlations:

1. Those children born to the mothers who had been able to emotionally cope and come to think positively about the future, were far more emotionally secure, cried less, slept more peacefully, and were generally healthier.
2. Those children of mothers who were unable to come to terms with the loss of their husbands were more emotionally insecure, with a tendency to fret, sleep fitfully and cry much more frequently. These babies were also less physically healthy and inclined to be colicky.

Emotional health and development begins in the womb. And very much in the mind of the mother.

Emotions — The Range — Negative and Positive

Because of our twenty-first-century tendency to accentuate the negative in education and training we have tended also to focus on the baby's negative emotions. We thus have a tendency to 'deal' with them, so that our overriding concerns are with anger, frustration, violence, crying, sulking, irritability and stubbornness.

It is far more beneficial to focus on the more positive emotions, and their development in the baby: happiness, enthusiasm, exultation, calmness and joy resulting in smiling, laughter, expressions of physical positive energy, and similar expressions of peacefulness.

Much research has been done on the full range of facial expressions, and there are surprisingly many.

Your baby is as expressive as the most talented Shakespearean actors!

The baby has an entire 'troop' of different 'muscle artists' waiting to etch the infinite possible variations of expression on the canvas of the face. These artists-in-waiting are, specifically, waiting for the parent and the parents' friends and acquaintances to give examples of what can be done, in order that the baby may mimic and rehearse the expression of the full gamut of emotions available to his human brain. Without such encouragement and stimulation your baby's face will remain a relatively blank slate. *With* such stimulation and encouragement your baby's face will become as muscularly flexible, fit and expressive as the face of any Shakespearean actor!

Expressing Emotion

In many Westernized societies the expression of emotion, both 'negative' and, surprisingly, 'positive', has been relegated to the realms of immature and inappropriate behaviour, and has consequently been frowned upon and disallowed. This can be extremely dangerous, for it inhibits the body's natural release mechanisms, and builds up unnecessary tension throughout the system.

It is important to let your child cry or weep when he is emotionally or physically hurt, to be alone when he needs to work something out; and to be physically exuberant and noisy when he is ecstatic.

Consider the full range of emotions to be very much like the body. The 'Body Emotions', like the 'Body Physical', need to develop maximum strength, maximum flexibility and maximum stamina.

Once again children need examples from which to learn and to mimic. They *do* and *will* understand the full range of emotions (even the negative) if they are expressed, treated as natural, and dealt with appropriately.

I remember with fondness those occasional times when my father

became sad, frustrated or angry. In such times he would go into his workshop, turn up Bach's organ music to full volume, and hammer out some new creative project. He would always return refreshed. As a very young child I learnt the invaluable lesson that such moods *do* arise naturally; that they can be mightily expressive and creative; that they do not necessarily lead to violence and destruction; and that, like any natural storm, they do pass ...
As your child becomes more mature, and as his foundations become more secure, you can explain to him that his upper brain (left and right cortex) can 'talk' to his lower brain; that part of the brain developed early in his evolution, and where emotions tend to reside, and that the two of them can 'get along'. This is best exemplified in the 'count to 10' scenario, where an inappropriate emotional reaction needs to be calmed down before the Intellect and the Emotion mutually decide on the appropriate course of action.

In developing emotional intelligence and strength, love is once again the password. The child's understanding of his own uniqueness, of the multi-ordinant nature of perception and reality (see *Radiant Thinking*, page 123) and of many of the principles and areas covered in *Brain Child*, will all greatly enhance the development of emotional intelligence, stability and strength.

THINGS FOR YOU TO DO

 Remember that smiling is a lot easier for the musculature of the face than frowning — the zygo maticus major muscle is your 'smiling muscle', and when it is active, it not only gives your face an easier task than when frowning, it also sends a fountain of positive chemicals to your brain. Give your child an easier life! If you smile at your child a lot, you will soon see him smiling back at you and at other people. Just think what an advantage this is going to be for him in later life. He will sail through job interviews, challenging situations, and he will make peace with people when an argument or even violence might seem more likely. The list is endless … People who smile sincerely are perceived by others to be more open, warm, friendly and confident. Smiling also takes far less muscular effort than frowning, releases floods of 'positive chemicals' into the bodily system and simultaneously directs the brain towards more positive thoughts.

Make sure that your facial expressions reflect as many of the different emotions as possible, emphasizing the positive. During baby talk (see page 265) we humans naturally go through many of these expressions. When your baby is very young, spend time in face-to-face contact. You will soon get a response. It's true to say that you get back what you put in.

Gather around your baby, expressive, emotional, energetic, enthusiastic, happy and loving acquaintances and friends. Allow them as much face-to-face and eye-to-eye contact with your baby as possible. This is great when friends and relatives want to hold and make a fuss of him. The more they inter-react with your baby, the more response they get. The happier everyone is!

Whenever possible, allow your baby to express all his emotions, guiding him, where appropriate, to behaviour that gains maximum benefit from, and understanding of, the behaviour. For example, if your child has a temper tantrum about something and loses control, let him go through with it and get it out of his system. Be a rock. As difficult as it can sometimes be, particularly in public, try not to modify his behaviour or calm him down (unless he is about to damage himself or other people physically). Equally, try not to get upset yourself; just be there for him. When the storm clouds have passed and it is appropriate, have a gentle chat with him, without apportioning blame,

brain child

about what happened. He may have been frightened by his own behaviour and he needs to be reassured that this was normal.

Teach your child about the importance of showing caring emotions towards others. By your own example, show how you care fondly for your friends and relatives. Show concern and love for them. This way, your child will imitate you and show the same feelings for his own friends — especially when they are in difficulty. If this approach is his model, he will be less likely to bully others or through inaction arising from uncertainty about how to act be complicit in group bullying. This is partly how children become moral beings and how ethical behaviour prevails in a group, such as in the school playground. The child comes to believe in his own behaviour and others will imitate him. The group then becomes moral (see also Schools, page 311). One other major path to morality is when the child realizes how precious and amazing he himself is and others around him are. When the child values himself and others he will naturally direct his behaviour towards care and compassion and the protection and nurturing of that which is valued and held precious; himself and everyone else. It should be noted here that instructing and ordering people to be ethical or moral often produces exactly the opposite result.

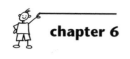

chapter 6

memory

---- ☆ ----

Your baby's memory has a potential to become the greatest database in the known Universe. As we saw in the Brain Cell chapter (see page 3), the physical capacity of his brain will have the potential to store over 'one followed by ten and a half million kilometres of noughts,' pieces of data or memories. This number is a million million million times greater than the number of atoms in our known Universe, and is, in terms of your baby's expected life span, functionally infinite.

---- ☆ ----

This giant Memory Muscle, like all other physical muscles and mental skills, can be nurtured, grown and strengthened by appropriate exercise and training.

Human memory, and therefore your baby's, operates on three fundamental principles:

1. Your child's brain will remember anything that is appropriately ASSOCIATED.
2. Your child's brain will remember anything that is OUTSTANDING.
3. Your child's brain will remember anything that is appropriately (by number and time) REPEATED.

Association

Your baby's brain is, in reality, a gigantic Association Machine. Association is the tool by which your child makes links and connections between the multitudinous different items in her growing Universe. All your baby's initial spoken vocabulary, language learning, initial reading, understanding of pleasure and pain, and knowledge of the nomenclature and nature of the human beings, pets and other objects in the world around her, are a function of this primary mental and memory tool. Watch your baby, or any child, and you will see the process in constant dynamic action: ball links with play; spoon links with food-to-mouth; furry toy links with comfort and friend; hot stove links with pain; smile links with happiness; and so on, literally ad infinitum.

LARISA AND IVAN'S STORY

A wonderful story indicating the power of association and its effect on memory, thinking and logic, is told by Larisa Curiel, Mexican mother of Ivan. She tells the story in her own words:

'A coche papa'

My son is no longer my little baby, with one year and nine months now he is my precious little boy.

He loves playing, dancing and singing. And one of his favourite games now is to pull one of his sleeves till he hides his perfect little hand inside it and turns to me saying: 'No 'ta mano, mama'. Which means, 'there's no hand in here mummy'.

When I look at him with a big surprised face and ask: 'Where is it? Ivan.' He smiles and says: 'a coche papa'. 'It's in daddy's car.' And not only his hidden hand is in daddy's car, but everything that isn't where it's supposed to be, is in daddy's car.

My husband and I wondered, 'why is everything in daddy's car?' and laughed a lot with his response.

So one day, out of nothing, we finally figured out why he was saying that.

Some days before he started saying 'a coche papa' as an answer to where things were, we came back from a weekend car trip to our house. The day after, when Ivan asked me to put on his favourite music during lunch-time as I always do, I said to him: 'your CDs aren't here, baby, they are in daddy's car'. We forgot to take them out of the car and daddy was at the office at the time.

It was a simple answer to a simple question, but he got it, and registered it in his mind.

So when something is not there, it must be 'a coche papa'!

This association story indicates that already by the age of one year and nine months a baby has developed a strong memory, strong associations and immaculate logic based on his current database of knowledge as well as having developed a delightful sense of humour.

Understanding the prime importance of the memory principle of association will enable you, the parents, and other mentors of the child, to strengthen her Memory Muscle considerably. Understanding this principle also provides a more profound understanding of, and insight into, the multiple intelligences, many of which are associated by nature, (see page 21) the multi-ordinant nature of words (see Radiant Thinking, page 123) and the theory underlying the multi-faceted thinking technique of Mind Mapping (see page 75).

LOCATION

A major sub-division of Association is *location*. Research has shown that what is known as the *contextual* effect, is significant in improving memory.

This effect simply means that we remember things by the surroundings (i.e. multiple associations) in which they take place. You will observe your child continuously doing this, often going so far as to remember only something when the context is recreated.

One of the most common and surprising examples of contextual memory occurs when adults are sitting in the living room and suddenly have a strong desire for some particular item to eat or drink. They walk into the kitchen, and stop, embarrassed to realize that they have totally forgotten why it is they are standing there! No matter how hard they try to remember *while they are in the kitchen* their attempts are fruitless. However, when they return to the living room (the context and multiply associative environment in which the original thought was 'placed') they recall it immediately.

Outstandingness

Your baby's brain will remember anything that is outstanding or unique. This quality of memory is known as the Von Restorff Effect, after the German psychologist who discovered that for survival purposes, the human brain is designed to pay attention to and remember things that are different from, and therefore stand out from, the normal environment.

THE PRIMACY EFFECT

 A sub-division of the Von Restorff Effect is the Primacy Effect; a law that states that your child will tend, increasingly, to remember those 'first time' experiences. The first time she flies in an aeroplane. Her first 'crush'. Her first major injury. Her first First Prize.

The early years of life are filled with many such primacies, which is why people tend to remember more from the beginning of their lives than the middle. The middle tends to become relatively routine, and therefore the opposite of *outstanding*, and therefore not especially memorable.

THE RECENCY EFFECT

Your child's brain will tend to remember more clearly the 'last time'. She will remember the last holiday; the last meal; the last time of seeing the best friend; the last time of seeing Grandma and Grandpa; the last pocket money; the last time they saw some person or pet who died; the last lesson of the day in school; the last ice-cream; the last time she saw you.

THE SENSES

The Von Restorff Effect is made more emphatic the more senses there are involved. All great memory systems, especially those devised by the Greeks, known as the mnemonic systems, were based on associations that linked outstanding images in multi-sensory ways. The current World Grandmasters in Memory use identical systems. People will often recount that their first memories were of exactly this nature.

TONY'S FIRST MEMORY

My own first memories were at the end of 1944 and the beginning of 1945, during the closing stages of the Second World War, when I was between two and two-and-a-half years old. I remember vividly standing between the thick velvety curtains in our living room, sandwiched between their warmth and texture and the cold panes of glass that looked out on to our back garden.

Coming over the horizon, accompanied by an increasing rumbling roar that eventually shook the foundations on which I was standing, came a giant squadron of Royal Air Force bombers. To my young eye they looked mysterious, fantasmagoric and awesome.

Shortly after the flight of the bombers, my second and equally vivid memory was of the shrill and tantalizing whistle of a doodlebug, which thundered overhead and which, as was their wont, suddenly went silent before plummeting to earth, one knew not where.

After the mandatory few seconds of silence, the doodlebug struck earth some few hundred yards from our house. The impact sent tremors through the building, and the force of the explosion shattered the thick and corrugated glass of our front door. The glass had been bomb-blown into our front hall and now lay shimmering iridescently on the hallway floor. I remember looking with delight and enchantment at this shimmering cascade of reflected and refracted rainbows and beautifully clean-cut edges. I picked them up gently, as one would a delicate animal, already knowing at that early age that glass and sharp edges were dangerous. The texture of the glass, the beauty of the multi-coloured light, and the magic of the whole splintered fairyland are etched as vividly in my mind today as the reality was in my eyes at the time.

These first memories emphasize the significant role that association, Von Restorff, and the multiple senses play in the child's and all memories.

It is also interesting to note that very little fear was associated with either event, as the giant network of adult associations associated with pain, war and death were not yet known to me. It is very often an error of the adult to assume for the child networks of negative connotations and fear that she does not possess.

Repetition and Review

Your child learns by repetition, loves repetition and *needs* repetition. During the first three years of vocabulary, reading and language learning, these repetitions may need to number in the tens to hundreds.

When your child's memory is more matured, the principle of *five* well-spaced Von Restorff repetitions will be more than adequate to ensure that the memory transfers from short-term memory (STM) to long-term or life-time memory (LTM).

A general guideline here is to review shortly after the learning period or daily event has occurred; to review one day later; to review a third time one week later; to review a fourth time one month later and to review a fifth time three to six months later.

The reason why so many adults report that their memories are failing as they get older is not because the memory *per se* is failing; it is because none of the principles outlined above is being applied. If they were, memory would consistently improve with age.

With your child's memory you have the possibility, by appropriate nurturing, to make it mighty, and have it increase in power not only every year of your child's formative years, but also throughout her adult life.

THINGS FOR YOU TO DO

 Apply the Law of Association in all your child's learning, especially vocabulary and language learning, reading and general knowledge. You can prompt this learning by asking questions such as: 'What does that make you think of?' Try getting your child to draw a Mind Map of associations (see page 75).

brain child

Stimulate all your child's senses, thus ensuring that she has more memory 'grappling hooks' with which to capture the information swirling around her. It is well known that smells provide particularly strong grappling hooks. In adults a smell re-encountered even decades after the first time can immediately connect the person with the original association. Encourage your child to notice smells. For example, smell flowers when you are walking, sniff the salty sea breezes when you are on holiday and savour the smell of fresh bread when you are at the baker's. Decades later, one of these evocative smells will trigger a strong memory of that childhood day in your grown-up child and reconnect her with her past.

Provide regular new experiences throughout the child's life, thus guaranteeing a greater number of primacies, and therefore a greater number of memories. These can include new subjects, visiting new places, meeting new people, exploring new ideas, tasting new foods, and experimenting with different activities. Make sure that the recencies in your child's life are primarily positive, especially partings. If the partings are in any way unpleasant or negative, the recency effect will guarantee that for the duration of the time between the last meeting and the next, the dominant memories and emotions will be negative and stressful. If the partings are pleasant and uplifting, the dominant memories between parting and meeting again will be positive and child-enhancing.

As soon as your baby can pick up a pen, introduce her to Mind Mapping (see page 75). A Mind Map emphasizes association, location, and Von Restorff, and is a wonderful and playful way to introduce the child to the magic of her own mind and to the power of her memory. Help your child to come up with her own version. Supply a stack of recycled paper and a pack of coloured felt-tip pens and see what happens! Some suggested themes are: My Holiday; My Pet; My Family; My Life; My Friend; My Grandpa, etc. (See the Mind Maps called My Friend Sally and This is Me.)

Explore your own memories, especially the more outstanding ones, and check whether the memory principles in this chapter apply.

Apply them in future!

Make memory your hobby, and apply your findings to your child's ongoing learning; especially her school work — everyone concerned (you, her teacher, her) will be surprised and delighted at her progress.

Have regular reviews with your child. These can take the form, as many families encouragingly practice, of 'end-of-day reviews', in which each member of the family takes turns to relate the highlights and thoughts of the day. Photograph albums and videos are also excellent review tools — it is important to remember that these need to be reviewed on a regular basis in order to have the five-times repetition rule locked in.

Some families keep a special memory book for each child. This is an album containing photographs, certificates, memorabilia, cuttings, souvenirs, drawings — creating a life record of everything that the child has done.

Play memory games with your children, especially those in which you uncover 20 or 30 items, leave them exposed for a minute, and then cover them again, the task being to remember as many as possible, and, in the more sophisticated forms of the game, to remember also their location and relationship to each other. Other memory games to try are: My Aunt Went To Paris, in which each person memorizes a lengthening list of imaginary items that this lady bought in Paris; Pairs (also called Memory), in which a pack of cards is laid out face down and each player takes it in turn to temporarily turn over two cards at a time. The players have to memorize where the cards are and then find pairs, which they keep. The person with the most pairs wins. Invent memory games that involve numbers. For example, see who can remember the longest number/binary number. Alternatively, devise sensory memory games in which each of the different senses is emphasized (the smells of different flowers, the tastes of different foods, the sounds of different birds/animals/musical instruments, etc.).

Visit the website www.worldmemorychampionship.com, which posts the latest news flashes on memory, memory techniques developed by those involved in memory games and competitions, news of forthcoming competitions, and the latest world rankings.

TATIANA'S STORY

The value of such games is wonderfully illustrated by the story of Tatiana Cooley. On 5 February 1997, at 9.00 a.m., the first American Memory Championships were about to start. As Tony Dottino, the co-organizer of the event and I prepared to launch proceedings, a breathless and bright-eyed girl came panting to the door, and asked enthusiastically if she was still in time to enter. I asked her why she wanted to, and she replied with gusto: 'I couldn't think of anything I'd rather do than spend a Saturday in New York playing with my memory!'

She was in!

As the memory competition progressed, Tatiana gradually eased ahead of competitors who included IT (Information Technology) company executives, college professors, top college students, students of memory, national newspaper journalists, teachers and psychologists. As the competition progressed, Tatiana's performances improved, and in the end, having surmounted hurdles such as the memorization of numbers, giant shopping lists, complex poetry and decks of cards, Tatiana emerged as the first National US Memory Champion.

In an impassioned and moving Championship Speech, Tatiana explained how, as a little girl of less than three years old, she had 'fallen in love with memory'.

The reason for this blossoming love affair Tatiana attributed to her father. Tatiana's earliest memories of her childhood were of playing mental and physical games of all sorts, especially memory games. These included speed association games, memorization of 20 or more covered objects on a table, which were uncovered briefly, covered again, and then to be recalled, and many other memory games involving words, numbers, situations and stories.

Also, whenever they went anywhere together, which happily was quite frequently, Tatiana's father would say such things as 'Tatiana my love, can you see that train? How many carriages does it have?' And so saying he would point to an exceptionally long trans-national cargo train that had as many as 73 carriages. Little Tatiana would count them and triumphantly announce the accurate number.

Tatiana counts train carriages

brain child

Some one, two or three weeks later, at 'random' moments, her father would say 'Tatiana, do you remember when we went into the countryside a little while ago and saw that train? Can you remember how many carriages there were?' and increasingly, knowing that 'the game was on' Tatiana would come up with the correct answers.

By playing such games, Tatiana's father was not only improving her memory, he was making her more interested in the world around her, expanding and stretching her senses, and regularly encouraging the development of her majestic imagination. Play such games with your child.

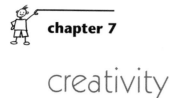

creativity

Connecione

Leonardo da Vinci, arguably the greatest creative genius of the last millennium, devised a number of principles by which he lived his life, and which were designed to develop a good mind. One of his prime principles was Connecione: the realization, while observing, studying or learning anything, that *'everything connects to everything else'*. In other words, there is an association, in some way, between any one thing and every *other* thing.

It is interesting to note here that in searching for brain-improvement principles, Leonardo had touched on the extreme similarity between memory and creativity. He had revealed, without commenting upon it, the fundamental theory on which memory systems are based. In so doing he had opened the way for the first proof that the capacities of the baby's and adult's brains are infinite.

The process of creativity: linking any item (a) with any item (b) to produce the new 'creation' (c) (apple + head = gravity; electricity + metal = light) is identical to the memory systems used by the Greeks, all mnemonists, all memory grandmasters and all memory champions. In these systems the memorizer has a long list of words, or map, or route locations with images placed on them. The new item to be memorized is simply associated with the existing pre-remembered image, and a new more multi-sensory and imagistic image is created, which, when triggered, gives immediate recall of the item to be remembered.

Everything connects to everything else

As the images selected by the memorizer to be permanent are obviously personal choice, and therefore 'random', and as that which is to be memorized could be *anything*, it becomes immediately apparent that the memory systems must be based on the underlying truth that, exactly as Leonardo discovered for Creative Thinking, 'everything must in some way connect to everything else'. For this to be the case in both memory and creativity, the organ that can operate this system effectively must itself be able to connect anything with anything else. How many 'things' are there that could be used as the permanent memory images? How many different 'things' are there which could be memorized? Obviously, the answer in both cases is infinite. And what is the organ that is required to perform this exercise involving an infinity of infinities? The Human Brain!

We thus have simple proof that your baby's brain is, from one perspective, an Infinitely Capable Association Machine; that its Memory and Creativity work in very similar ways, and that exercising one of these two giant mental skills will automatically exercise the other.

Two of the prime ingredients of creativity, and with which the baby is born as a birthright, are *imagination* and *association*. These fundamental tenets need to be nurtured throughout your Brain Child's formative years. Knowing of their existence and of their primary role in creativity sheds light on many commonly asked questions, as well as many perplexities that often accost the young parent's mind.

Creativity and IQ

These two crucial elements of the multiple intelligences (see page 21) are often confused with each other and sometimes, to the untrained mind, can be seen as opposite and antagonistic intelligences. They are, of course, not, and should be trained simultaneously and synergetically.

When IQ tests are administered to young children by untrained overseers, two of the prime strengths (and indeed requirements) of the creative thinker: *originality* (seeing things in ways that no one has seen them before) and *multiple perspectives* (seeing things from many different angles) can lead to the child being given lower marks than deserved.

Two examples will serve to illustrate:

In the first, a 10-year-old boy was given an IQ test in which there were many multiple choice questions, he being obliged to select the correct answer from a choice of four.

One of the questions had four consecutive cubes, in each of which was a different image, with its name underneath; in the first square was an image of the *sun*; in the second an image of the *moon*; in the third an image of the *earth*; and in the fourth an image of a *lemon*. The young boy was asked to select the 'odd one out'.

The expected and 'obvious' answer was number four, lemon.

The young boy immediately chose (and speed is another major factor in creative thinking) number three, the earth.

His IQ was 'marked down' because on this question, as with many others, he had failed to see the obvious and 'logical' answer. In fact many of his answers, as with this one, were so bizarre that the testers actually began to wonder whether he was suffering from some form of mental retardation.

As a result they brought him back to the clinic, and went through his answers one by one, asking him to explain why he had selected as he had. His responses were startling and, to many of the psychologist interrogators, humbling. On the question in question, when they asked him why he had selected 'earth' instead of 'lemon', he looked at them with amazement in his eyes, and responded with sympathy for their lack-of-perception in his voice: 'because it's the only blue one!'

His answer revealed a big knowledge of space, dimension and colour and an intellectual process that was far more complex and creative than the more simple solution for which his relatively uncreative thinking testers had been waiting. His brain was obviously thinking in new and creative ways, very similar to those recounted in the story of Calvin and Spaceman Spiff (see page 241).

The second test was similarly a multiple choice picture test, this time including colour, no defining key words, and being administered to a 10-year-old girl.

In the first square was a picture of a large pile of coal; in the second a yellow daffodil; in the third a shovel; and in the fourth an empty fire-place. As with the little boy, she was asked to select the 'odd one out' and to indicate which one it was by putting an 'X' through the image. She crossed out the picture of the 'coal'. Again, like the boy, her IQ was downgraded because she had missed the obvious logical answer: number two 'daffodil'.

When asked why she had answered certain questions in the way she did, she said, referring to this one: 'Oh, I thought the correct answer was supposed to be 'daffodil', but it was such a pretty picture I didn't want to spoil it.'

Her response was as beautiful as her thoughts, displayed a wonderful creative and spiritual intelligence, and was worthy of an upgrade in her IQ score.

The Dilemma of the Expensive Christmas Toy and the Cardboard Box

One of the infinite possibilities of a cardboard box

Another manifestation of the child's limitless creative abilities, and of our adult trained-away-from-the-child-thinking occurs regularly at birthdays and other present-giving times.

Loving parents and relatives often go to extreme trouble (not to mention expense) to find the latest new toy that has bright colours and a number of working parts. What causes adult confusion is the fact that the child will, with all his senses, devour the toy in a few minutes, and then discard it. For the next hour, day and often week, the child will then play with the box!

Why?

brain child

The answer becomes blazingly obvious when we consider the Einsteinian curiosity of your brain-child's brain (see page 3) and its requirement for infinite creative thinking possibilities.

The beautifully coloured toy often has a rigid structure, only a few working parts, and often only one or two functions or uses. It may be battery-operated and just be for looking at. Time for the young super-scientist's brain to check, absorb and spit out? No time at all ...

But what about that box?! Just think of the possibilities for the child's creative imagination: it could be a boat; a car; a spaceship; the entrance to a giant cave; a sled; a hideaway; a house; and so on ad infinitum, each one of the possibilities itself opening up the possibilities for infinite adventures of the imagination. Adventures on which can be met those wonderful Fantasy Friends (see page 66). Also infinite opportunities for that necessary solitude and isolation which only the untrammelled imagination can provide. Throughout the modern world there is a great cry for more people to be thinking 'outside the box'; to think of ideas beyond the norm. Your child will help you realize that it is just as easy to think 'outside the box' *inside* the box.

TUBE TRAIN EINSTEIN

One day I was travelling by tube. I had been making the same journey for a number of months, knew the time it took, and had established a reading/working/resting/people-watching routine.

On this particular day I was sitting behind a mother and her very young daughter. Half way through the journey I noticed, with some alarm, that the train seemed to be travelling faster than usual, and seemed still to be accelerating. I rapidly went into panic-thought mode, envisioning us hurtling increasingly faster out of control towards a demolition destination.

As my mind was being gripped by a rising fear, the little girl in front of me, who had obviously become aware also of the train's speed, turned to her mother, and grabbing excitedly on her sleeve said: 'Mummy, wouldn't it be amazing if this train could keep going faster, until it was going so fast it could take us into the next day, because then when we got home we could tell Daddy what was going to happen tomorrow!'

The mother's reaction was to turn around and shout: 'Don't you ever say stupid, crazy things like that to me again! Now be quiet, sit still, and speak to me only when you have something important to say.'

The little girl retreated into her shell, the genius who had already, before her first days at junior school, launched her imagination into those wonderful realms that had so intrigued all the great physicists of the nineteenth and twentieth centuries. Had she been encouraged appropriately, I am sure we would have seen her as one of the Nobel Prize winners in the early part of this century.

THINGS FOR YOU TO DO

Realize that at the beginning of his life your baby will have fewer bits of information than an adult in his Giant Association Machine. As a result he will need to make associations that are 'informationally further apart', and will often therefore come up with ideas that will astonish adults with their originality. Encourage and reward your child for such insights.

When observing and judging your Brain Child's behaviour, always bear in mind the blue planet and the yellow daffodil, and investigate the process rather than the result. If we adults had been practising this for a few thousand years, we would already be in possession of insights and awarenesses that it will probably take us the rest of the twenty-first century to come to.

brain child

Provide your child with toys that stimulate, expand and encourage the development of his imagination, rather than toys that bore and restrict. Look around your home for playthings — there's no need to spend a lot of money on toys (see the Mind Map called Your Child's Creative Environment). Used yoghurt pots, egg cartons, washing-up bottles, measuring jugs, and a plethora of other kitchen items can be used in the child's imaginative play. There is no need to make suggestions, just provide the raw materials and let the child use his imagination. Older children like to be provided with paste, scrap paper, brushes, etc. so that they can make more creative projects. A large collection of cardboard loo rolls and clingfilm rolls can be taped together to make an exciting marble run, for example.

Play association games with your child. From quite an early age, your child will delight in 'silly word associations' and this will develop his sense of humour, too. Word jokes and puns are a special delight for the young child, because they trigger original and startlingly new image connections in the brain that spontaneously produce a smile or a laugh. Word-plays that appeal to the senses and anything remotely 'rude' are among the favourites! I knew one little girl, for example, who always loved it when adults, in any context, said the word 'bottom', because for her it had only one humorous, very visual, and 'naughty' association.

Read the Chapter on Synergy (see page 99), and apply it to developing your child's positively synergetic imagination.

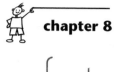

chapter 8

fantasy friends

―――――――――――――――――――――― ☆ ――――――――――――――

The question of fantasy friends is another one of those areas that, like nature-nurture and IQ versus creativity, has generated a lot of heated and often unnecessary debate.

―――――――――――――――――――――― ☆ ――――――――――――――

Every brain is born to fantasize, as the marketing, sales, sex and fashion industries know full well. Your child's brain, in its still relatively pure state, is able to fantasize in an incredibly vivid manner, similar to that idealized by the great creative artists, and typifying a 'state of innocence' to which they all say they try to return.

In your child's brain, the 'production' of fantasy friends is a process identical to that used by the great writers of fairy tales such as Lewis Carroll and Antoine de Saint Exupery, the great writers of the great novels including Dickens and Dostoyevsky, and the producers and creators of the immortal films and videos quintessentially epitomized by Walt Disney and his 'fantasy friends' Mickey Mouse, Bambi, Donald Duck and Hiawatha; and Brain of the Year Gene Roddenberry, the creator of *Star Trek* and his fantasy friends Captain Kirk, Uhuru, Mr Spock, the Borg, Scottie, Jean-Luc Picard, Whorf, Data, 7 of 9, Jakote, etc. These latter have become the 'fantasy friends' of tens of millions of adults, many of whom live their lives mimicking fantasies of these characters under the clan name 'Trekkies'.

Fantasy friends have the following advantages:

1. They exercise the multiple dimensions of your child's imagination.
2. They provide your child with virtual characters who can act out variations on real life situations the child is 'trying to figure out'.
3. They act as companions with whom the child can discuss intimacies.
4. Fantasy characters, like pets, 'always understand'.
5. Fantasy friends provide real, not just imagined, companionship. Research has shown that the brain reacts identically, on all levels including molecular/muscular, to a real image perceived by the eye in the external world, as to an internal image perceived by the imagination.
6. They train your child happily to be alone with her thoughts, simultaneously developing creative intelligence, intra-personal intelligence, and inter-personal intelligence.
7. They boost confidence, as good friends always do.

THINGS FOR YOU TO DO

Welcome the fantasy friends to your family circle, even going so far as to set places, where appropriate, at the dining table. If you have older children who are likely to ridicule the child and her fantasy friend, take them on one side and try to get them to hold back by reminding them that they probably once had one too when they were younger. Alternatively, get them to join in the fantasy too. The same applies to the Tooth Fairy and Father Christmas.

When your child, directly or indirectly, introduces you to her fantasy friends, ask positive and probing questions such as 'and does your friend have brothers or sisters or other friends or pets?' Such questions will often reveal a treasure-trove of additional fantasy characters. In instances where such characters do not exist, the child will often spontaneously generate them with a speed and originality for which many best-selling authors would trade fortunes! This gives you another wonderful opportunity to record/transcribe your child's genius, while at the same time teaching and encouraging her to become, in the most natural way imaginable, a writer and story-teller. Many of the immortal fairytales, including Alice in Wonderland and The Wind in the Willows, were the result of family story-telling.

Realize that Shakespeare's statement 'all the world's a stage' applies even more significantly to the internal world of your child's imagination. Let your child be protector, producer, director, actor and audience.

Realize that most of the great fairy-stories for children were written by mothers and fathers, uncles and aunts, and family relations and friends; tap this limitless vein of creative wealth and create a Family Fairy-Tale Group.

This is an easy and delightful thing for you to do, and is best done in the following way:

Create a family ritual of telling group fairy-stories. A good way to do this is for one person to start a fantastical tale, speaking for a maximum of a couple of minutes, and leaving the tale suspended at some high point of drama such as a fantasmagoric space creature zooming out of the sky 'and then ...'

At the 'and then ...' it is the next person's turn, whether that be mother, father or sibling, to carry on the story in as an imaginative way as possible.

While this process is continuing, a tape-recorder should be recording the entire procedure and narrative.

When the story is complete, it should be transcribed and edited by the whole group.

When the editing is complete, the revised transcription should be transferred to the 'Fairy-Tale Book' using large print, and containing ideally no more than three sentences per page.

Opposite each page should be an image/illustration of a character, scene, impression or emotion, drawn by one or more members of the family. Each member of the family should have an equal number of illustrations in the finished product. The book should be completed, bound, dated and numbered, and included in the child's library.

Mind Maps are an ideal tool for overviewing the entire story: all characters, settings, plots and themes. For example, see The Hat Adventure Mind Map. In this story there are six chapters. In Chapter 1, Mrs Montgomery buys the hat in a posh shop, wears it at the races and then leaves it on a train. It eventually finds its way to the Lost Property Department. In Chapter 2, Miss Matilda buys the hat from a charity shop (it was unclaimed from Lost Property), decorates it with beautiful flowers and wears it to her best friend's wedding. Unfortunately she leaves it behind and someone gives it to a little girl called Susie. In Chapter 3, Susie keeps it in her dressing-up box and then decorates it to wear in the school play. It gets left in the playground and the school caretaker gives it to Miss Batty. In Chapter 4, Miss Batty sticks a couple of blue feathers on to it and wears it as a special gardening hat. It gets left out in the rain and in Chapter 5, old Fred finds it. He adopts it and wears it every day. It is hung on a peg and gets sat on by the cat. Eventually it gets thrown out. In Chapter 6, some tramps find it and it is worn by Tom at a tramps' party, where it is much admired by all.

The book can be read as part of those 'Special Treat Books' which are read repeatedly. When reading, the parents should point to each word with a finger, thus encouraging the child to recognize words with which she is already familiar, and thus helping her naturally to learn to read. The parents should also encourage the child to 'read along' as they read out loud.

The parent should regularly compliment the child on her own involvement in the creation of the book, thus introducing the child seamlessly to the fact that she is a creator, an artist, and a writer – not just any old writer, but a writer of books! By the time the child is seven years old, she can easily be the author and co-author of 10 or more books. Imagine the ease with which she will transfer these skills to writing the short essays required in school.

Next, when the time is ripe, explain to the child that the external and internal Universes are, to the brain, of equal weight, and that the creative geniuses have been able to perceive each with identical clarity, and to draw from each with equal reward.

As your child is learning to balance her brain, to balance her multiple intelligences, and to enhance her ambidexterity, so she should learn to balance the time put into and rewards drawn from these parallel Universes.

brain foods

---- ☆ ----

When we think of food, we traditionally think only of standard nutrition. Good standard nutrition (see page 316) is, though, only one of four necessary brain foods. Each of these brain foods is equally important, and is totally necessary for your baby to survive; without any one of them he will die. They are Oxygen, Nutrition, Love, and Information (ONLI):

---- ☆ ----

OXYGEN

Make sure that your child gets as much exercise and as much good oxygen as possible throughout his embryo stage and his early years (and make sure you do too!). Oxygen is a vital and energizing fuel and the more aerobically fit both mother and child are the more the brain will be fed with 'high octane' nourishment. Think of your child's brain as a super-formula-one racing car. Your baby's blood is the petrol. If you or your child are aerobically unfit, your super-formula-one brains are receiving, *every second of your life*, a weak burst of low-grade petrol. If, on the other hand, you are both aerobically fit, your super-formula-one brains will receive, again for every second of your life, a large burst of the highest-grade fuel. Your baby and you *need*, if your brains are going to operate at their highest capacity, the best supply of oxygen possible.

NUTRITION

You and your baby's million million brain cells require a large part of their energy and physical robustness from liquids and foods you drink and eat. It is essential, therefore, that, as with oxygen, you supply your million million brain cells with the best possible energy and body-building nutrition. Make sure that your diet is varied, fresh, and contains all the vitamins, minerals, proteins, carbohydrates and fats you need (for more information see page 316).

LOVE

Happily the Universe has designed you and your baby's brains to survive and thrive on love! Love is therefore not just a 'nice' thing; it is utterly necessary for survival. Studies have shown that without it we die. The brain feeds on love as a bee suckles on honey. It can take a limitless supply. Offer it!

Love is one of the four 'foods' your baby's brain needs if he is to survive. And here we are talking not only about personality and emotional development but about the very growth of the architecture of the brain itself (see Brain Development, page 11). A tale of two baby monkeys will illustrate …

The Tale of Two Baby Monkeys

When Jeepers was born in a zoo, his mother paid him the normal monkey mum's attention, carrying him everywhere clinging to her, grooming him, 'clipping him one' when he was a nuisance, chattering at him and with him and suckling him whenever he wanted a meal. They lived in a community cage with other monkeys, and soon Jeepers was scampering around happily with the other baby monkeys.

Creepers wasn't so lucky. His mother died soon after he was born and Creepers was left in a cage in which there were only older male monkeys. The keepers fed him at regular intervals, but there was no other monkey to cuddle him, chatter to him, groom him and care for him. He would sit alone all day, relatively still and silent, looking miserable.

About a year after his birth, an infection swept through the zoo and sadly both Jeepers and Creepers died. A psychologist interested in monkey behaviour did autopsies on both monkeys' brains. He found to his amazement that Jeepers had a well-developed mental nervous system, much like an oak tree — millions of branches intricately interconnecting. Creeper's mental nervous system, on the other hand, looked like a withered tree. It had simply not developed.

Love allows the brain and the body systems to open out, to function well, to receive, to explore, and to develop.

INFORMATION

Information is a Brain Food. Your baby's brain will actually grow more interconnections and become more complex the more appropriately stimulating the environment is. Nature is one of the best sources of information, so the more time with this other 'mother' the better for your baby. Child-friendly museums, exhibitions and galleries are also superb Brain Foods. Other major sources of information are your answers to your child's questions and your provision of an environment that is rich in knowledge from all fields of human endeavour and exploration. You can now see, from your child's physical brain-patterning needs, why it is so important to have dendrite-stimulating books, videos and electronic media as part of your child's room, study and general environment (see Paradise and Curiosity, pages 159 and 221).

An excellent way to remember the four essential brain foods is the acronym/mnemonic ONLI. You only (onli!) need these four brain foods in order to develop a fully functioning and healthy brain for your child.

THINGS FOR YOU TO DO

Apply all of the recommendations in this chapter and love your baby with all your body, all your heart, all your mind and all your soul.

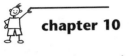

chapter 10

Mind Mapping®

The Mind Map is the natural expression of the way your baby's, and indeed the human brain, works. The Mind Map is, literally, a 'Map of the Mind', which utilizes the main elements of:

Memory
Association
Location
Outstanding – Von Restorff
and which marshalls all the skills of the left and right cortex.

The Mind Map also allows and encourages the accelerating flow of creative and innovative thoughts based on the multi-ordinant nature of words and reality (see also Radiant Thinking, page 123), and therefore allows your child's brain to express in a simple yet intricate manner the infinite expression and expansion of her own individuality.

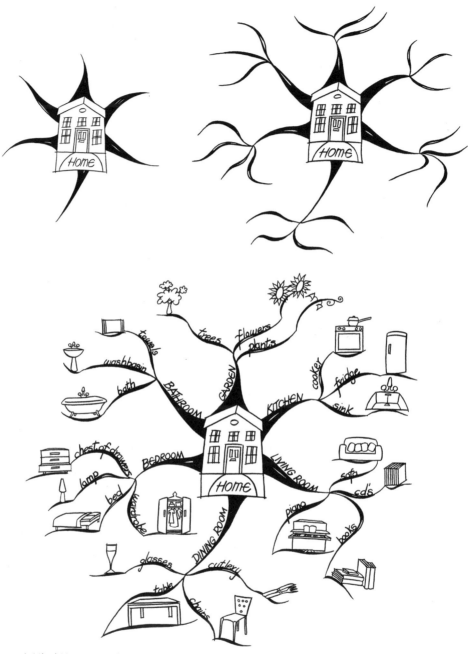

A Mind Map expands and branches out as it is formulated

brain child

Similar to a road map, a Mind Map will:

1.   Give an overview of a large subject/area.
2.   Enable you to plan routes/make choices and let you know where you are going and where you have been.
3.   Gather and hold large amounts of data.
4.   Encourage problem-solving by seeing new creative pathways.
5.   Enable you to be extremely efficient.
6.   Be enjoyable to look at, read, muse over and remember.
7.   Attract and hold your child's eye/brain.

Mind Map Guidelines

1.   Take an A4-sized sheet of blank, unlined paper and turn it sideways-on (landscape). Draw a picture of your main topic in the centre. Try using at least three colours and draw in a thoughtful, enjoyable fashion — to get your brain working. If you are Mind Mapping your home, for example, you might draw a picture of a house.
2.   Draw some thick, curved, connected lines branching out from your central image. Allocate one for each of the main ideas you have for your main subject. For example, if you are Mind Mapping your home, each branch might represent a room or a theme. Choose a different colour for each line. Use a different colour for each main idea and use a range of felt-tip pens, from thick highlighters to fine-tipped varieties.
3.   Write the key words, one per branch, (for example, Kitchen, Bathroom, Bedroom, Living room, etc), using matching colours. The branches can start out thick and become thinner as they radiate outwards. These branches are your main sub-topics.

4. Next, draw more little branches radiating out from these main ones. For example, from Kitchen you might have the following branches: cooker, fridge, dishwasher, cupboards, sink, table, chairs, etc. Add branches to the branches, like a real tree, but make sure that they are all connected.

5. You can now branch out further if you want to, making the writing smaller each time. You could establish a hierarchy of lettering styles — capital letters for the main ideas, underlined lower case for the next most important ideas and small letters for the third category.

6. Draw pictures where necessary to imprint your thoughts and help you think. This also uses both sides of your brain.

At this juncture, you may be thinking that this is a bit advanced for your baby/child's brain. Nothing could be further from the truth. Because the Mind Map *reflects* the internal functioning of your Brain Child's brain, it is far easier for a very young child to understand a Mind Map than any other form of noted information.

A charming story (with a sting in the tail!) will illustrate.

THE IT MANAGER'S STORY

In Colorado, a young computer engineer, Brent, was the proud father of a three-year-old girl who, apart from one continuing and notable exception, 'was his little angel'. The singular exception had been triggered by Brent's very compassionate approach to marriage and child-rearing. He had proposed to his wife, who also worked, that they would each come home early on alternate nights, and would individually spend extra time with Christina while also, where possible, helping out with family and housekeeping tasks.

Brent had ended up with early Tuesdays, which coincided with the day when shopping needed to be done. He felt that this would be a good opportunity to spend co-operative and functional time with Christina, as she could help him do the shopping.

However, Christina decided that she did not like shopping, and did not want to accompany her father on the trips. This was obviously not possible.

As a result every Tuesday, Brent had to haul a screaming little banshee around the supermarket, cringing from the stern and disapproving stares of other shoppers, who probably assumed that he was an uncaring, vicious and brutal example of how not to be a parent!

This mini horror-story went on for a number of weeks, Christina demonstrating her powers of persistence in sticking to her attitude and opinions.

On the next Tuesday, Brent, in one of his breaks, was musing on what to do about this increasingly untenable situation. Running through the considerable shopping list that he had to buy that evening, he decided to convert it into a Mind Map, festooning it with images of the foods and products to be bought. As he developed the Mind Map, the idea formed in his mind that it would be a wonderful gift for Christina, and that it might in some way entice her to consider shopping in a slightly more positive light.

Little did Brent realize the magnitude and implications of what he had just done.

That evening he took Christina, once again howling, to the entrance of the hyper-market, and there handed her the multi-coloured, illustrated Mind Map (see the Mind Map called Christina's Shopping List).

Brent thought that Christina would simply like it as a colourful object.

He had underestimated Christina!

She surveyed the map intensely, and then, holding it in front of her like a steering wheel, pointed to the drawing of carrots and looked at her father imperiously while stating: 'Carrots!' Then, like a little guided missile, she directed Brent through the mazes of the market to precisely where the carrots were. As soon as the carrots were selected, weighed, placed in the bag and put in the trolley, Christina pointed to the drawing of potatoes and, in the same manner, proclaimed: 'Potatoes!' Once again she led her father directly to where the potatoes were on display. This procedure continued for half an hour, with

Christina pointing eventually to every object on the Mind Map, and leading Brent upstairs, downstairs and throughout the entire complex of the shopping centre with unerring precision and accuracy. He reported that he was amazed by her performance, not only for her instantaneous ability to recognize and name every item on the Shopping Mind Map, but also by the revelation of the fact of which he had been completely unaware: Christina's three-year-old brain, despite her dislike of shopping, had totally memorized the architecture, structure, design and location of hundreds of different objects in the hypermarket.

Brent reported that in subsequent weeks Christina could not wait for Tuesdays and 'shopping!' with a different Mind Map each week as both her guide and confirmation of her own genius.

The 'sting in the tail' mentioned at the beginning of this story refers to the fact that as the weeks progressed, Christina became more and more enamoured of shopping. It became such a passion for her because of the way in which the Mind Map had released her intelligence and allowed her to display her memory, knowledge and skills, that whenever her parents asked her what she would like to do, the only answer she ever gave was: 'Shopping!'

The reason why the Mind Map *is* so effective for young children is that it allows their brains to see known images ('a picture is worth a thousand words') and their associations and interrelationships without the 'interference' of grammar and semantics. The Mind Map immediately gives the child the 'whole picture', while allowing her simultaneously to cluster those items that are more closely connected to each other.

The Mind Map has been called 'the Swiss army knife for the brain', and for the young child is a wonderful tool to allow her to 'open up' and explore the realms of memory, learning, creative thinking, analysis, preparation for school work, review and self-expression.

THINGS FOR YOU TO DO

Mind Map in your Brain Child's presence, so that she can become accustomed to and able to mimic Mind Maps and the Mind Mapping process. Start off with simple subjects, such as planning an outing or a party.

Make sure you have a plentiful supply of Mind Mapping materials.

Use Mind Maps to summarize any subjects your child is interested in or is formally learning. This can include information that is fun to organize such as 'My Pet', or that needs thinking out such as planning a school project on 'The Norman Conquest'.

Use Mind Maps to help your child discover a reflected sense of her being. This being is magnificent, artistic, colourful, connected, integrated and whole. Making a Mind Map of her Self will help this process.

Copy Brent's shopping style and make shopping trips a Mind Mapping Adventure that everyone can enjoy and from which everyone can learn.

Use Mind Maps to summarize and illustrate the family's storybooks.

As your child grows, keep a developing Master Mind Map of herself. Place an image of the child in the centre of the Mind Map, and have major and growing branches that you can add to for: Interests; Hobbies; Friends; Stages of Growth; Accomplishments; Family; School; and Thoughts.

part two

uniqueness

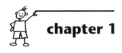

chapter 1

uniqueness — physical

---☆---

Since the beginning of time there have been an estimated seventy thousand million (70,000,000,000) human beings on earth, each one astoundingly different from all the others. There will never be anyone like your baby. He is now at the head of Nature's thrust of evolution towards greater intelligence, exploration of knowledge, accomplishment and understanding.

---☆---

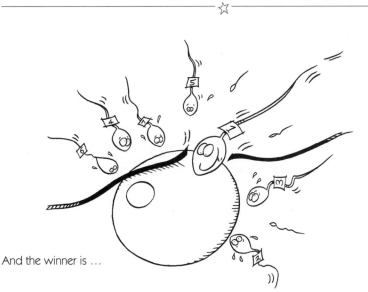

And the winner is ...

☆

Your baby is, physically, astoundingly unique. With the fantastic mathematical permutations and combinations available because of the genetic variations contained within each father's sperm and mother's egg, it is possible, with the current human race, to create more than three hundred thousand million million million (300,000,000,000,000,000,000,000) babies, each of which is physically unique and easily distinguishable from every other one.

If we take the current population of our own planet, which is six thousand million (6,000,000,000) unique individuals, the possible number of unique human individuals would be fifty million million (50,000,000,000,000) planets-worth of individuals all like ours, with no two individuals the same.

☆

Your baby is one in infinity; one in eternity.

THINGS FOR YOU TO DO

Treasure your unique jewel.

Frequently point out your child's uniqueness to him, in a positive way. For example, 'I've never known anyone else with your ...'

Explain, with illustrations, about the uniqueness of fingerprints, eye pupils, faces, DNA and thoughts, etc.

Ask your child to point out the uniqueness he sees in you, members of your family, friends and your pets.

brain child

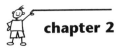

chapter 2

uniqueness — mental

---☆---

'We can't understand it. We gave our two children the same upbringing. We gave them the same basic diet. We gave them the same education. We sent them both to the same school, where they had the same teachers and studied the same subjects. We listened to the same music. We played with them the same games. We took them to the same church, where they were taught the same religion. We taught them the same values and gave them the same idea of what were the proper social behaviours. We treated them equally and loved them equally.'

'And yet they are SO different!'

---☆---

How many times have you heard parents exclaim, in wailing tones, the above dirge (have you ever done it yourself?).

The reason why we have for so long been confused by this apparently nonsensical and certainly counter-intuitive result of our teaching, nurturing and parenting is that we have been looking from the outside-in with gross perceptions and assumptions, rather than from the inside-out with the minute microscopic eye that clarifies perception.

Consider the *real* situation; what *really* happens in the child's developing Universe.

THE LITTLE SISTER'S AND LITTLER BROTHER'S STORY

Let us take an imaginary nuclear family consisting of a mother, a father, a seven-year-old girl and her five-year-old brother. Let us look at it first from the little girl's point of view.

At every family breakfast, lunch and dinner where the four of them sit down to dine together, she is the only one who, throughout the tens of thousands of meals they will have together, will never see her own face, seeing only the faces of the other three. To measure the significance of this, consider how important the faces and the expressions of those with whom you have been are to your memory of the times you spent with them.

In addition, she is the only one who is a little female sitting at a table with a large female, a large male and a considerably smaller male.

She is the only one who goes to school feeling the emotions she feels and thinking the thoughts she thinks, and is the only one who sits in whatever seat she sits in, in whatever class she attends, seeing that class only from that seat's perspective. Think of the difference that sitting at the front, back, sides or middle of a class or lecture room makes to your memory of that class.

'How can our children be so different?!'

brain child

She is the only one who has the special relationship she has with her teachers, and is the only one who feels the way she feels about the different subjects she is learning. She is also the only one who has the friends she has and who relates to them in the very special and private ways in which friends relate.

She is the only one who has the fantasy friends that only she in the Universe could create, and she is the only one who has the dreams, fantasies, fears and hopes that only she will ever have.

The Universe is bombarding her eyes with a million million unique photon video packages per second; her ears with million-molecule percussion messages; her nose with a million-faceted palette of aromas and smells; and her skin with a never-ending symphony of atomic information. Only she will ever sense these magical particular messages from the cosmos.

Every micro-second of every day sees her as the only one at whatever point in the Universe she is currently inhabiting, seeing and reacting to the kaleidoscopic uniqueness of possibilities for interpretation and reaction that her unique and constantly varyingly being gives her the privilege of experiencing. She is infinitely different from anyone who has lived, is living or who will ever live. She is also, in a very big sense of the word, Alone.

Consider now the little boy.

At the thousands upon thousands of meals that he will share with his family, he is a little male sitting at a table with a giant male, a giant female and another larger female. He, like his sister, is the only one who will see only the faces of the other three members of the family, never his own.

He is the only one who will interpret the things said to him in the way that only he can interpret them, and he is the only one who will go to the 'same school' as his sister and will experience it as not the same at all.

He will sit in his classes in his special seat seeing everything from his unique physical and mental perspective. He will experience the 'same teachers' who will not be the same teachers at all. The male teachers will be the same sex as him, the female teachers the opposite sex. The 'same teachers' will be different. They will be two years older. Those 'same teachers' will relate to him in ways very different from the ways in which they related to his sister. He will be the only one who had his sister attend the 'same school' before him, leaving her trail of memories and influences that will affect him in myriad subtle and unique ways. He will be the only one with his friends and the only one who throughout his entire school year will never see his face or his body in any of the interactions or games with which he is involved.

His senses gambolling with the Universe will, like his sister's, take place in the playground that only he will ever know as he knows it.

He, like his sister, would be the only one with his dreams, his fears, his passions, his loves and his hopes. He will spend his early life, and indeed his entire life, being the only intrepid explorer of the Universe as seen from the second-by-second kaleidoscoping viewpoints that make up his special being.

There is not one micro-second in one day, week, month or year of his life in which he sees anything from the same perspective as his sister or anyone else.

He is utterly, fantastically, infinitely and preciously unique. And Alone.

THINGS FOR YOU TO DO

Be concerned only if your children are not different! Differences may be harder to take on board if the children bear a strong physical resemblance to one another. You may have a deep-seated expectation that they are similar mentally as well as physically. They will never be.

Nurture, treasure, cherish and honour your child's growing individuality and differentiation from all others. Emphasize the differences between your children, point out how much they see things from different perspectives and celebrate those differences. Doing Mind Maps will emphasize differences and similarities. For example, if two children each does a Mind Map about Cats, when they compare their results, they will find both differences and similarities. Notice how each child has a particular 'take' on the subject. Encourage children to see things from another person's point of view and notice how you are also seeing your own viewpoint too.

See also Mind Mapping, page 75, Creativity, page 58, Radiant Thinking, page 125 and Part V — The Senses, page 191.

brain principles

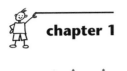

chapter 1

mimicry

☆

The brain is designed to learn by copying. This is true both for all humans and all other forms of animal life.

☆

In the last century of the second millennium, the human race made the tremendous blunder of thinking that copying was cheating and that cheating was wrong. This was especially true in Western countries, when hundreds of millions of just-flowering minds were crushed in their pursuits of knowledge and creativity by having their main learning tool, mimicry, ripped from them.

This is especially true in music (see an extensive discussion of this point on page 248) and art.

Recent field surveys I have conducted show that by the age of fifteen, 95 per cent of all children believe that they both cannot sing well and that they have a fundamental genetic incapacity to draw and sculpt. These conceptions are manifestly untrue as the extended discussions in Part VI, Chapter 5 on Art, page 244 and Chapter 6 on Music, page 248 well document.

Realizing this natural tendency of the brain to mimic can add considerable depth of understanding and meaning to the parent/child relationship.

Parents will notice that the baby/child is by far the greatest 'copying machine' ever invented, putting to shame our greatest mechanical duplicators. Your children will copy *everything*, including language, gestures, older sisters and brothers, animals, the noises of machines, all sounds of nature, friends, teachers, and most importantly *You*! This they will do utterly objectively, and with dazzling precision and accuracy, even when it involves words and expressions that lead parents to exclaim 'but we *never* say *that*!'

When the child grows into the pre-teen and teen years, once again understanding of the mimicking principle can allay many worries and fears. Parents often become overly concerned about the heroes and heroines their young children are choosing, especially rock and pop stars, because of what appears a valid worry over the association with 'sex, drugs and rock 'n roll', which seem to have negative connotations.

The 'copying' process

brain child

It is important first, however, to question what the child is *actually* mimicking. A closer analysis will probably reveal that it is not the drugs at all but it is the fact that the heroes/heroines are many of the things to which the child aspires: stars; famous; sexy and sexual icons; rich; world travelled; talented (many of them *are*); leaders. Beethoven, Mario Lanza, Frank Sinatra and The Beatles were all 'rock stars' in their day!

These are all desirable qualities, and can be encouraged in the child by understanding and supporting the *positive* aspects of those he mimics.

THINGS FOR YOU TO DO

Encourage your child's mimicking abilities in as wide a range of activities as possible. Girls will tend to mimic their mother's activities while boys will tend to mimic their father's. Hence, if the mother is the one who does most of the cooking, the daughter will stand by her mother in the kitchen copying her technique with a wooden spoon and mixing bowl. If you want to avoid sex-role stereotyping in your child it is important to share roles with your partner so that your child sees you both carrying out the broadest possible spectrum of activities (both mums and dads can mend cars as well as make cakes).

Mimic your child! Just for fun — try copying what your child is doing. For example, if he is lying on the floor making a complicated layout of bricks, cars and Lego pieces, lie on the floor too and join in. He will feel that you are literally communicating on his level and may even feel flattered that you want to learn about what he is doing. When the child is experimenting with his super-operatic-potential-voice, try to sing along and push the boundaries even further than your child. If you do this, he will not only mimic you, he will immediately join in the game, repeating exactly what you have done and then adding to that. Similarly, with dance and body movements, your child will take you through a post-graduate aerobic and yogic flexibility training session of the most supreme quality!

 Allow your child to benchmark (copy from the best) with abandon. This comes in handy when your school-age child needs to do a project. For example, if it is a historical project and he needs to find a picture of one of the kings or queens of the past, find a reproduction of a painting in a reference book and suggest he copies it. Don't do what so many do — download images from the Internet.

 Explain to your child (and copying can be done at a very early age) that copying is one of the best ways to learn, and that it's always good to copy the best and then to add your own interpretations. Reiterate that there is nothing to be ashamed of in copying. The only 'bad' sort of copying is when you sneak a look at someone else's answers in a test instead of relying on your own learning, memory and resources (rely on your own brain!).

 Demonstrate such behaviour yourself. In helping your child learn all the skills he can, use the Mimicking Brain Principle as a major learning tool.

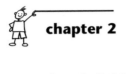

chapter 2

synergy

---☆---

One of the most encouraging pieces of news from the current explosion of new information about your baby's brain, is that it is not, as was previously thought, arithmetic in its prime functions. In other words, your baby's brain does not simply think in an additive fashion, ploddingly adding just one thing to another and then one other thing to that sum.

---☆---

Your baby's brain is SYNERGETIC. In a synergetic system one plus one equals two plus $(1 + 1 = 2+)$. In such a system the '2+' can equal 3; 5,224; multiple millions or infinity.

A very good way to grasp this concept is to think about the common and very necessary habit of daydreaming. In daydreaming you take 'one', yourself, and add 'one', another person. With that simple one-plus-one combination, your synergetic brain can fantasize all day and all night, all week, all month, all year, and in some cases for a lifetime, creating the most fantastic Shakespearean love stories, tragedies, and comedies.

The synergetic principle of brain functioning is further confirmation of the brain-cell findings that your baby's brain has an infinite thinking potential.

And the news gets even better. The synergy principle suggests that your baby can go on building positively synergetic spirals of thinking and learning throughout her life, and that memory and creativity will similarly continue to grow and flourish.

This contradicts the centuries-long previous belief that both these skill areas diminished through life. How often have you heard people say things such as 'I'm not going to learn anything new for the moment, because my memory's full up, and I'm saving the precious few remaining spaces for the really important things!'. Or others explaining that creativity is like a giant but limited container from which you take until it is empty.

Such positions also held that as time goes on all mental functions become gradually more difficult, and slow, virtually stopping in middle and old age.

The Synergetic Principle puts an end to all this unfortunate rubbish, and gives rise to a new Mental Formula:

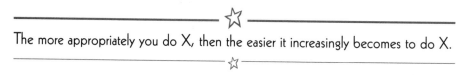

The more appropriately you do X, then the easier it increasingly becomes to do X.

In this formula X equals any major mental skill. Thus: 'the more appropriately you create, the more easy creativity becomes' and 'the more appropriately you remember, the more easy memorizing becomes'.

The Synergetic Principle also demonstrates that as the child builds her own synergetic thinking structures, she will become increasingly unique, designing giant Universes of thought that will be like no other child that has ever lived, is living or will ever live.

There is, however, a downside to the Synergetic Principle, and this can be discovered by looking at the standard computer-company acronym: GIGO – 'Garbage In Garbage Out'.

This was thought to be true for the human brain, but it is not. The situation is even *worse*. For with the human brain the acronym has to be adjusted to: GIGG – Garbage In Garbage GROWS. Misinformation or inappropriate data finds a nice little nesting place in the brain and multiply. In a synergetic system what is the potential for this multiplication? INFINITE!

(See Uniqueness, page 83)

Thus as well as being infinitely creative, your baby's brain has the potential for being, similarly, infinitely destructive.

The good news in this bad news in the general good news is that your baby's brain is not *designed* to be self-destructive. It only becomes so in one situation, and that situation has three necessary conditions for it to trigger:

1. Your child's brain has to have been given the wrong formula.
2. Your child has to believe in that incorrect formula.
3. Your child has to act on that incorrect formula.
   (See the Synergetic Learning Spirals Mind Map.)

A simple illustration of this principle is as follows: imagine a muscularly strong, very flexible and extremely aerobically fit, athlete who gets stuck in a quicksand or swamp. Imagine also that the athlete believes that the best way to get out is to put massive effort into the struggle to extract herself.

What will happen?

She will sink!

And how?

Fast!

The irony here is that the stronger, fitter, more flexible, more intelligent, more creative, more dedicated, more passionate and focused that individual is, the faster she will go down, because she is putting all that power and energy into exactly the wrong process, and therefore producing exactly the opposite result to that desired. Many of the great failures and tragedies in life come not from lack of effort but from extraordinary effort innocently directed in ways that are exactly opposite to the brain's intended function; in other words to the hyper-enthusiastic application of the incorrect formula.

From this you can see that it is essential that throughout its early stages, your baby's/child's brain is fed with Correct Formula Food, Correct Mental Formula Food!

Brain Child is designed to provide you with those correct formulae.

THINGS FOR YOU TO DO

Let your child know that her thinking and creative abilities are infinite and will never run out. Explain that knowledge and skills are built up during life like the bricks that are used to build a tall tower. The ones at the bottom are just as important as the ones at the top.

Constantly remind your child that her memory is extremely powerful, has a capacity to store anything and everything that she wants to remember and that if she uses it well it will continue to get better as she progresses through youth and into old age.

Appreciate that the synergetic nature of the child's brain means that she will become increasingly individual and unique, becoming more and more different from you, other members of the family, and everyone else. This growth to uniqueness is to be both greatly desired and greatly encouraged. There is an unfortunate tendency in some families for parents to expect their children to be like one or other (or both) of themselves. This may be based on physical, not mental, similarity. If not, perhaps they are expected to be like Uncle Nick or Auntie Lucy. This is placing unfortunate restrictions on a child. The gene pool is wide and deep and your child is most likely to be 'like himself' and needs to be appreciated for this.

Make the brain your hobby, and constantly hunt for the Correct Formulae. Share them with your child. Some examples of incorrect and correct formulae for your child can be seen in the following table:

INCORRECT FORMULA	CORRECT FORMULA
Thinking she is stupid	Thinking she is bright
Using only half or one particular aspect of the brain	Using the whole brain
Taking notes in one colour	Taking notes in many colours
Taking notes in lines	Taking notes in Mind Maps
Thinking that memory is linear, hard work gets worse with age	Knowing that memory is based on Imagination and Association and can be improved throughout life
Thinking of images as childish	Thinking of images as childlike
Thinking that food is not particularly important	Knowing that a correct diet is vital for physical and mental health

Thinking that children similarly raised should be similar	Knowing that every child is a unique Universe unto herself
Thinking that the child should be 'kept under control'	Knowing that the child should be given as much freedom for learning and self-expression as possible
Thinking that copying is cheating and cheating is wrong	Knowing that mimicry is the foundation on which we learn and is good
Thinking that the brain is additive	Knowing that the brain is synergetic
Feeling guilty about failure	Knowing that 'failure' is a necessary part of learning and is the springboard for success
Thinking that things have one meaning	Knowing that all things have infinite meanings
Thinking that truth-saying is weak	Knowing that truth-saying is strong and a necessary survival mechanism
Thinking that nature cannot be changed	Knowing that your child's brain is born to change
Thinking of the baby as weak and helpless	Knowing that the baby is astonishingly strong and mentally incredibly bright
Thinking that one is either left- or right-handed	Knowing that everyone is by nature ambidextrous
Thinking that shoes are good	Knowing that feet are better!
Thinking that questions can be stupid	Knowing that all questions are intelligent
Thinking that most people are genetically incapable of good art and music	Knowing that everyone is capable of good art and music
Thinking that babies should not be taught to read	Knowing that babies love to be taught to read

TEFCAS

---☆---

Your baby's brain operates on the TEFCAS principle, which is applicable to all the learning that your baby will do throughout his life.

---☆---

The TEFCAS principle is more from the realm of physics than the realm of psychology, and concerns what *must* happen in the physical Universe as your baby learns.

T is for Trial. Trial can be spelt 'Try-al' because it refers to the fact that your baby must first *try* anything if it is to learn at all. Walking is a particularly good example, although language learning, manual dexterity, and social skills, etc. are all equally apposite.

In the art and science of learning to walk, your baby will go through hundreds of thousands to millions of trials before finally succeeding. This emphasizes that each trial is an experiment, and must be considered as such – one more episode in a giant game of exploration.

Without the trial and its attendant risks, no learning can ever take place. *Your baby is therefore a risk-taker by design!*

In his thirst for learning, your baby is a natural risk-taker

E stands for Event. When your baby tries, there will by 'physics definition' be an Event (and let us take for purposes of illustration, a baby who is approaching the first time he stands). Let us imagine that our baby has worked out that holding on to something is probably a good idea, has grabbed on to a loose tablecloth, and in attempting to pull himself up has pulled the tablecloth, some loose cutlery, and a small carton of orange juice down. This is the Event – the physical reality that occurs as a result of the Trial. Each trial *could* give rise to a million million different events, but in the end gives rise to only one prime Event.

---- ☆ ----

From this it can be seen that 'failure' is not part of the formula that the Universe gives to your baby. Each trial and event is simply another step in the learning process towards the ultimate goal. It is therefore essential that your baby/child be encouraged to learn without the 'fear of failure' hounding his every effort.

---- ☆ ----

F is for Feedback. Feedback is the response the Universe gives to your baby as a result of the trial and the event. The feedback pours in through your

baby's senses, in the form of sights, sounds, smells, tastes, and touch. This fact emphasizes the importance of guaranteeing that your baby's senses are continuously developed, and that the primary sense organs, including the skin, are as 'free' as possible.

In our example our baby will have heard the clattering of the cutlery and the splash of the orange juice, will have seen all the items and the tablecloth falling to the floor, as well as having seen the changes in perspective as his own eye-level both rose and then fell, would have smelt the orange juice, will have felt the tablecloth and its sudden instability, and will have been aware of mother earth gently reminding him by a gentle bump on the behind, that loose supports are not the best idea when trying to learn to stand!

C stands for Check. Having received all the feedback, our baby's massively developing brain will register the literally million million bits of data it has just been given, and will check them against all the previous learning trials, and the desired goal.

On the basis of these deliberations your baby will:

A is for Adjust. Your baby will adjust his behaviour to one thing and one thing only: his *goal*. And what is his underlying goal? To stand, of course, but even more deeply to:

S stands for Succeed. Yes! Your baby, as you always intuited, *is* a 'Success Mechanism'! (See Success, page 109.)

Having completed the TEFCAS process (and this can sometimes be a split second, sometimes a few days) your baby will begin the entire process again by embarking on the next trial. To watch and assist with this process and his development is your magical and mystical privilege.

THINGS FOR YOU TO DO

 Observe the TEFCAS process-in-action in everything your baby learns, including walking, taking apart (not 'destroying'!) objects, talking and socializing, etc.

 Make sure that the 'fear of failure' is absent from your child's learning processes. Parents who say 'be careful' all the time are not helping their child to be safe; they are destroying his self-confidence. Children's playgrounds are good places to witness this sort of stunting behaviour.

In conjunction with encouraging his curiosity (see page 221) encourage and develop the use and application of the Scientific Method for your child, of which TEFCAS is a major demonstration.

chapter 4

success

---- ☆ ----

Your baby is a Success Mechanism. Your baby is born to succeed. Your baby is born to be a success story.

---- ☆ ----

Until nearly the end of the last century, it was thought by many educationalists and psychologists that the brain operated on a trial and error basis. This was a subtle mistake, for it surreptitiously obliged us, for centuries, to consider life in terms of 'mistakes', 'errors' and 'failures', the opposite of what we now know to be the more appropriate approach.

If the brain *were* a 'trial and error mechanism', you and I would have been born, would have tried and tried and tried, leading us to error, error, error, error, error, error, error, error, error, and within a few minutes it would have all been over! But this was not the case. We tried and tried and tried and tried, and the result was success, success, success, success, success, success, success, success, success, success, success, success, success, and then Error! Check! Adjust! Success! Try again! (see TEFCAS, page 105).

Your baby's brain is thus a Trial and Success Mechanism. This switch of emphasis from error to success has profound implications, which are most vividly illustrated in an educational experiment that reveals what is known as the Pygmalion Effect.

The trial and success mechanism

A standard form of this experiment involves giving, at the beginning of a school year, the new teacher of a class of 10-year-old children their IQ scores. The list is presented in descending order, the top IQ (probably around 150) being placed at the top, and the bottom IQ (probably around 85) being placed at the bottom of the class list. The teacher is informed that this is not considered particularly important, but that it is given purely for interest's sake.

At the end of the school year, the children's academic performance and 'social' or behavioural performance is tallied, and then comparisons made with the IQ list as given to the teacher.

At first glance the results appear dispiriting: there is often as much as an 80 per cent correlation between the excellence of the IQ and the excellence of the academic and social performance. This seems to imply that there is little that the teacher or the parent can do, and that the basic ability of the child (Nature) overrides the home and educational environment (Nurture).

The sting-in-the-tale of this experiment is that the original IQ list was in fact exactly the opposite of the truth! In other words the child with the highest IQ was placed at the bottom of the list, and the child with the lowest IQ at the top of the list with the highest IQ number next to her name.

What, then, was the cause of the extraordinarily high correlation?

Not, obviously, the IQ of the child. It was the expectation of the teacher. If the teacher expected the child to do well for whatever reason, there was an 80 per cent greater probability that she would do so. Similarly, if the teacher expected the child to do poorly, there was an identical 80 per cent probability of that child doing poorly, regardless of her latent IQ.

How is it possible for a really bright child to so rapidly approach the bottom of the class? Easily! Imagine, for example, that you are a very bright young child and that the teacher thinks of you, for whatever reason (IQ list or not) as *not* bright. When you make imaginative comments in class, how will they be interpreted? As stupid! And when you honestly achieve a perfect mark in a test, how will that be interpreted? That you cheated! And knowing increasingly that you are thought of by the teacher as stupid and dishonest, what will your opinion of that teacher be? And what will your reaction and actions be? Obviously negative, disruptive and destructive. You will have been drawn innocently into a major and damaging self- and other-destructive cycle (see Synergy, page 99).

If the parent and teacher expect 'error', 'mistake', and 'failure' that is what they will tend to get. If they expect 'success', 'accomplishment' and 'excellence', that is *also* what they will tend to get.

The Pygmalion Effect gets its name from George Bernard Shaw's play *Pygmalion*, adapted into the stage and film musical *My Fair Lady*. We shall here look at the play as a 'tale of brains!'

The fundamental plot revolves around one brain, Professor Higgins, who knows how to speak and teach the King's English, and Eliza Doolittle, a Cockney barrow-girl, who does not.

──────────────── ☆ ────────────────

Higgins believes that he has the knowledge; believes that he can teach Eliza 'proper' English; wants to do so; and believes that Eliza is capable of learning. Eliza wants to learn; believes she can learn; accepts that Higgins has the appropriate knowledge; and believes that he has the skill to teach her.

──────────────── ☆ ────────────────

All around them, the other people (brains) mock, deride, scoff and scorn, all to no avail. Higgins and Eliza are successful because they had the immaculate formula boxed in the previous paragraph.

As in the educational experiment, what was expected of them by each other was achieved because they believed in each other. The sceptics' expectations were not realized because they were not accepted.

You will know intuitively that the Pygmalion experiments and Shaw's metaphor himself were a correct reflection of reality.

Picture a five-year-old daughter who has just given her parent one of her first drawings. Imagine that the parent responds by saying: 'What a horrible, disgusting, ridiculous, useless little drawing. I don't like it. You'll never be any good at art. You needn't ever bother giving me such rubbish again!' Imagine now the child's reaction: what will her posture transform into? What will the expression on her face become? What will her eyes be like? What emotions will be erupting within her? A slumped and withered

brain child

posture; a shattered and perhaps even frightened face; downcast and tear-filled eyes; disappointment, hopelessness and despair.

Rewind your internal video, and imagine the parent responding enthusiastically in the following manner: 'Thank you! Thank you! What a lovely gift! How kind you are; how generous you are; how clever you are. Come and sit on my knee and tell me all about it – what do these colours mean? What do these shapes mean? You *are* becoming a good artist – please do me another one!'

Upright and poised posture; all organs and bodily functions elated, open and flowing more efficiently; face radiant, eyes sparkling; and emotions erupting with happiness, love and hope.

Your baby's brain is a Success Mechanism. It feeds on success and your assumptions, expectations and celebrations of that success. Be successful in making this so!

THINGS FOR YOU TO DO

 Make sure that you and your child are 'locked in' to the Buzan/Pygmalion Formula: you must have appropriate knowledge and wisdom to impart; you must wish (love!) to impart it; you must want your child to receive it; and you must believe that your child is eminently capable of learning whatever you teach. Similarly your child must have faith in your knowledge; must believe that you can teach it; must want you to teach it (you must nurture the soil very carefully here); and must believe in her own massive aptitude for learning.

Go shopping or to any public place where parents and young children are regularly together, and observe the number of negative versus positive responses those children get for every aspect of their behaviour. Sadly you will find that there is a

15-to-one negative–positive dominance, for example:

1 'You're a naughty girl!'
2 'Be quiet!'
3 'Don't touch!'
4 'Don't run!'
5 'Don't play with your food!'
6 'You're bad!'
7 'You're an idiot!'
8 'That's stupid!'
9 'Stop making that horrible noise!'
10 'You are a nuisance!'
11 'How many times do I have to tell you before you get it through your thick skull ...?'
12 'Stop fidgeting!'
13 'For goodness sake, sit still!'
14 'You're a pain in the neck!'
15 'Nobody's interested in what you have to say!'

With the sixteenth positive,

16 'Ah, we love you!'

Try to use positive language with your child at all times. This can be particularly challenging if she misbehaves in public. If you find any of the above phrases on the tip of your tongue, try holding back for a moment and redirecting her behaviour in a more positive and less restrictive way. It is of course important to find a balance, as there will be times when it is in the child's best interests to act quickly. Afterwards, try to help the child understand that there are certain boundaries of behaviour.

Monitor your own vocabulary for positive and negative effects on the child. Similarly monitor your own 'self-talk' and adjust it where appropriate towards the positive.

brain child

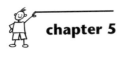

chapter 5

persistence

---☆---

In the early 1970s I underwent a paradigm shift in my thoughts concerning Persistence and its relevance to human thought and activity.

---☆---

Up until that time, having been trained in a wide range of intellectual skills, especially English, Logic and Mathematics, I considered persistence in a very negative light, prescribing to it such expressions as: 'dull'; 'thick-headed'; 'stubborn'; 'pig-headed'; 'bull-headed'; 'dogged'; and 'dim-witted'.

I was horribly wrong.

I came rapidly to realize that Persistence was a vital intelligence, and that it was in fact the engine of learning, thinking, and creativity. It was the 'T' in TEFCAS (see page 105).

Indeed my subsequent and ongoing study of the great geniuses confirmed this. In biography after biography the leading artists, scientists, athletes and leaders of all kinds named Persistence, the ability to keep getting up when knocked down, the implacable commitment to continue striving towards a goal regardless of the setbacks, as the single defining characteristic that made them leaders in their field.

This was most succinctly summarized by Thomas Edison, the inventor of the light bulb and telegraph, and the most prolific inventor of modern times, with an average of one new patent per every two weeks of his life! Edison is also famous for his oft-quoted statement on the definition of genius: 'Genius is 1 per cent inspiration; 99 per cent **perspiration**.' What Edison was pointing out was that it is possible for any normal brain to have great ideas. The genius is the one who has the dedication and commitment to persist towards the inevitable goal of making that vision and dream become a reality.

Edison knew what he was talking about.

THE THOMAS EDISON STORY

 In inventing the light bulb, he had been inspired by a vision to 'light the planet at night', providing the human race with, should they wish it, 24 hours of 'sunlight'. He proclaimed to his family, friends and the world his goal, claiming that he would do it by passing the then generally unknown and mystical force of electricity through objects in order to create heat and light.

Trial after trial eventually led Edison to illumination

brain child

He was mocked and scorned.

Edison went through innumerable substances, eventually having tried over 5,000 different experiments without success. He had to endure mounting criticism and censure, and when he was well on his way to his 10,000th trial, still without a notable success, the censure had reached such a pitch that even his closest family and friends considered having him committed to an insane asylum.

Thomas earned himself a temporary reprieve by pointing out to his mass critics that he was the only person in the world who knew of so many thousands of things that didn't work, and therefore he was the closest person in the world to finding the single thing that did!

As he approached his 10,000th trial, the light dawned.

From that day to this, the light bulb has been the symbol for inspiration and genius. It is the appropriate symbol for genius, and therefore, by Thomas Edison's definition, is also the appropriate symbol for Persistence.

So what was the event in the early 1970s that transformed my own thinking about this crucial aspect of human intelligence? It was, as you will by now realize not surprisingly, a profound lesson-by-demonstration taught to me by a five-year-old girl.

OLIVIA'S STORY

The scene is a small tree-lined street nestled near the heath in the writer's and artist's community of Hampstead in North London, England. The time is late Saturday morning; the day balmy and scented with apple blossoms.

I had strolled a few houses up the street to pay a casual visit to my friends Gerard Benson and his wife Joan. Gerard was not at home, but Joan, who was a concert pianist, was, and she invited me into the spacious downstairs room, which was dominated by a large rectangular antique table. Around the table sat four of Joan's female friends. I was invited by one and all to join them both for morning tea and for conversation, which as I had entered had turned to the nature of freedom, the definition of feminism, the nature of male/female relationships and best practices for bringing up children.

The discussion had already become intense, and as the tea in the teapot cooled the heat of the debate rose. The level of emotion and intellect was high, the members of the 'debating chamber', in addition to Joan and myself, consisting of a BBC television presenter, a novelist, an English scholar and a Cambridge don.

The debate had become a raging inferno of thought, and words probably unknown to Webster and Roget, in combination with quotes from every imaginable 'great thinker' were being hurled around the table like grenades.

After half an hour had passed and many brilliant arguments voiced, no one had yet managed to convince anyone else to change an opinion. The individual frustration felt by proponents of an idea that was not gaining acceptance raised the heat of the debate even further.

As it was reaching a climax, and as temperatures and blood pressures were continuing to rise, the hanging curtain that separated the room from the garden silently opened, and there stood, unannounced and generally unnoticed in her entrance, Olivia.

Olivia was a five-year-old girl who was dressed beautifully in the hippy-child-style of that time: a puffy-armed white blouse and a full length, autumnal-coloured Indian cotton dress that reached down to the ground, the hem just revealing the protruding toes of her bare feet. Her long brown hair fell to the base of her spine, framing a face that could only be described as 'grimed cherub'.

After the few seconds it had taken her hazel eyes and focused brain to absorb the physical and mental environment, she glided, again generally unnoticed, to the left of the chair of the lady sitting to my left.

In Olivia's right hand was a crumpled white bag that contained her treasures of the morning — her weekend ration of sweets. With her head reaching only just above chair

brain child

level, she raised the bag of sweets to adult-sitting-in-a-chair elbow-level and said: 'do you want a sweet?' There was no reaction, as the offeree was intently and totally committed to the ongoing debate.

Unperturbed, Olivia stood, motionless, like the Statue of Liberty, still holding up the little white bag, and repeated, in exactly the same tone as previously: 'do you want a sweet?'.

Again she went unnoticed and after a brief hesitation, again, she repeated the request: 'do you want a sweet?'.

This continued roughly for another 12 identically intoned repetitions, at the end of which, acting almost as if she had been hypnotized and not quite knowing consciously what she was doing, the woman muttered: 'Oh yes, thank you' and unseeingly and unconsciously dipped her hand into the bag, taking a sweet, and putting it into her mouth as she continued to make the points that were crucial to her ongoing argument.

Having accomplished her task, Olivia glided clockwise around the table, and placed herself identically next to the next woman.

Once again she asked: 'Do you want a sweet?' and once again she was not noticed. Once again she repeated and once again she was not noticed. Once again, as the intellectual missiles continued to be hurled around the table with increasing ferocity, Olivia began her almost mantra-like intonation of: 'Do you want a sweet? Do you want a sweet? Do you want a sweet? Do you want a sweet? ...'

And once again, the fire-branding debater succumbed after 15 repetitions, again taking the sweet almost robotically from the proffered bag. By this time I had begun to become intrigued, slowly realizing that something quite extraordinary was taking place in this Hampstead home. I kept one part of my attention on the debate, in which I, like the others was arguing 'brilliantly' while simultaneously failing to make any headway, and the remaining (and growing!) part of my attention on Olivia and her Pilgrim's Progress.

Two down and four to go!

Olivia approached the third lady, and proceeded with the identical routine, achieving an identical result. By this time I was mesmerized, and as I listened to the screaming intellectual bansheeism of our august adult group, I simultaneously listened to this extraordinary and obviously irresistible incantation from this genius Brain Child. 'Do you want a sweet? …'

Olivia's chant began increasingly to sound like the fundamental base rhythms of the double bass or digeridoo, while the violin and cello sections screeched out of control.

As numbers three, four and five inevitably fell to the intoxicating offer, I began to hatch a wicked plot to foil this master schemer.

When Olivia finally glided to my left side, I pretended to pay no attention whatsoever to her, and mentally tolled off the mounting number of her repetitions. I thought that she would stop at around 20 and then I would challenge her. Instead she continued and continued: 'Do you want a sweetie?' to me until, by the time she had reached 36 repetitions, I decided it was time to pounce.

Turning around in my chair, I gave her my total and passionate attention, exclaiming with a loud voice, blazing eyes, and hands outstretched over her like giant cranes descending upon her offering 'YES!! I WANT THE WHOLE BAG!!!!!'

At that moment the transformer was transformed! As I looked triumphantly and exultantly down at Olivia, I was greeted with a smile; one of the most extraordinary smiles I have ever experienced that instantaneously told me that I had been easily outfoxed by a thinker of gargantuan proportions.

Olivia's smile was utterly angelic and open, admitting, willingly, that she had been 'sussed'. At the same time, and far more importantly, that smile contained one of the most impish gleams imaginable. That impish gleam was the product of her realization that although I had sussed her scheme, she had won. She had gained my attention. I had focused upon her, had focused far more than any of the others, and had taken a sweet!

brain child

Mission accomplished, the tiny mastermind left as noiselessly and unobtrusively as she had entered, leaving the debate to rage on unabated and her vanquished competitor sitting stunned by the magnitude of what had just occurred.

I sat, the raucous sounds of the still-inflamed debate fading into a background din as my mind filled with thoughts about the significance of what I had just experienced. For more than an hour, six highly trained and highly educated intellects had presented, passionately, an incredible range of arguments and rationales for the points they were attempting to make, and in order to bring about change in thinking and behaviour of those they were addressing.

Not a single thought or behaviour had changed one iota.

While all this incredibly intense yet utterly unproductive behaviour had been going on, the seventh mind, with a similar mission to adjust thinking and influence behaviour, had succeeded perfectly with every single member of the group, while every one of those individual members had singularly failed with every other one.

Children can be very persistent when they want something

The debate eventually subsided to a gentle simmer, and after a light lunch of white wine and salad the guests went their separate ways.

At least one, however, was changed for life. I began to put Olivia's lessons into practice, arguing less and persisting more. And succeeding more. With far less effort, and always keeping in my mind that extraordinary morning and that amazing smile as a constant and eternal guide and provider of amusement.

I have observed, and as the genius biographies confirm (it is interesting to note that contemporaries of the geniuses almost invariably describe them as being like 'big children') that all children are like Olivia, and use persistence like ultimate artisans as a tool to learn, to accomplish multiple tasks, and to satisfy basic needs.

Young children, on a daily basis, regularly outwit their 'more educated and powerful' adult masters.

Consider the typical example of a multiple-degreed, athletically skilled, 1.90-m (six-foot three), 90-kg (two-hundred-pound), business-leader father, who comes home in the early evening to be greeted by his three- and four-year-old daughters, who, after the initial hugs and greetings say:

'Dad, can we have an ice cream?'

'No' (distractedly)

'Dad, we want an ice cream.'

Persistence is a vital tool that a child must develop

brain child

'I said No.'

'Ohhhhhhhhhh, *go* on Dad, we want an *ice* cream'

'I said No, now stop asking.'

'Daaaaaaaaaaad, pleeeeeeease, we want an ICE CREAM'

'Stop pestering me and leave me alone. I said no.'

After a moments pause and reflection.

'Go on Daaaaaaaad, pleeeeeeeeeeeeeese, we want an ICE CREAM'

'I said No and I mean No.'

Again, after a slight pause, some tactical leg hugging and heart-movingly pleading looks, the Olivia-like mantra begins:

'**We** want an **ice** cream, **We** want an **ice** cream, **We** want an **ice** cream, **We** want an **ice** cream, **We** want an **ice** cream, **We** want an **ice** cream, **We** want an **ice** cream, **We** want an **ice** cream, **We** want an **ice** cream, **We** want an **ice** cream, **We** want an **ice** cream, **We** want an **ice** cream, **We** want an **ice** cream, **We** want an **ice** cream, **We** want an **ice** cream.

'**ALL RIGHT, ALL RIGHT! But only this once!**'

Child's brain 1 – Adult's brain 0!

Persistence is a vital (it can even be an endearing) quality that is an essential survival tool to your child. It needs to be encouraged and developed.

THINGS FOR YOU TO DO

Observe persistent behaviour in babies and children, keeping a record, where feasible, of the approaches and techniques they use, of the number of times they will repeat in order to achieve, and how often, in the end, they get what they want. Remember that this technique is begun early when the hungry baby keeps up his wails until the very moment you actually begin to feed him.

Make your own child your Persistence Teacher! Watch and listen to him and see how he goes about things. Then try his techniques out for yourself. You could even try them out on him! For example, try 'Put on your shoes, put on your shoes, put on your shoes' or 'Time for your bath, time for your bath, time for your bath' and see what the result is. If you do try this tactic you must speak in the calmest possible tones, leave gaps in between requests and say 'Please'. If this doesn't work, leave the shoes off. Don't get angry, otherwise the child will have 'won' by winding you up.

Make sure that your attitude towards Persistence is positive, nurturing and guiding. A useful way to view Persistence, especially when it is a child aggravatingly directing persistent behaviour towards you, is to look at it as a mini-Shakespearean theatre. You and the child are the main protagonists in the play, and the child is, in a very real sense of the concept, using your own brain as a training and honing device for the strengthening of its own Persistence. Some of the plays you observe will be worthy of the London or Broadway stage, and will provide you with first-class entertainment, whereas before they might have provided you with nothing but angst and frustration.

Guide inappropriately persistent behaviour into a positive direction. For example, if your children nag you for an ice cream just before dinner time, when it will ruin their appetites, just promise to let them have one after dinner — and then keep your promise!

Reward appropriately persistent behaviour. You can do this by simply offering words of praise and encouragement. Remember that your approval counts for much, as far as the child is concerned. It is not always necessary to offer material rewards, though sometimes you may feel that they work better. For example, small treats and privileges might be appropriate.

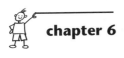

chapter 6

radiant thinking

Each one of your Brain Child's thoughts is like a starburst, a supernova of radiating thought-associations, with the possibility of extending to infinity in an infinite number of directions.

Your child radiates thought-associations like a giant supernova

A Game For You to Play

To understand the nature and realize the significance of this, it is a good idea to play an association game. It is more effective to do this in groups of four, and it is better to do it all at the same time. If this is not possible, do it at different times and make a comparison later.

The object of the game is to print the word 'LOVE' in the centre of an unlined page, outline it with a heart, and then draw 10 radiant spokes, with hooks at the ends.

Give yourself and your three co-players the instruction to do the exercise 'intuitively' and as fast as possible. Print clearly on each of the 10 lines, the first 10 associations, no matter how wild, crazy or inappropriate you think they might be, that come into *your* head when you think of the concept 'LOVE'. Do NOT compare words yet.

When you have *all* completed your 10 first associations, the object of the game is to look for any words that are common to all four of you in your group. To be 'common' a word must be *identical*: it must be spelt in exactly the same way. Thus if *you* have 'chocolates' and one of your partners has 'chocolate', this is *not* counted as the same.

When you have discovered those words that are common to all four of you, next check those words that are common to any three of you, those that are common to any two, and finally calculate the number of words remaining that have no commonality at all.

Before you do this exercise, estimate what you think the scores will probably be in the following box:

	NO. OF WORDS IN COMMON			
No. of people	4	3	2	1
Prediction				

At this stage of the game it is best to check your results before reading on.

THE RESULTS

Educationalists and psychologists, the general public and myself, were asked to predict, having been given the design of the game, what the results would be. Almost unanimously the predictions were a few words common to four, more words common to three, a lot common to two and almost none 'left over'.

How wrong we all were! The common results when looked at over, for example, six groups, were as follows (*see table*):

	NO. OF WORDS IN COMMON			
No. of people per group	4	3	2	1
Group 1	0	0	0	38
Group 2	0	1	2	33
Group 3	1	0	0	36
Group 4	0	2	2	30
Group 5	0	0	1	38
Group 6	1	1	1	31

radiant thinking

A staggering average of *far* less than one word common to any four individuals, and a *vast* majority of words that were common to no one.

And just to make it all the more astoundingly unpredicted, if a word *were* common to all four, and therefore apparently meaning the same to all members of the group, it was taken and placed in the middle of a page, and a similar exercise was done on *it* with the same four people. The result on the 'same' word was as different as the differences on the original word 'LOVE'. In other words even the 'sames' at a deep, personal level, were comprehensively different!

How could this be?!

The answer lay in the realization that the brain works in a radiant multi-ordinant (many-hooked/multi-associative) way.

Before your baby is born she begins to build her database, grasping with all her five senses the torrents of information that pour into her receiving, curious, and ecstatic fledgling brain. By the time she is three years old she has accumulated a database larger than that of any library on the planet. You might worry at this rate that the child's brain might soon be 'full up', as many people mistakenly think their own is.

Don't worry!

Your baby's brain can store a million million million of Universes-of-atoms-worth of information – it will *never* fill up!

Data that is already in your Brain Child's brain at any given moment in time can be considered as its current database, storage, memory or library. At any age, no matter what its colossal numerical value is, it will always be microscopic in relation to the storage capacity that as yet remains unused – your Brain Child's remaining potential.

Each one of the nodes or nexuses of information in your child's brain is as multi-ordinant as was the word 'LOVE' in your own brain. *Every* word, *every* number, *every* image, *every* smell, *every* taste, *every* note of *every* tune, *every* sensation is its own ultimately dense central core of meaning waiting to explode into the Big Bang Universe of its own meaning.

Look back at the basic word association game. Each word you put down surrounding the word 'LOVE' can itself have 10 or more associations. Each of those can have 10 or more and so on and so on ad infinitum in all 360 degrees of the circle, and, *more* than that, off every point of the surface of the meaning-sphere.

This means that every thought your Brain Child has, will in many significant ways, be different from those of yours, her siblings, and every other person in the world. Suddenly, armed with this new information about your child's brain, paradigms begin to shift: the nature of the bulk of your child's learning becomes suddenly clear; the nature of understanding and the appropriate networks of its structure are revealed; the nature of *mis*understanding and the nature of dissimilar associations become understandable, often humorous, predictable, and stress-reducing in their inevitability; the foundation structure for the note-taking technique of Mind Mapping is suddenly revealed; the nature of memory and recall becomes vividly apparent; as do the nature of forgetting and the 'missing link'!; the wonder, amazement and awe that most parents experience at the astonishing learning capacity and rapidly developing individuality of their children is confirmed as entirely appropriate. Joseph Chilton Pearce's description of the child as magical is upheld.

This new realization about the multi-ordinant nature and infinite capability also helps to explain just *why* it is that any two children brought up in the 'same way' *must* by the laws of multi-ordinant and infinite association, grow up to be so utterly different. Two stories help to illustrate this point.

GOD LEADING A SNOT

God leading a snot

In the first, a class of five-year-old children in Sunday school were asked by the teacher to draw a picture from the Lord's Prayer. One little girl drew the illustration above. The teacher, not understanding the principles you have just discovered, became angry and publicly chastised the child for not drawing a picture from the Lord's Prayer as requested. The little girl was obviously humiliated and was reduced to tears. Tragic, as it was a picture from the Lord's Prayer — one of the best I have ever seen! The drawing was a picture of God leading a 'snot' into temptation!

Investigation rather than pre-judging your child's Associations will be rewarding for everyone.

brain child

THE CLOUDS' STORY

The second story concerns a young boy of eight who had fallen in love with the subject of Geography. As a result he was consistently top in all his Geography tests. One day the Geography teacher asked the pupils to write an essay on the types and forms of clouds. The young boy enthusiastically went back home and as it was a warm day with a sky three-quarters filled with billowy clouds, he lay down on his back in the garden, watched the clouds drifting by and fantasized. Within no time at all his daydreaming mind was seeing all forms of structures, scenery, scenes and fantastic creatures gliding across the sky of his imagination. Inspired, he transferred this fantasy world into a short and imaginative story, which he dutifully handed in as his essay. He was particularly happy with his effort, and when it came time for the essays to be handed back and marks to be given, he was anticipating his usual top-of-the-class mark.

The teacher, as expected, selected his essay for reading to the class. But rather than with the imaginative enthusiasm that the essay deserved, the teacher read it with total sarcasm, rolling his eyes with the introduction of each new creature, and eliciting howls of derisive laughter from the boy's classmates. He was totally nonplussed and mortified, and had no idea why the teacher had read it in this way, why his classmates had been so amused, and why he had been given zero as a mark.

He told me that from that humiliating moment on he came to associate Geography with beautiful dreams that were crushed for no known reason and with deep emotional pain. He immediately rejected Geography as an interest and sank to the bottom of the class.

The grown man explained to me that it was four years later, again while in a daydreaming state, that the realization of what had happened suddenly dawned on him. By 'forms' the teacher had meant the distinguishing characteristics of clouds such as cumulus or stratus.

A beautiful misinterpretation by a child and a brutal unexplained, intentional and feigned misunderstanding of the child's understanding had destroyed a love affair between a child's brain and the fascinating

Universe of an entire area of human knowledge.

Now let's look on the sunny side.

In the light of our new awareness of the astounding uniqueness, not only physical but now, even more dramatically, mental, it is worth pondering how we human beings react to unique things, especially stones and minerals. If we find an utterly unique, or even extremely rare, mineral, what words do we use to describe it? Quickly run through your own thoughts …

The words most commonly used are the following:

RARE
GEM
PRECIOUS
INVALUABLE
PRICELESS
JEWEL

We apply these words to inanimate objects. Your new-born baby is already *far* more unique (and yes things *can* be far more unique) than any gem will ever be. How much *more* appropriate to apply these words to your Brain Child (and while you are at it, apply them to yourself and your loved ones as well!).

Your baby's brain has enough power to light up an entire city

THINGS FOR YOU TO DO

Observe how the multi-ordinant nature of words and the brain's Radiant Thinking networking capacity works in your baby's language and reading development.

brain child

Similarly your child's understanding and memory.

If you are brave, try the following experiment, as one senior IT executive did: place the word, or the picture of 'Mummy' or 'Daddy' in the middle of a page, and place 10 branches off it. Tell your child that 'anything goes'. Have her put down the first 10 (or fewer if appropriate) associations that come to mind when she thinks or feels around these concepts. The results can be intriguing, not to say alarming.

In the case of the IT executive, he was 'inordinantly' (most inappropriate word in the context of this chapter!) proud of his son, festooning his desk with pictures of him and them together, and regularly telling proud stories to friends and colleagues.

The results of the association game shocked him to the core.

His little boy had found only four key words associating from the centre: AWAY; WORK; MONEY; SMACK!

How did these words evolve? Being a typically busy senior executive, he arose at 5.00 a.m. and was gone by 6.00, well before his child awoke and arose.

'Mummy, where's Daddy?'

'Already gone.'

'Where?'

'To work'

'What for?'

'To earn money ...'

Again, being a dedicated executive, the father regularly came home just before the children's bedtime. In a typically tired and irritated mood, his son's activities of the day, especially the more 'naughty' ones, were recounted, resulting in the physical admonition.

And so to bed!!

See also Memory, page 46, Mind Mapping, page 75, Uniqueness – Mental, page 87, Reading, page 254.

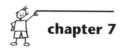

chapter 7

truth seeking

———————————————— ☆ ————————————————

Your baby's brain is a Truth-Seeking mechanism. And it is this for one very simple reason: survival. If your baby does not know, on the gross level, that fire burns and that sharp things cut, and on the more finely tuned level the subtle aspects of the real world, its chances of survival are massively reduced. Your baby's brain is thus instinctively wired like a universal Sherlock Holmes, to hunt out the truth in order to increase its own chances of living successfully.

———————————————— ☆ ————————————————

He thus checks everything, including everything you the parent do, and sieves it through his massively powerful brain, checking, checking, checking with his logic, his senses and his intuition just how congruent you are.

(If you are getting concerned or nervous at this moment, remember you did exactly the same with *your* parents!)

This is why children (and indeed most adults) can bear all manner of destitution, pain and disability yet are still most hurt when someone does something that they consider unfair, or when they are cheated or lied to.

Being thus obliged, as a loving parent, to tell the truth, one immediately gains a double benefit from the activity.

Firstly, when the brain is telling the truth, the body is more open, all senses operate more sharply and keenly, and stress is greatly reduced. The baby and child pick this up on many levels, mimic it, and benefit massively from it.

Secondly, because telling the truth gives you less to remember, your own memory is thus less burdened and operates more flowingly and accurately.

Indeed it is interesting to note that most of the world's great geniuses saw their life's goal as 'searching for the Truth' whether it be in the sciences, the arts, philosophy or religion. Sir Isaac Newton, rated in the Top 10 All-Time Geniuses in every such list, wrote in the margin of one of his papers while at Cambridge: 'I have three friends: Aristotle; Plato; and the Truth'.

And Shakespeare said: 'Time's glory is to calm contending Kings; To unmask falsehood, and bring Truth to light.'

Telling the truth is usually a straightforward matter. It can, however, be a much more complex affair that directly relates to consistency of message, discipline, behaviour and emotional stability, as the following story will unfold:

AUSTIN'S STORY

At the age of four Austin, his parents, and his and their lives seemed ideal. Austin was a good-looking, athletic, charming, happy and attentive child; his mother, Diana, was the successful director of a major national management group; and Austin's father, Keith, was a leading medical specialist, who was also the director of a major hospital. They lived in a spacious country house with delightful grounds and a large swimming pool, and happily led a social and cultural scene.

One year later poison had entered their lives. I received an urgent call from Diana and Keith, explaining that Austin had evolved into 'a little monster'. He had become rude, aggressive and increasingly violent, and was now virtually out of control. They had tried many different approaches to cure the problem, but to no avail, and the situation was now so out of control, and so potentially dangerous that they were reluctantly considering, against all their instincts and desires, having Austin committed to a psychiatric ward.

I naturally offered to do whatever I could to help, and one early balmy summer afternoon I visited them, and the three of us sat by the swimming pool, sipping tall fresh fruit punches laced with ice, and discussing Austin's extraordinary decline and increasing delinquency.

In the middle of the afternoon, Austin returned from school, where once again he had apparently been causing havoc. As he walked in, I was surprised to see not a scowling and snarling psychopath, but a little boy similar to the one I remembered from a year ago, though slightly larger. Austin said 'Hello', and rather aggressively asked for a fruit punch like ours, with lots of ice and two straws.

For ten minutes he behaved perfectly normally, sipping contentedly on his drink and wandering around looking at the flowers.

As he finished his punch, he sidled over to our table, and when he was standing next to us, suddenly and mightily sucked on both straws, creating a loud, drain-like gurgling sound that rattled our collective ears.

'Austin! Stop that!' said Diana.

And Austin did. For 20 seconds.

And then, having exhaled totally, he once again inhaled mightily, making an even louder and more disgusting 'schluuuuuuurrrrrrrrrrp!'.

'Austin! I've told you once! Now stop it!' said Diana.

And once again Austin did stop.

For 20 seconds.

And then, once again, the total exhalation and yet another mighty inhalation through the thundering straws.

'Austin! O--n--e mooore time . . .' said Diana threateningly, waving her finger pointedly at him.

And, of course, Austin obliged with one more time!

'All right Austin!' said Diana 'that's IT! Keith!' said a now-livid Diana 'you tell him!'

Keith, momentarily taken aback by the sudden responsibility thrust upon him, quickly recovered and, glowering, turned towards Austin and said:

'All right son, now it's me! Quit!'

And Austin did.

For 20 seconds.

And then, calmly, methodically, and without a trace of fear, came the inevitable and next monstrous schluuuuuuuuuuuuurrrrrrrrrrrrrrrrrp!

Keith, who was a big, commanding, strong and athletic man, then glowered more ferociously and fell into exactly the same trap as his wife had done:

'All right son that's enough! One more time ...'

And of course, Austin obliged!

By this time I must admit that I was surreptitiously rooting for the boy! My own internal man-child was saying 'Come on kid, you've got 'em on the run!' By this time Keith was now really furious, and turning to Austin he said, with an ominous and threatening finality in his voice:

'All right Austin! That's IT! One more time and you are going to get hit! And you know I mean it!'

This threat had more of an effect on Austin than the previous ones, and he momentarily quit. I kept my peripheral eye on him as Keith and Diana exasperatedly explained that this was yet another example (though mild) of his cantankerous delinquency and insubordination. While this was going on, Austin, like a master hunter, was massaging the space between us and him, sometimes sidling closer, sometimes farther away. When he had come innocently in to within a metre or so, he moved approximately 15 metres (50 feet) away, and suddenly, without warning, schlurped with even more vigour than he had done before!

Keith instantaneously leapt up from his seat. Austin had been prepared for this, and had already run to the far end of the garden. Keith, observing this, subsided into his

truth seeking

seat, saying with relief: 'Ahhh, it's OK now, we won't be able to hear him any more.'

And there, at the far end of the garden, schlurpping away in the distance, stood the little Mohammed Ali of the Mind, Austin — total 'victor' of the mental battle.

Diana, Keith and I had been discussing the episode for some few minutes when suddenly, 'out of the blue' I was hit, full force on the pressure point in my shoulder, by a perfectly directed, and malicious-in-intent, karate punch from the five-year-old miscreant.

I turned to Austin and, like his parents before, said: 'Austin! Stop it!'

And stop it he did, for a micro-second, before hitting me full-power again in exactly the same spot. A five-year-old with energy, direction and good technique can hurt any adult. It hurt!

This time I grabbed Austin by the shoulders, looked him straight in the eye and said: 'Austin, I don't want you to do that again. I don't even want you to want to do it again. But if you do, you'll turn this into an unpleasant game of consequences: when you hit me, I will hit you in exactly the same place on your shoulder, but just a little bit harder each time. So the choice is yours.'

Austin thought only briefly, and then wound up and smacked me again, once again in the same place. I immediately grabbed him, explained that I didn't want to do what I was going to do but that that was the arrangement between us, and so hit him on the corresponding spot on his own shoulder.

Austin thought for slightly longer, looked me straight in the eye, and again hit me, hard.

I immediately grabbed him once again, explained that I didn't want to do it, didn't like doing it, and would quit as soon as he did, but that the deal was the deal and therefore I would hit him again as agreed. I did.

Austin thought about this even more deeply but nevertheless decided to continue, and whacked me again. Persistence! (See page 115.)

This time I once again grabbed Austin and explained to him the following metaphor: 'Austin, if there is a large boulder falling towards your foot, it doesn't know

brain child

about your foot and doesn't care about it. You obviously know about your foot and care about it. If you don't move your foot the boulder will land on it and crush it. If you don't want your foot crushed you must move it to save yourself. The promise you and I have between us is just like that boulder. The promise doesn't know about you or know about me, or care about you or care about me. It simply says that if you keep hitting me I will keep hitting you, no matter how much we care for each other, and that if we don't stop we'll both end up in a bloody mess on the ground. So I have to hit you again, although I don't want to.' As soon as I had exchanged hits, I held him gently but firmly, and said: 'I don't want to continue doing this because I like you. I'll quit if you quit. It's a promise.'

Austin strolled away, thought about this for some minutes and then came at me as if to hit again, but instead said: 'Do you want to go for a swim?!'

'Sulphuric Acid in the pool!' was my first thought! I said: 'Yes' but explained that I wanted to have a little half-an-hour lie down first and then we'd go swimming. I lay down in the shade, with one concealed eye checking, and to my amazement observed Austin sitting cross-legged some little distance away from me observing me. When Keith came towards him heading in my direction, Austin raised his hands and said: 'Shsh! He's resting.' At precisely the 30-minute mark, his little face was next to mine saying: 'You promised!'

With that I leapt up, saying: 'Yes! I did!' Gathered him in my arms and leapt into the pool with him. He played ecstatically, and for the rest of my stay with them, behaved like my guardian angel, trying to make sure that my every need was catered for. We became 'best friends'.

What brought about this sudden change in Austin's behaviour? And more importantly what was it for which Austin was so desperately searching?

Quickly review Austin's Story, and decide what you think his goal was (a clue is that most people immediately get an 'obvious' answer — and it's wrong!)

What Austin was searching for was not attention. This he had by the barrel-full.

What Austin was searching for was MEANING and TRUTH.

truth seeking

Austin, with his infinite and brilliant creative intelligence had unwittingly thought his way out of reality! It was only when there was a formula that enveloped him with both love and no way out, that he became centred, directed and happy.

Think, from the brain-new-to-the-planets-point-of-view about the meaning of what his parents had said. When Diana said: 'Stop it!' It really meant: 'There is no time limit, and if you use your creative imagination you can do it whenever you want.'

When Diana said: 'That's it!' It really meant that '*wasn't* it'!

When Keith said: 'All *right* Austin! That's IT! One more time and you are going to get hit! And you *know* I mean it!' It meant: 'If you can think of a creative interpretation of what I've said, you won't get hit. And what's more son when I say I mean it, I *don't* mean it!'

Extrapolating from Austin's point of view, what did *anything* mean when his parents said it? Whatever he could creatively interpret it to mean. When Diana and Keith said: 'Austin, we love you!' in Austin's Universe what did that mean? NOTHING!

Austin was like a little spaceman on the spaceship 'Meaning' who had been cut off, and was drifting away in space totally isolated, without the oxygen of 'Truth', in an increasingly blank Universe where nothing meant anything, or everything meant nothing.

Imagine yourself in such space. What would be your first and immediate reaction when you realized you had been set adrift from the spaceship? Obviously, pure utter and stark terror. It was that terror that drove Austin to the frantic behaviours he was increasingly exhibiting, as he tried desperately to find meaning, to be aware of parameters, to, know literally, where he stood and where he therefore was.

Unintentionally and unwittingly Keith and Diana had been lying to Austin. They had all suffered the consequences.

THINGS FOR YOU TO DO

Make truth a beacon in your relationships with your child. For example, if you say to your child: 'We are going to the park at 4 o'clock', when 4 o'clock comes round, go to the park. Do not stall the child further with excuses after the deadline has arrived (because you are breaking your promise and not living in Truth). Mean what you say and do what you say you are going to do. That way, your words will have meaning for your child and he will trust you. He will learn that Truth is worth something, that people can be trusted, and that he can trust himself. His integrity as a person will develop.

Observe parents' admonishing and 'threatening' behaviour in public with their children. Count how many times they mean what they say, how effective what they say is, and how often children, unfortunately to their own disadvantage, win the battle of wits. You may well be dismayed by what you witness.

Check the same with owners and their dogs!

Reward your child's honest behaviour. For example, if he says 'Mum: I'm sorry but I've spilt my cereal on the floor', say: 'Thank you for telling me, now let's clear it up together before the dog/baby gets at it' as opposed to: 'Oh you clumsy child! Why can't you sit still and stop wriggling, then you won't drop things.'

Always remember that your child's probability of surviving is by definition increased the more accurate information that baby's brain has about the environment. This includes the physical, social and conceptual worlds. The more you can present and reinforce truth, the more completely successful will your child be.

part four

development and environment

From Cygnet to Swan: An Overview of Brain Child

Your Child's Creative Environment

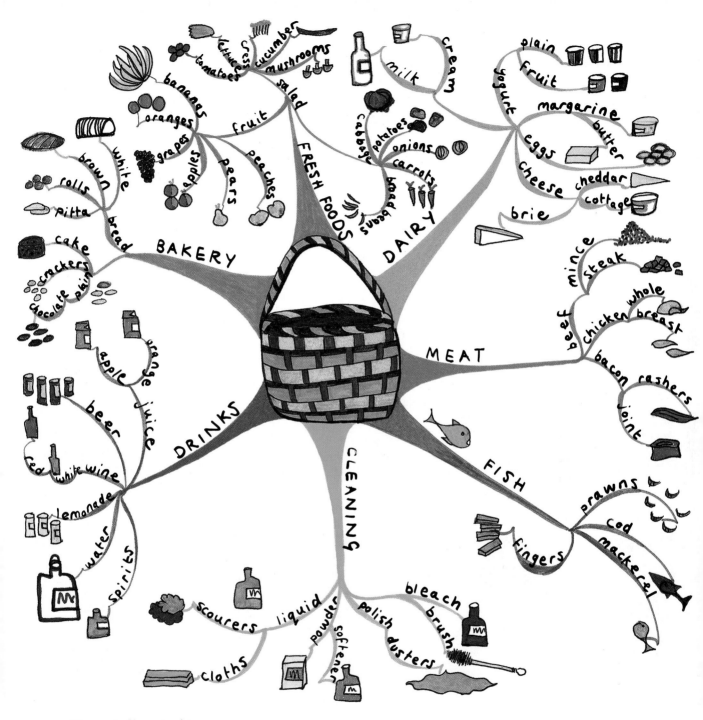

FRESH FOODS
- salad
  - cress
  - lettuce
  - cucumber
  - tomatoes
  - mushrooms
- fruit
  - bananas
  - oranges
  - grapes
  - apples
  - pears
  - peaches

DAIRY
- milk
- cream
- yogurt
  - plain
  - fruit
- margarine
- butter
- eggs
- cheese
  - cheddar
  - cottage
  - brie
- cabbage
- potatoes
- onions
- carrots
- broad beans

MEAT
- beef
  - mince
  - steak
- chicken
  - whole
  - breast
- bacon
  - rashers
  - joint

FISH
- fingers
- prawns
- cod
- mackerel

BAKERY
- bread
  - brown
  - white
  - rolls
  - pitta
- cake
- crackers
  - chocolate
  - plain

DRINKS
- orange juice
- apple
- beer
- wine
  - red
  - white
- lemonade
- water
- spirits

CLEANING
- scourers
- cloths
- liquid
- powder
- softener
- polish
- dusters
- bleach
- brush

Christina's Shopping List

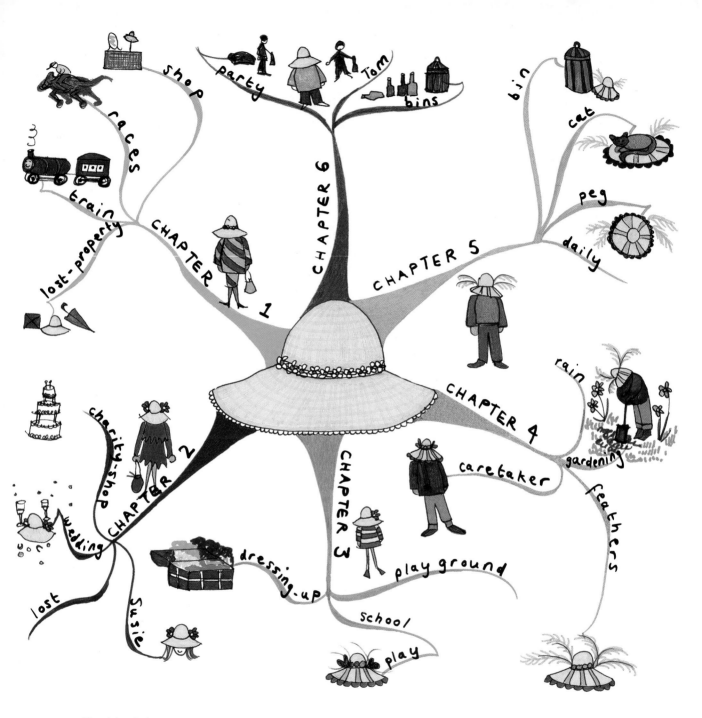

The Hat Adventure

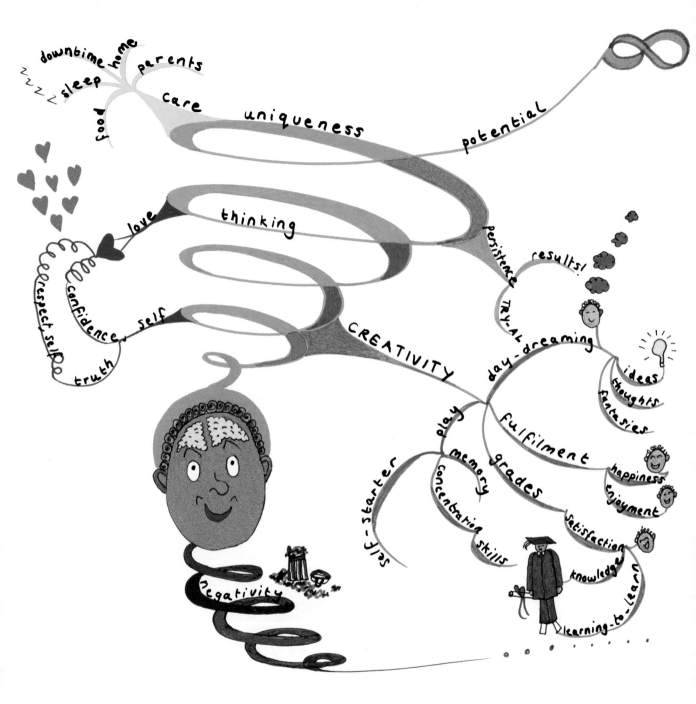

Synergetic Learning Sprirals

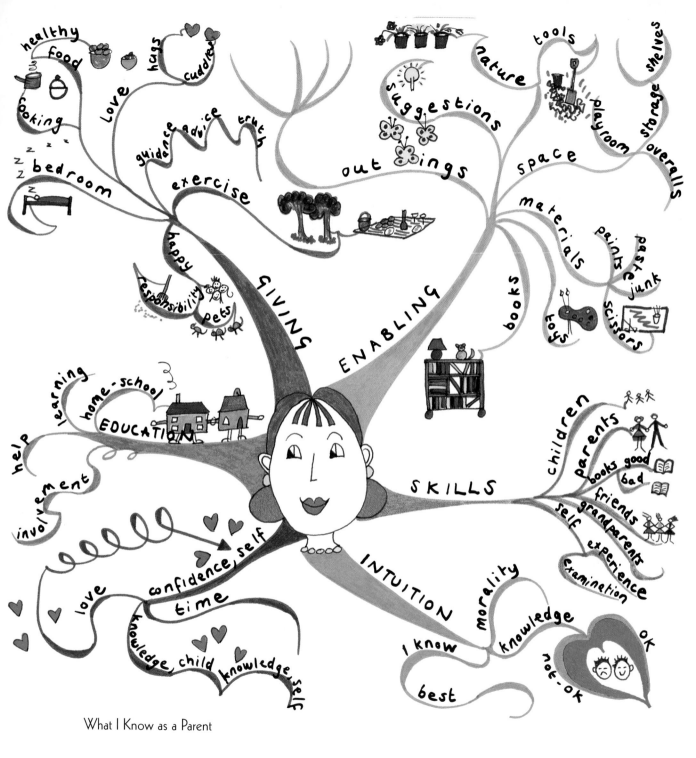

What I Know as a Parent

books

pillow

sleep

z z z z z z

marbles

shoot

bookcase

READING

PLAY

friends

SCHOOL

maths

2÷2=4

homework

lunch

playground

READING

happiness

love

FAMILY

togetherness

Harry Potter

Roald Dahl

CLIMBING

tree

frame

This Is Me

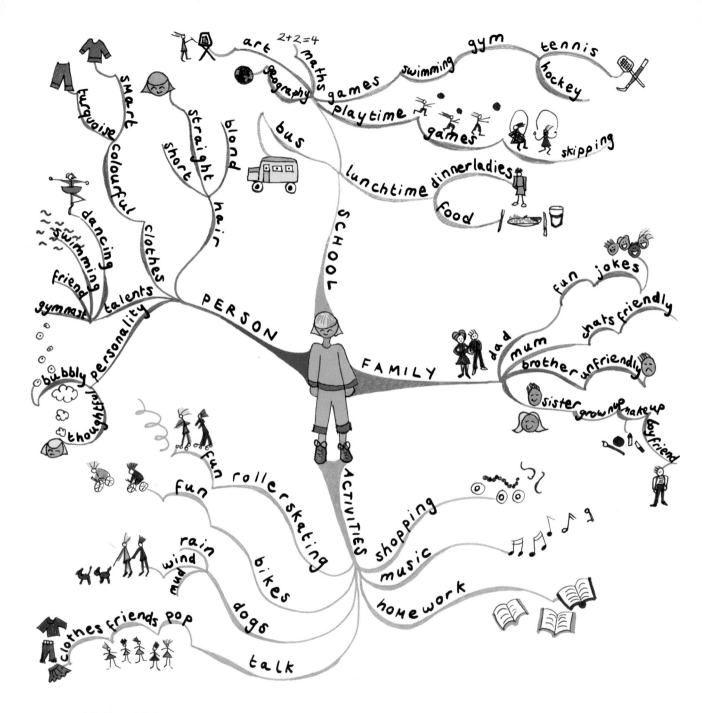

My Friend Sally

chapter 1

nature—nurture

☆

The nature—nurture debate (are all mental, physical, personality and social traits and skills determined by genetics and therefore immutable and inevitable, or are they the result of education and training?) raged throughout the twentieth century, and unfortunately for much of that time was a simple and entirely inappropriate dyadic debate: either one or the other. It has now become (as indeed it has always been!) blazingly obvious that both play a role. The question, of course, is to what degree does each contribute?

☆

Brain Child holds that the genetic potential for the average child is a universally large template with individual variations such as those to be found in thumb prints. On this gigantic instrument an infinite variety of 'melodies' or 'tunes' of intelligence and behaviour can be played, and it is these that are determined *entirely* by the environment.

Extreme examples will make the case vividly clear:

1. Raise your child in a Spanish-speaking environment and she will speak Spanish. Perfectly. Raise that same child in a Chinese-speaking environment and she will speak

Chinese. Perfectly. Genetics have nothing to do with the language the child learns. Environment is everything.

2. Expanding on the language example, surround your child with the languages of mathematics, music, art and physical culture, etc. and the child will learn these languages. Keep your baby's brain totally isolated from them and she will learn nothing at all. Genetics has nothing to do with the 'yes' or 'no'. Environment is everything.

3. Feed your child on the diet of a Sumo wrestler, and her body will become Sumo-esque. Deprive your child of the proper nutrition, and she will become skeletal and all her organs, especially her brain, will be stunted in their growth. Genetics has nothing to do with this. Environment everything.

4. Force your child to use the wrong mental formulae and she will increasingly self-destruct. Encourage her to use the appropriate mental formulae and she will increasingly self-create and self-generate. Genetics have nothing to do with this. Environment everything.

5. Deprive your child of light for three years, and the development of her visual system will be terminally stunted. Genetics have nothing to do with this. Environment everything.

6. Feed your child poison and she will wither. Feed your child appropriate nutrients and she will flourish. Genetics have nothing to do with this. Environment everything.

Of course, nature plays its part. The colour of our hair and eyes, many of our physical characteristics, and indeed the very brain itself are designs of Nature that are unique to each one of us. It is what we *do* with them and how we use them that determines our nature! The sad arguments of those who observe that all children are extraordinarily different and who therefore conclude that parents 'seem to have little impact on their temperament, intelligence and development' and that 'the basic biology and psychology of the mind is fundamentally set in stone' are both irresponsible and in abnegation of the responsibility and privilege of introducing a new, probing, and infinitely adaptive and adaptable intelligence to the wonders of the Universe.

brain child

THINGS FOR YOU TO DO

Nurture! Take the approach that everything and anything (positive) that you can do for your child can and will make a difference. Think of yourself as a force for positive influence in your child's life. Care for your child with love. Give yourself over to your child while she is young. Your efforts will be rewarded many, many times over. Common wisdom has it that anything that you do in the first five years of the child's life, will bounce back in the teens.

Check your own personal history and identify the numerous influences — physical, mental, people, social, environmental and spiritual — that changed and/or transformed your life. Most people, especially the Greats, report that it was exceptional love, kindness or attention that encouraged, motivated and/or transformed them. Others note that it was some marvellous vision when they were a child that 'set their hearts and minds' on becoming the next example of what they had seen. Torvil and Dean, the 'Bolero' Olympic Ice-dancing Champions saw the great Russian skaters the Protopovovs, and wished to 'be like that'. Mohammed Ali, one of the two greatest pound-for-pound-boxers in pugilistic history, saw Sugar Ray Robinson, the middle-weight phenomenon, and decided that he 'wanted to be like that'. And who was Sugar Ray Robinson? The other of the two greatest fighters in history! It's not only the 'greats' who have a role to play here. Everyone can remember at least one 'great teacher' in their lives, who made a lasting positive impression on them, who had time for them and from whom they learnt something important.

chapter 2

play

'Should we let our children play more and send them to schools that encourage playtime, or should we curb playtime, and send them to schools that concentrate on the "more important" aspects of learning, encouraging them to get high academic marks and test scores?'

This question is increasingly asked by perplexed parents caught in what appears to be a Catch-22 situation between a vague intuition that play is somehow useful, and a real awareness that academic success does correlate with success in the 'outside world'.

As with the arguments about IQ versus creativity, Nature versus Nurture, and handedness, the flaw in this argument lies in its dichotomy of 'either/or', and its failure to realize that very often doing two things can take *less* time and be *more* productive than doing one of those things alone.

Let's take a step back from the tussle of the dilemma, and look at what play means in general, and to you in particular.

Envision yourself watching puppies gambolling or kittens mock-fighting or playing with a ball of string. What are your emotions? What does your face do? What does your body do? Is the experience pleasant? If so, how?

Remember the times in your childhood when you played with friends or at school. Did you look forward to those times? Why? What kind of games did you play? What kind of benefits did you derive from the play? What did you learn? How exercised were your multiple intelligences, your cortical skills, your mind and your body? Did you look forward to play and playtime? Do you *still* look forward to play and playtime?!

What the Dictionary Says

Even the minimalist *Pocket Oxford Dictionary* devotes nearly an entire page to 'Play'. As you read through just some of these definitions, and through the subsequent list of similes for play from *Roget's Thesaurus*, think about how these words and concepts make you feel, and consider whether or not the *application* of these words and concepts to your child's life would enhance that life and make it more full, productive and joyous.

From the *Pocket Oxford Dictionary*

PLAY v & n   1. Have free movement within limits, alight or be visible or have effect here and there, sport, frolic, toy, trifle, amuse oneself, engage in games of fun or mimicry or acting or make-believe, perform on musical instrument, (*light, smile, water, gun, ~s on sea, lips*). 2. v.t. Take part in (game) move (piece) or produce (card) or select (person to ~) in game, act (drama or role), act like, show oneself to be, perform piece &c. on (musical instrument). 3. n. Light movement, activity or operation or scope for it, freedom of movement or space allowing it, recreation, ~ing of game, dramatic piece, (*the ~ of light, fancy, &c; come into ~* begin to operate; so be *in full ~; make ~* act vigorously; *at ~; in ~; go to the ~,* attend theatre); *~ fair,* act honourably; *~ fellow,* companion in childhood; *~ ground,* school recreation-ground; ~ the game, keep the rules esp. those of a code of honour; *~ the man,* act with courage & resolution; ~ hard in game, do one's share in talk or action; (*-fully*), frolicsome, jocular.

From *Roget's Thesaurus*

pleasure, interest, delight, entertainment, labour of love, recreation, refreshment, relaxation, sport, fun, good clean f., good cheer, joviality, jocundity, merriment, game.

Of *course* play is essential – *Brain Child* considers it to be the ultimate learning tool.

THE STUDIES

Parents' intuition and common sense have always favoured play. Happily a growing number of studies now confirm that cultural wisdom.

Researchers at Baylor College of Medicine in Houston, Texas, have reported that the availability of toys in infancy is already related to the child's developing IQ at the age of three. In addition the Baylor Study reports that children who do not play, develop brains that are as much as between 20 and 30 per cent smaller than those of their more playful counterparts.

brain child

This research is supported both by that of Dr Glenn Doman (see page 255) and Dr Kathleen Alfano, a Child and Play Psychologist, who demonstrates her point by showing brain scans of normal children and neglected children (these latter from Romanian orphanages where the young victims of the war were left to sit all day, often tied, in their cots). In her scans, Dr Alfano shows the brightly coloured neural pathways of the normal children, and the noticeably dark-patch-dominant scans of the neglected children.

Dr Alfano's research has also shown that children who play more, with plenty of movement, will be happier, more successful at their school work and better able to develop skills they will need later on in life.

Her research points out the fallacy of the either/or argument cited at the beginning of this chapter. The answer is both/and: play and learning. Dr Alfano's research has also produced identically positive results to that of Dr Doman's, especially concerning the vital importance of movement in the baby's development. She has shown that movement is vitally important as an element of play because it emanates from the same part of the brain as other aspects of learning, thus showing a direct support for the idea that physical activity is essential in stimulating mental ability (mens sana in corpore sano again). Her researches showed a striking example of a child learning to read who had trouble linking words with the letters with which they began. This child was given movement exercises similar to those recommended by Dr Doman, the result being a statistically significant improvement in the child's ability to link (A) with apple, (B) with baby, (C) with child ...

It is interesting to note that in the animal kingdom, the human baby is the one privileged to have by far the longest childhood. Mother Nature has wisely allowed the child's developing brain to spend a maximum number of years in the presence of siblings and adults, exploring, experimenting and playing with the infinite behavioural options that will help it secure its survival.

Mother Nature's gift to your child is that 'ultimate tool' for developing and realizing our infinite potential through the most serious, important, delightful and precious of all human activities: PLAY.

WARNING! MISCONCEPTIONS ARE ABOUT ...

Despite the tidal wave of parents' traditional and current intuition, and despite the mounting evidence from researchers such as Dr Alfano, there are still some who are trapped on the negative side of the Dyadic Dilemma. They have neglected the full value of positive play, and have chosen to interpret 'play' to their and every child's disadvantage, as meaning only 'frivolous', 'trifling', 'half-hearted', 'amateurish' and 'insincere'. They have similarly interpreted play as both lack of seriousness and the opposite of 'work'. They should have had young Oliver (see page 236) as an advisor before starting off on their misdirected course!

As a result of this misdirected thinking, many school systems in the 'developed' world, especially in America and England, are drastically cutting down or even eliminating entirely from the school curriculum, playtime. This is based on the argument that when children are in school they are there to learn, that play is frivolous and irrelevant to learning, and that therefore 'play' should be excluded from the curriculum.

This is obviously a catastrophe for the child and for society at large, for it eliminates from the child's learning 'vocabulary' and experience all those things that you mused upon when answering the questions at the beginning of this chapter, including and in addition to the following catalogue of advantages, which reveal just why play is the ultimate learning tool:

THE MULTIPLE ADVANTAGES OF PLAY

1. Physical Play

   Physical play is the ultimate 'training ground' or gymnasium for the body, involving the child in activities that develop the three main and necessary physical attributes:

   (a) Aerobic Fitness

   (b) Muscular Strength

   (c) Bodily Flexibility

   In addition, physical play helps develop the vital bodily attributes:

   (a) Co-ordination

   (b) Balance

   (c) Speed of multi-sensory perception

   (d) Speed of multi-sensory reaction

   (e) Overall exercise including large doses of laughter, which is considered by many in the medical professions to be one of the greatest all-round exercises as well as one of the greatest releasers and reducers of stress and generators of overall health.

2. Mental Play

   The advantages of this sort of play are covered fully in Mind Sports, page 278. In summary, mental play involves and develops the following skills: analytical, strategic, creative and global thinking; concentration; memory; independence; interdependence; and self-reliance.

3. Play in General

   Play in general helps, in addition to all the previous advantages mentioned in points 1. and 2, the development of the following skills for your Brain Child:

(a) Leadership/followership. Many forms of children's play, often generated spontaneously by young minds who obviously know the value of both aspects of the leadership game, involve follow-the-leader-type activities, in which the leader is constantly changing as a function of the game.

(b) Friendship. It is often through play that we find those other individuals who share the same interests, approaches and delights in things as we do. Your child will be the same.

(c) Social relationships. In play, the entire range of social relationships is exposed, can be experimented with, and the most successful approaches to them woven into the fabric of your child's behaviour patterns. In play this often involves various forms of trading; an excellent preparation for the business and professional worlds.

(d) Win/lose. Many children's games involve winning or losing. Repeated practice in each of these areas teaches your child how to react appropriately.

(e) Mimicking. Play offers your child limitless opportunities to develop mimicry (see page 95). Dr Alfano also observed that a lot of play is imitative and tells the stories first, of a two-year-old girl using a toy kitchen coffee-maker as a Cappucino machine, making the appropriate steam-hissing noises as she did so, and second, of a three-year-old boy who, while playing with a barbecue set, fetched a little paint brush in order to paint the food with oil, after which he wiped his hand on his apron in exactly the manner in which he had seen his father do.

4. Rest and Solitude

Very often, when a child is at play, there will be sudden 'lulls in the action' where the child is sitting in silence by a stream or a pond, not being found by the 'seekers', far ahead or far behind in the walk, run or chase, lolling on the branch of a tree, or simply being alone in silence surrounded by friends as they rest, doze, travel or watch the clouds in the sky together.

These largo movements in the symphony of play are as important as the allegro movements.

To realize the significance of these times, consider for yourself, dear reader, where *you* physically are when you come up with those bursts of creative ideas, wonderful fantasies, solutions to problems, or sudden bursts of recall. The most common answers are:

In the bath

In the shower

On the loo

Walking in Nature;

Long-distance running,

Skiing or swimming

Driving

On long-distance flights

In bed before sleeping and on waking

While dreaming

While listening to music

While watching water

What is common to all these responses?

The fact that in such situations, the brain is usually RELAXED and ALONE. It is primarily in these situations that great thoughts and acts of creativity are generated, as evidenced by the millions of poems not only written in such situations but *about* them, and by the great scientific discoveries of Archimedes, Kekulai, Newton, Robert-the-Bruce and Einstein, which came about as a result of lolling about in the bath, drifting off to sleep under an apple tree, dozing in front of the embers of a fire, sitting in solitude watching a spider spin its web and daydreaming about travelling to the ends of the Universe on a sunbeam!

It is thus that the wonderful oases of rest, which are part of your child's play activity, are a vital part of the development of his composure, imagination, stress reduction and relaxation, creative thinking and humanity.

Work Versus Play

Once again, educational theorists in the late centuries of the last millennium found themselves thinking that they had to *either* work *or* play.

The twenty-first-century solution is neither to work nor play, nor to do some work and some play. It is to do only one thing, and that is to do them both at the same time! As Heraclitus' co-philosopher, Plato stated 'life must be lived as play ...'

Those human beings who have most regularly realized this are, not surprisingly, the great brains. One of the most common observations (and sometimes complaints!) about their behaviour, was that their capacity for work seemed boundless and that their energy for activities related to their vision was like an unstoppable tidal wave.

Rembrandt, the artist, was known to be able to exhaust one group of colleagues and friends in the morning, another in the afternoon, and a third group in the evening and into the early hours of the morning! Similar energy related to work was reported of Madame Curie, Alexander the Great, Mohammed Ali (they often had to throw him out of the gymnasium!), Beethoven, Pablo Picasso, Maria Montessori, Queen Elizabeth I and Thomas Edison – to start a list of geniuses that could go on for thousands.

(When the truth about the work/play relationship is fully known, we will be changing the familiar proverb to '*all work makes Jack a very bright boy!*')

What was their secret?

Simple. They considered their work to be play, in all the wonderful definitions and extensions of the words expounded in this chapter. Work was not a drudged necessity separated from their real life; it was the essence, the focus, the joy, the play (in the Shakespearean sense) of their lives. They were, in every sense of the word, the Players. Their laboratories, their art and writing studios, their battle fields, their theatres, and the world on which they lived was their Stage. Their Playground. Their Kindergarten. Their Paradise.

THINGS FOR YOU TO DO

Play! Make time in your own life for 'downtime', 'nothingtime' — when you are not actually 'doing' anything. Reserve time every day for daydreaming. Don't fall into the trap of feeling that every moment of your life has to be filled up with purposeful activity. Not only will you benefit yourself but you will understand how important it is for you, and therefore how very, very important it is for your child, for whom to play is to live and to live is to play. Play is your child's work.

Aquire the best-quality toys for your baby. 'Best' in this instance obviously means those that will stimulate and challenge the full range of his cortical skills and multiple intelligences. Don't waste time and money on toys that rely on batteries or have limited function or purpose. Avoid toys that are for 'watching' rather than for 'doing'. Choose instead those that engage the child's imagination.

Introduce your Brain Child to Mind Sports at an early age (see page 278).

Make the home, in the best senses of the word, a playground (see Paradise, page 159). Arrange your living space so that there is as large an area as possible reserved for play, where your children's belongings are stored and where it's OK for him to make a mess and to leave unfinished projects out.

Bring Nature into your home and your children into Nature. Reserve a corner of your child's play area as a 'Nature Corner'. Here, make a beautiful arrangement of plants, flowers, leaves, shells, stones, twigs, branches, seaweed and objects that you have found together. You can keep this as a permanent fixture that changes gradually according to the seasons. Bring back finds and trophies from your walks in Nature to create an ever-changing tableau. Make it a fixture in your day to take your child out for a walk in the park, the local wood, or in the fields.

Make sure you provide your children with nature's ultimate playmates – pets (see page 298).

chapter 3

paradise

☆

The overwhelming desire of any 'current generation' is to leave the world a better place for their children, this being the next step in the conceptual and philosophical evolution of the human race towards Utopia; towards the deep-rooted idea of Paradise.

☆

I had always assumed that the word 'paradise' came from the Ancient Greek, and that it meant heaven or Utopia. To my surprise and delight I discovered that it came not from the Greek, but from the Arabic and that it was a much more basic, tangible word.

'Paradise' means 'garden'!

It is interesting to note that in many religions Paradise is actually described as a garden, as in the Garden of Eden; that one of the fastest-growing hobbies around the globe is gardening, with an explosive growth of garden centres, which are themselves becoming expanded into social, eating and meeting places; that another of the fastest-growing businesses is the florist, with flowers becoming the main trading currency for love and affection; and that the name we give to the schools to which we send our two- to five-year olds in the most delicate stage of their intellectual, physical and social growth, is the kindergarten – from the German kinder (child's) garten (garden) – the Child's Garden.

Brain Child strongly recommends that you introduce your child to Paradise as soon and as often as possible.

In the full context of this discussion, 'Garden' means 'Nature', and it is nature that I suggest you select as one of your baby's/child's primary godmothers.

With what you now know about your baby's different intelligences, her senses and their development, her need for stimulation, and her insatiable curiosity and thirst for new knowledge and experience, contemplate the advantages of your child's brain and body being exposed to the following:

1.   The myriad different concerti and symphonies of the song bird (it has been calculated that a single skylark sings the equivalent of 40 Mozart symphonies, all with different variations, per day).
2.   The constantly shifting skin-caressing breezes.
3.   The numberless textures of the earth, including its dryness, moisture, soil, plants, grass, rocks, sand and the many other feasts on which the Homunculoid feet feed.
4.   The aromas and fragrances of the blossoms and flowers that waft in never-ending aromatic combinations to delight the olfactory sensibilities.
5.   The eternally shifting variations and gradations in the light, producing constantly changing shifts in perspective and the second-by-second recreation of the shadow world.
6.   The million million-plus liquid diamonds that are constantly created and recreated in the running stream that flash starlight beacons to the eye as it babbles its own baby talk to your baby's brain.
7.   The gently undulating reflection of the world and sky that embrace the reflected face of the child as she contemplates herself and an upside-down world on the mirroring surface of a pond.

8. The 'black-belt martial art' exercises presented by the dancing penumbra of mayflies, challenging the eye, as they dart, dance, combine and separate, to follow any one of them for more than three seconds.

9. The breathtakingly intricate and infinitely varied and coloured designs of the insect world, most gloriously exemplified by the eye-enthralling butterflies.

10. The aromas of nature in heat, especially grasses.

11. The ever-changing clouds, their drift, glide, scurry and billowing, creating for the child's mind's eye an eternally changing theatre of worlds and landscapes in which more different animals and beings roam and play than the sum total of all those that inhabit the earth.

12. The 'laser show' of sunlight seen by the head reclining at the base of and under the canopy of the protecting tree and its tinkling leaves.

13. The flight of birds, their hovering, swooping, arcing and gliding, and the 'achieve of, the mastery of' these ultimate acrobats of the air.

14. The vast awesome night sky, with the Universe pouring its starlit history into the waiting eyes of the child at a phenomenal 186,000 miles per second while the moon hangs near and globally by, raising questions of Science and Romance.

And just think. Instead of all this, your child could be watching television!

THINGS FOR YOU TO DO

Make Mother Nature part of your child's Mastermind Group (see page 187).

Make your home and environment a Paradise; Paradise your home. Apart from bringing Nature into your home, take the trouble to make your home beautiful and cared for. Make it a delightful place to be, where the imagination can flourish and where people want to spend time. Make your home colourful and cosy. Organize your possessions so that they are easy to find and easy to care for. Remove all extraneous clutter from your life. Give away things that no longer serve you, whether in use or beauty.

Make sure that your child does not become one of those adults who sits in an aeroplane asking others, who are in the window seats watching the magnificent and moving vistas of the clouds and continents, to 'shut your shade so that I can watch the video'. Make sure your child is one you have encouraged to keep wonder alive, and who watches the incredible 'video' of the passing oceans and continents, of which the window is the screen.

See Pets, page 298 and The Mastermind Group, page 187.

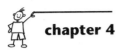

chapter 4

development stages

---⭐---

Babies go through three major developmental stages: Motor Skills; Physical
Development and Mental Development.

---⭐---

Motor Skills involve the gross motor skills such as supporting the body
weight on the legs, and fine motor skills such as the more delicate operations performed by the hand and fingers. Physical growth and development refers to the development of the senses, sleeping and feeding habits,
teething, grooming and task-oriented behaviour. Mental development
involves language learning, memory, general awareness and the development of intelligence.

As you know, each child grows at his own very individual pace. The following charts are based on general statistics, and allow you to check your baby's
own progress against the standard norms. Whether your baby is behind,
level with, or ahead of the average, continue to encourage his developments
on *all* levels.

1 month

Check-ups: Regular visits to doctor for first 6 months.

Feeding: Most babies drink 3–4 oz of milk per feed.

Senses: Prefers sweet smells, soft fabrics. Calmed by high voices and soft music.

2 months

Health: Dress baby in multiple layers because internal-temperature control is not mature yet.

Senses: Eyes sharpen and track moving objects. Loves to stare at faces.

Sleeping: Colic may set in but will usually disappear by the third month.

3 months

Feeding: Anticipates feeding by smacking lips.

Senses: Coos and smiles when talked to. Lack of response may indicate a hearing problem. Eyes should be aligned and able to focus on one object instead of two.

4 months

Feeding: Some babies may begin eating puréed solids like cereals. Balance between solids and milk will vary, depending on child's preferences.

Health: May catch a cold because of low immunity. See doctor if symptoms persist.

Senses: Sees in colour, adjusts to different distances and perceives depth.

Gross motor: Jerky movements smoothen as nervous system and muscle control improve. Most actions are reflexive, like sucking and bringing closed fists up to mouth. Thrusts arms and legs. Head flops backwards if unsupported.

Language: Small throaty sounds may turn into cooing sounds by end of first month. Responds to voices.
Memory: Some babies may start to expect feeding at regular intervals.
Tips: Use simple, lively phrases and address baby by name.

Fine motor: Opens and closes hands carefully. May hold object for a few moments.
Gross motor: Legs start to straighten from inward-curving new-born position. Struggles to raise head. Some reflexes fade near month's end.

Awareness: Begins to make simple associations — if he cries, he gets picked up. Awareness of outside stimuli increases.
Language: Communicates mainly by crying. Noises are more vowel-like, such as 'ooh-ooh' and 'ahh-ahh'.

Fine motor: May swipe at dangling objects. Should move both arms equally well when lying on back.
Gross motor: Pushes down on legs when standing on firm surface. Learns to bounce. May raise head and chest when lying on stomach. Kicks gain force, as flexibility in hip and knee joints develop.

Awareness: May respond to mirror image by smiling. Stops sucking to listen to parent's voice.
Language: Whimpers, squeals, chuckles, gurgles at back of throat. Stimulated to make sounds by hearing others talk.

Fine motor: Reaches with arms. Clenches rattle and puts it in mouth.
Gross motor: May learn how to shift weight from side to side and flip over. Upper body and arms strengthen; child may sit up with support. Often leans for balance.

Awareness: May sense strange places or people.
Language: May babble routinely to himself or to others. May raise voice as if asking a question.
Memory: Distinguishes who's who in his life. May recognize mother in a group of people.
Tips: Engage child in face-to-face talk. Mimic his sounds to show interest.

development stages   **165**

5 months   **Feeding:** Babies ready for solids may try iron-rich baby foods like green vegetables to promote growth. Easily distracted during breast-feeding. Some babies may be ready for weaning.
Sleeping: May sleep through the night, with two naps during the day.

6 months   **Feeding:** May be down to 3 meals a day, plus nutritious snacks.
Teething: Cuts lower-central incisor around the sixth or seventh month. May have a gum swelling, crankiness and irritability. Teething rings should be made of firm rubber and should not be frozen.

7 months   **Feeding:** Watch for allergic reactions to new foods. Weight gain slackens as a result of increased mobility.
Senses: Sees as well as a teenager and locates sounds accurately.
Sleeping: Usually sound, but may be disturbed by pain or hunger.

8 months   **Feeding:** Spills less when drinking from a cup. To prevent choking, give foods that are mashed or soft enough to swallow without chewing.
Sleeping: Learns how to stay awake. Over-stimulation may make settling down difficult.

Fine motor: May swap object from hand to hand. May hold bottle.

Gross motor: Developing better control of trunk, head and neck. Raises head and holds it up while lying on stomach. May also rock like an aeroplane. Grabs feet and brings them to mouth when resting on back.

Awareness: May drop object just to watch parent pick it up. Looks at where object falls from and where it lands on the floor.

Language: Watches mouths intently and tries to imitate inflections. May utter consonant sounds like 'm' and 'b'.

Memory: May anticipate a whole object after seeing part of it.

Fine motor: Reaches out when sitting, often in a raking motion.

Gross motor: Rolls over in both directions. Maintains balance while sitting due to stronger abdominal and back muscles. May move forward on stomach, pushing with legs.

Awareness: May perceive cause and effect: wave the rattle and it makes a noise.

Language: Learns to make new sounds by changing shape of mouth.

Tips: Try to phase out baby talk and use more adult language with the child.

Fine motor: Clasps hands and enjoys banging objects together. May grab for a toy with one hand.

Gross motor: Supports entire weight on legs, likes to bounce. Sits with light support from pillows. Pivots when sitting to reach objects. May get into sitting position by pushing up on arms.

Awareness: May sort toys like bricks by size.

Language: May make several sounds in one breath. Recognizes different tones and inflections.

Memory: Improves memory by playing hiding games and by observing the comings and goings of others. Remembers that a jack-in-the-box pops up at the end of a song.

Fine motor: Learns to open fingers at will and drop or throw objects.

Gross motor: Co-ordination improves, and child may start to crawl, often pushing backward at first. Some babies scoot across the room on their bottoms.

Language: Starts to imitate a broader range of sounds. Responds to familiar noises by turning head and torso.

Tips: Remembers how to respond to specific phrases: raises his arms when he hears 'so big'.

development stages   **167**

9 months   **Check up:** Visits doctor for check-ups and immunizations.

             Sleeping: Anxiety over separating from parents may cause trouble at bed-time. Relaxes by sucking thumb, cuddling soft toys or rocking.

10 months   **Feeding:** Most babies this age need between 750 and 900 calories a day, more than half from breast milk or formula.

             Grooming: May pull off hat and enjoy using soap.

11 months   **Feeding:** Able to hand-feed himself an entire meal by end of year. Prefers soft or crispy foods.

             Grooming: May help in undressing, especially pulling off socks.

12 months   **Check up:** Has one-year medical examination to check weight gain, motor skills.

             Feeding: Insists on feeding himself, however messily. May pick up spoon but misses mouth often.

             Sleeping: May resist having naps and going to bed.

MOTOR SKILLS	MENTAL DEVELOPMENT
Fine motor: Puts objects in containers then takes them out. May finger holes on a peg board and enjoy toys with moving parts like wheels or levers. **Gross motor:** Near the end of the first year, baby may begin to pull up on furniture and stand. Learns how to bend knees and sit down after standing.	**Language:** May respond to his name and other words, like 'no'. Listens intently to conversations. May say 'ma-ma' and 'da-da'. Likes to imitate coughs. **Memory:** Notices when someone leaves the room and anticipates their return.
Fine motor: May hold crayon and try to scribble. Intrigued by tiny things. **Gross motor:** May walk while holding on to furniture. May let go momentarily and stand without support. Sits confidently.	**Awareness:** May be able to determine heights and edges of objects. **Language:** Adds gestures to words: waves when saying 'bye-bye' or shakes his head while saying 'no'.
Fine motor: Likes to turn pages, often not one by one. Fascinated by hinges and may swing door back and forth.	**Language:** Imitates word sounds as well as actions. Learns the meaning of words by hearing them used in different situations. **Tips:** Games like peekaboo and pat-a-cake stimulate baby's memory skills.
Gross motor: Children walk at about their first birthday, although some start earlier or later. First steps will be shaky; stumbles, and an occasional bump, are very likely.	**Language:** May babble short sentences that only he understands. Shows more control over intonation and inflection. May say two to eight words like 'bow-wow' or 'hi'.

AGE	PHYSICAL DEVELOPMENT
13 months	**Feeding:** Expresses definite likes/dislikes of foods. **Health:** Feet may turn outwards. During the second year, hip ligaments tighten and straighten feet. **Teething:** By now, some babies have cut two upper front and two lower front teeth. Arrival of first molar can cause pain.
14 months	**Feeding:** Needs about 1,000 calories a day to sustain proper growth. May drink less milk, but solid foods cover nutritional needs. **Grooming:** May co-operate by lifting arms and legs when undressing, or even comb own hair.
15 months	**Check up:** Visits doctor for mid-year testing of vision, hearing, reflexes. **Sleeping:** Morning nap becomes shorter but may still need afternoon rest. Cot bumpers can protect baby's head if she moves around at night.
16 months	**Grooming:** May outgrow shoes every three months during the second year.

Fine motor: Points with index finger. Accurately picks up small objects with thumb and index finger.
Gross motor: May walk with feet wide apart, toes pointing out. Uses arms for balance when walking.

Awareness: By imitating adult actions, she learns that objects have functions. Uses toy telephone like a real phone.
Language: May not say full words yet but gestures to complete idea. Says 'ba' and points to ball.

Fine motor: Holds two or three objects in one hand. Turns containers over to dump contents.
Gross motor: May stoop to pick up toy and carry it across the room.

Awareness: Understands that she can make things happen by her actions.
Language: Enjoys rhymes and jingles. Expresses needs mainly through gestures: brings books to parent to read.

Fine motor: Builds small towers of blocks and then knocks them down.
Gross motor: Climbs stairs on hands and knees; descends by crawling and sliding. Pushes or pulls a toy while walking.

Language: May follow simple commands like 'come here'. Points to familiar objects when requested. Recognizes names of major body parts.
Tips: Develop associations by giving word labels to everyday objects and activities.

Fine motor: Puts round peg into correct hole. Tries to fit things inside each other.
Gross motor: May try to kick ball but steps on it instead. Walks sideways and backwards. Quickens pace when excited or being chased.

Language: May say six or seven words clearly. Enjoys word games and singing songs like 'Pop Goes the Weasel'.

17 months

Feeding: Dawdles during meals; prefers bland to sharp flavours.

Sleeping: Often gets over-tired and may have trouble falling asleep. More than half of children 1 to 2 years old fuss when it's time for bed.

18 months

Check up: Visits doctor for mid-year examination.

Feeding: Spoon may reach her mouth more often by mid-year. Steer child away from sugary foods that can cause early tooth decay.

Grooming: May indicate when nappy is wet. Enjoys taking off shoes and socks, unzipping slippers.

Sleeping: May bring stuffed toy or pillow to show she is ready for bed.

19 months

Feeding: Blows on food when it's hot. Should be drinking 16 to 32 oz milk a day, which provides most of the calcium needed for bone growth.

Grooming: May brush teeth; washes and dries hands with help. Check water temperature before putting child in bath.

Sleeping: Sleeps fairly well but may have a bad night now and then. May try to climb out of bed.

20 months

Feeding: Learns food talk like 'more' and 'all gone'.

Grooming: Encourage child to undress completely on her own. Can't buckle or lace shoes yet.

Sleeping: Nightmares may disrupt sleep occasionally.

Fine motor: May roll ball to others and pick up objects in motion. Throws balls. Drinks from cup.

Gross motor: Has more control over stopping and turning when she walks. Likes to push buggy, rather than sit in it.

Language: May start to use words to express needs: says 'up' to be held. Enjoys pointing at pictures in books. May understand more words than can say.

Tips: Speak slowly and give child time to respond.

Fine motor: Sorts many shapes and drops them in matching holes. Takes toy apart and puts it back together. Unzips zips.

Gross motor: Keeps feet closer together when walking; gait becomes much smoother. May walk upstairs with parent.

Awareness: May grasp the idea of 'now'.

Language: Vocabulary explodes. Child starts learning as many as 12 words a day. 'No' is chief word. Points to own body parts or to pieces of clothing when asked. May refer to self by name.

Tips: Asking child simple questions stimulates decision-making process.

Fine motor: May stack three or four bricks. Loves to inspect new objects and places. Tries to climb out of bed. May take off socks and shoes.

Gross motor: Active and adventurous throughout the day. Walks, climbs, trots and runs whenever possible.

Awareness: May be aware of cause and effect but not of potential dangers. Realizes doors open and shut, but may not know to keep hands from getting caught.

Language: Focuses on words and objects that are central to her life.

Fine motor: Throws ball overarm instead of underarm.

Gross motor: May kick ball without falling or tripping. Likes to hang from bars by her hands. May climb onto an adult-size chair, pivot around and sit down. Running may look stiff; child may have trouble stopping and manoeuvring corners while running. Tries to jump with both feet, but may not get off the ground.

Language: Near end of second year, she learns that everything has a name and constantly asks, 'What's that?' May combine two words like 'all gone'.

Memory: May be able to recall a familiar object or person without seeing or touching it.

Tips: Do not pressure a child to speak. Acknowledge her body language but let child hear the words that complement the gesture.

21 months   **Grooming:** May be able to put on clothes with easy-to-manage openings.

Sleeping: Afternoon naps turn into rests: total sleeping time drops near the end of the second year. May try to delay bedtime with extra kisses.

Tasks: Some children put away clothes and toys.

22 months   **Feeding:** May give cup to parent when thirsty.

Grooming: May put on shoes, but often on the wrong foot.

Tasks: Tries buckling car seat-belt with parent's help.

23 months   **Grooming:** May put on simple garments but not differentiate between front and back.

Tasks: By the end of the second year, may open doors, unwrap parcels, help parents with chores.

24 months   **Check up:** Visits doctor for two-year checkup; may include blood test to check for lead poisoning and a skin test for tuberculosis. Meets the dentist for the first time.

Feeding: Can eat all kinds of foods. Encourage use of utensils.

Grooming: Some babies may be ready to start potty training, while others will need more time until their motor skills and bladder control improves.

Health: Watch for ear infections in toddlers. Signs include ear pain and fever.

brain child

MOTOR SKILLS	MENTAL DEVELOPMENT
Fine motor: May turn pages one at a time. Enjoys finger-painting and scribbling with big crayons. Loves to inspect tiny objects, especially insects. Shows hand preference. **Gross motor:** Looks down to dodge obstacles while walking. May walk up stairs, holding on to banister, both feet on one step.	**Awareness:** Improving memory skills may allow child to make right associations. Matches shoes with the correct family member. **Tips:** Explain safety in simple terms. Feeling the heat from a stove teaches the meaning and danger of 'hot' objects.
Fine motor: May put on shoes but often on the wrong foot. Tries to do up car seat-belt. **Gross motor:** Alternates easily between walking and running, sitting and standing. Likes to be pushed on a swing and enjoys other playground activities.	**Awareness:** Recognizes when a picture book is upside down. Learns to turn pages one at a time. **Language:** Enjoys listening to simple stories. May take the lead in conversations and use words to express feelings or ideas.
Fine motor: Likes to play with clay. May draw a crude circle if shown how. **Gross motor:** Shows greater co-ordination in movement. Often runs rather than walks. Can seat self at table and climb into car seat on own. May throw ball into a basket.	**Language:** May use words to express frustration or anger. At times, still relies on facial expressions or an occasional scream to communicate feelings. **Memory:** May follow simple directions, but attention span is fleeting. **Tips:** Have genuine two-way conversations with child. Try not to respond with 'uh-huh'. A child will recognize when you are not listening.
Gross motor: Moves with greater efficiency by end of second year. Child is sturdier on feet and less likely to fall. Some toddlers may walk up and down stairs by themselves; others may feel more comfortable crawling on steps. May enjoy dancing to music and learns how to move according to tempo.	**Language:** By end of second year, some children may have a vocabulary of more than 200 words. Mimics adult inflections and actions. **Memory:** May grasp meaning of 'soon' and 'after dinner …' but has limited knowledge of days and time.

AGE	PHYSICAL DEVELOPMENT
25–29 months	**Feeding:** Should be served whatever the family is eating, but a balanced diet may be hard to maintain. Sweets should not be used as a bribe to finish dinner. **Grooming:** Has become a creature of habit. May ask to go to the toilet, but accidents are very possible. Insists on choosing own clothes. May dress himself in easy, pull-on clothes. Loves to use Elastoplast for bumps and bruises. **Health:** Baby fat slowly disappears in the third year. Posture improves as muscles strengthen. **Sleeping:** May switch from cot to bed, which can create some difficulty in settling down at night. Maintain a regular time for bed, including nightly rituals like last kisses and storybook readings. Side bed-rails will prevent tumbles to the floor.
30–36 months	**Check up:** Sees doctor for annual check. Visits dentist every six months from two-and-a-half years old. May receive fluoride treatment. **Feeding:** Appetite still fluctuates; may skip a meal occasionally. Do not make a special meal. Encourage proper table manners, such as using utensils and sitting through entire meal. By third birthday may use a fork efficiently but often forgets to chew food well. **Grooming:** Child may express more consistently when he needs to use the bathroom. **Tasks:** A true mother's helper. Makes bed, cleans up messes. Needs supervision in the kitchen.

Fine motor: Child learns to co-ordinate movements of his wrist, fingers and palm. May unscrew lids, turn knobs, unwrap paper.

Gross motor: Constantly on the move. Loves to be chased. Enjoys going down slides, swinging and running around playgrounds. May pedal small tricycle. Learns to walk on tiptoe and may be able to stand on one foot. May count stairs and jump off the final step. Jumping on the spot still takes great effort and co-ordination.

Awareness: Starts to solve problems in his head. May understand number concepts like co-ordination (one dog, two dogs) and the process of classification (a cat is an animal).

Language: Vocabulary grows rapidly and child starts combining nouns with verbs to form three-to-four-word sentences. Begins to use pronouns, such as 'I' and 'me', and other parts of speech. May begin to ask 'why' questions. Pays attention to what others say, whether to him or to someone else.

Tips: To keep his attention, choose books that encourage touching and pointing.

Fine motor: Learns how to hold a pencil in writing position. Loves to draw with chalk and crayons. Imitates vertical and horizontal strokes, but may have difficulty making a cross with two lines. May use small scissors with parent supervision. Rotates jigsaw pieces and completes a simple puzzle. By the age of 3, child will have enough muscle co-ordination to play a simple musical instrument.

Gross motor: Walking becomes more adult-like with a heel-to-toe gait. Likes to try out new types of movement like galloping and trotting. May alternate feet when going up stairs. Capable of multiple actions when moving. May throw a ball while running or eat ice cream while walking. Bends over easily without falling. Kicks ball in an intended direction. May hit a baseball if it's placed on a stand. Pedals and steers a tricycle well.

Awareness: Understands relationship between objects. May sort out toys by shapes and colours. By the age of 3, has very one-sided reasoning and still cannot see an issue from two angles.

Language: May grasp two- or three-part command. Can follow story line and remembers many ideas presented in books. May correctly name colours.

Memory: Becomes more focused on activities like reading and drawing. May tell people his age but has no sense of the length of a year.

Tips: Do not expect child to use perfect diction. If he stutters, set an example by talking calmly and correctly. Slow down speech and try not to draw attention to his difficulties. Help child use words to describe emotions.

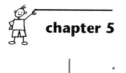

chapter 5

physical strength and co-ordination

☆

How physically strong would you estimate a one-day-old baby to be?

☆

Most people answer 'very weak', perceiving the new-born infant to be fundamentally both helpless and strengthless.

Nothing could be further from the truth.

If you give a one-day-old baby a rope, such that she can get her little hands and feet around, and if you gently lift (do this in a softly padded cot), many babies will hold on. If you want a good idea of how impressive this performance is, try it yourself!

Similarly to the question 'how co-ordinated is a one-day-old baby?' most people respond 'hardly at all'.

Again, how absolutely incorrect!

If, on the first day of her terrestrial life, you placed your baby in a large, warm, freshwater swimming pool, guess what the baby would have done? Swim! And swim well.

Your baby's muscles are therefore both strong and co-ordinated from birth onwards, and need constant movement, stimulus, exercise and nourishment to allow them to grow powerfully and naturally.

Is this what we normally do?

No!

For example, we take this little paragon of physical and mental genius, this mini Da-Vincian-in-waiting, to explore our planet, and become involved in the following tragi-comedy:

First we put hip-locking nappies on, over which we place thick, puffy trousers.

Next we put on a little t-shirt, over which we put another shirt, over which we put a little woolly jumper, topping all this off with a space-man-like jacket that has giant arms with connected and fingerless gloves.

Strapped in and ready for take off

At the bottom end we put on thick socks, over which we place hard-shelled shoes. At the top end we put a giant spaceman-like hat, which comes up over the hearing apparatus and crushes the visual apparatus.

We then place the poor little creature back down into the wheeled vehicles we use to transport our babies around on the planet, the perambulator (pram), baby buggy or kindervargen.

'Ah!' we think, 'light could damage the eyes', so over the top we place a giant hood: early training in tunnel-vision!!

Next we feel that the mini Da Vinci might fall out, so we strap her tightly around the gut. Next, wanting to simulate his musical creativity, we place little dingling bells on the side of the hood, which, as the pram moves, go dingle, dingle, dingle, dingle, incessantly.

Still not satisfied, and realizing that the multi-lingual human will be the more powerful Intellectual Capitalist of the future, we stick a gob-stopping pacifier into her mouth.

Finally, wanting to complete the nurturing of our young genius, we take a little piece of string and attach one end to the roof of the pram, and to the other end we attach a plastic or furry toy, which swings back-and-forth, back-and-forth, back-and-forth, numbingly and hypnotically.

AND THEN WE WONDER WHERE ALL THE DA VINCIS HAVE GONE!

We adults are, metaphorically, still in the pram! All we need to do is pull down the hood, take out the pacifier, silence the monotonous bells, undo the straps, take off the clothes, and leap free.

What we need to do for our babies is to make sure they are never restricted in them physically, or metaphorically, in the first place.

THINGS FOR YOU TO DO

The best transportation system for your baby is you. Wherever possible, carry your baby in your own embrace or in a sling. Slings have the advantage of keeping the baby in close contact with the parent. Some slings are designed to carry the baby facing outwards so that they can see what's going on. These are suitable after the baby is strong enough to hold her head up (see development chart, page 164). Toddlers enjoy being carried in a kiddie-carrier backpack. However, if your baby is particularly heavy and you need to use a buggy, buy one that allows your child as much physical and sensual freedom as possible. Little things can make a difference. For example, there is no need to have the buggy's rain cover on unless it is actually raining or

brain child

is very windy. These limit the baby's ability to see out. Do not put the buggy into the reclining position if he is not actually asleep. The baby likes to be able to see what's going on and once she can sit up properly, let her sit fully upright in the buggy rather than reclining. When your child is walking, let her walk (using reins), rather than making her sit in the buggy. Prolonged use of the buggy is more convenient for parents but makes toddlers lazy and unfit.

Locate baby swimming centres and discuss with trainers and other participating parents their success stories. Many local swimming pools arrange 'classes' for parents and toddlers. The best ones take the approach of offering fun 'splash' sessions, which graduate from relatively random play to more directed lessons in the art-science of swimming.

Babies are natural-born swimmers

Make sure you are an accomplished swimmer yourself. If you cannot swim, it's well worth joining an adult beginners' class and taking the plunge.

chapter 6

handedness

---☆---

In my travels to over 70 different countries in the last 30 years, I have consistently carried out a handedness field survey. I ask the audiences, and they range from kindergarten children to members of the general public, to university students and professors, to businessmen and political leaders, 'how many of you are right-handed?' and 'how many of you are left-handed?' Invariably 100 per cent raise their hands, 90 per cent-plus raising their right hands, to indicate that they are right-handed, and the remaining smaller percentage raising their left to indicate that they are left-handed.

---☆---

I then point out that this is a rather surprising admission on their part, as I have been with them for a number of hours, and have observed that all of them have two hands, and that most of them seem to be using them both exceptionally well in walking, balancing, talking, eating, greeting, holding, carrying, putting on and taking off clothes, opening and closing doors, driving, scratching and hugging! (It is interesting to note that 'right-handed' people will hold a knife in their right hand and a fork in their left. If you consider which is the more delicate and important activity, cutting or directing the food to the mouth and not the ear or nostril, they should perhaps consider themselves left-handed-dominant when dining!) For the final few centuries of the last millennium, most societies made two major errors:

1. They decided to consider left-handedness somehow inadequate and even evil, coining words and phrases such as: sinister; gauche; cack-handed; and their opposites, right; correct; and adroit, etc. In many societies 'left-handers' were scorned and rejected, and as recently as the last half of the last century, millions of 'left-handed' children were forced to use their right hands by methods including having their left hand 'strapped behind their back', more general punishment for the use of the left hand, and in the more extreme cases, beatings.

2. Realizing that there appeared to be a slight preference for one hand or the other, societies around the world made the fatal blunder of leaping from a relativistic continuum (60/40 or even as delicate as 51/49) to an either-or dyadic absolute: right or left. (100–0). This verbal classification formed a negative synergy that encouraged people to think that they were, for example, right-handed, and therefore to prefer slightly the right hand even more, which encouraged them to use it even more, thus confirming their thinking, and so on, until the ingrained mental imbalance had manifested itself as a physical imbalance and as a 'proof' of their assumptions about themselves.

This thinking/function *mal*function was funnily and disturbingly illustrated by an event in one of my extended seminars. After a weekend of rest and relaxation, one of the delegates returned from a skiing expedition with his left arm in a plaster cast.

Upon receiving sympathy and commiseration from myself and a number of the other seminar delegates, he attempted to allay our worries and concerns by cheerily proclaiming 'Oh, don't worry! I was lucky! I broke the arm I don't use!'

His unconscious exclamation emphasizes how deeply ingrained and fundamentally counter-productive such thought patterns can be.

The fact of the matter is that _all_ babies are born AMBIDEXTROUS. Regardless of whatever slight preferences they may have, their baby bodies are _designed_ to operate in a balanced, integrated manner. To confirm this all you have to do is watch their early muscular and co-ordinative development, especially in activities such as creeping, crawling, holding and climbing.

The Greats and Champions

A quick analysis of the history of both art and sports shows that those children who were able to maintain their ambidexterity throughout life were able to use it to massive advantage. In the arts, both Leonardo da Vinci and Michelangelo were known for their ambidexterity. It was reported that Michelangelo, when getting tired while sculpting, would simply change hands in order to give the other a 'rest' and would continue apace!

In sports the great batsmen in activities such as cricket and baseball were renowned for being able to spray balls to any parts of the field, and in baseball such all-time greats as Hank Arron and Stan Musual would actually change hands and stance from right to left or from left to right to confuse the pitchers.

In boxing the two 'greatest of all time', Sugar Ray Robinson and Mohammed Ali were both 'switch-hitters' and could advance or retreat with either hand or foot equally. The effect on their opponents was obviously doubly confusing because they never knew from where any move or punch was coming.

In modern Olympic training, especially in sports such as soccer, hockey, rowing and swimming, the top athletes are regularly trained, often for hours on end, to use their less favoured side in order to bring it up to par with their favourite side, and thus to give them both a more balanced muscular and bodily alignment, and a greater range of physical and athletic possibility.

brain child

To emphasize the underlying ambidexterity of the brain and the body, and the flexibility of the brain to adjust when necessary or when trained, results of work done with amputees have produced astonishing results. Within *three months* of losing a dominant hand, the remaining non-dominant hand has taken over all the tasks of the other, and performs them at virtually identical skill levels. This is confirmed most dramatically by hand-writing analysis, which instantaneously recognizes the writing as from the same (the word is ironic) 'hand'.

Even more amazingly, when both hands have been lost, again within a few months, the feet can be trained to do many of the activities that the hands once did. This includes the incredibly complex task of drawing and painting, outstanding examples of which I am sure you will have seen during the Christmas-card season. Even more amazingly, where people have lost, or lost the ability to use, both hands and feet, they have accomplished superb writing and artistic competence using only the mouth or the muscles of the neck.

What these studies demonstrate is that the brain of your child is prepared to express itself through any of its limbs or extensions, and that those limbs will readily adapt to whatever the brain demands.

In terms of the latent ambidextrous potential of your baby, the signposts point simultaneously in both directions!

THINGS FOR YOU TO DO

Make ambidexterity a game rather than a task. Play ambidextrous games with your baby/child including the following:

(a) Use eating implements in opposite hands from normal.

(b) Put on clothes while changing the order of which arm/leg 'goes in first'.

(c) Regularly throw and catch balls with the non-dominant hand.

(d) Regularly play racquet games with the non-dominant hand.

(e) Regularly brush teeth and comb hair with the non-dominant hand.

(f) Experiment by drawing and painting with the non-dominant hand.

(g) Teach your child to juggle, which is a wonderful balancing and ambidextrous activity.

(h) Arrange piano lessons for your child – think of the balance involved, the mental activity and agility required, and the smile on the face of the Happy Homunculus!

(i) Encourage your child to participate in 'balanced sports' such as dance, sculling, the martial arts, running and swimming, etc.

brain child

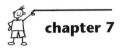

chapter 7

the mastermind group

---☆---

Consider the team gathered and the expense incurred in the running of a Formula One racing car: the team will consist minimally of engineers, aeronautists, aerodynamicists, fuel specialists, tyre specialists, computer specialists, psychologists, masseuses, doctors, bankers, accountants, lawyers, physiotherapists, security officers, marketing experts, scriptwriters, camera operators, press officers and meteorologists, to name but a few!

---☆---

The cost to run such an enterprise for a year, with the sole purpose of hurtling that piece of metal, fibreglass and rubber around an interminable track faster than any other similar piece of metal, is a staggering £250 million! Even with this astounding commitment of resources and fabulous expense, the machine breaks down on average 50 per cent of the 17 times per year when it is expected to perform.

Consider its body, composed of no more than one hundred working parts, and its 'brain' (its on-board control system) composed of a few million computer chips.

Consider now your human baby, with a body a *million million* times more complex and beautiful, and a brain infinitely more powerful. What kind of Mastermind Group do we assemble for it? And how much are we willing to invest in its function? Even with relatively little investment the human baby performs relatively immaculately not only for most of the 365 days of the year but for most of the 31,176,000 seconds in that same year, year after year.

The argument of *Brain Child* is that it is more important to assemble a Mastermind Group for every child born than for any Formula One car.

Take your pick from the following (or choose them all) recommended members for your child's Mastermind Group (Things For You To Do): a musician, an artist, a doctor, an athlete, a clown (as in a Shakespearean monarch's fool), a doctor, a polymath, an explorer, a Mind Sports Master or Grandmaster, an astronomer, a sports psychologist, an economist, a counsellor, a martial artist, a scientist, a physical trainer and a poet. You may have friends or family members who can be called upon to fulfil these roles, but do not worry if you cannot compile a complete team: a handful of willing participants will suffice. It is not an onerous undertaking – it could be a bit like being a godparent and many people are greatly flattered to be asked. There might be an occasion when your child needs to talk to an expert about a specific school project, say to a scientist about Galileo. It will be far easier if the child already knows this person and has an easy-going relationship with her. When your Mastermind Team lacks a real person for a specific subject, find the best-possible quality reference book in your local library.

It is surprisingly easy to find people in each of these categories who are willing to help if they know that the parents are committed and that the child, in the *Pygmalion* sense (see Chapter 4, page 110), is thirsting after the knowledge they possess.

brain child

If it turns out to be not possible or easy, virtual mastermind members can easily be found. These can manifest themselves as books, computer programmes, toys, websites, films, videos or CDs.

A broad and diverse Mastermind Group can provide a winning 'formula'

It is interesting to note that in the history of the great geniuses, one of the recurring and most common of themes is the Mastermind Group. Leonardo da Vinci, Isaac Newton, Queen Elizabeth I, Thomas Jefferson, Einstein, Beethoven, Picasso and Garry Kasparov were all surrounded by their modern-day giants in multiple fields. Alexander the Great, considered by most military leaders and strategic thinkers throughout history to be the greatest of them all, is particularly noteworthy in this context. His father, King Philip of Macedonia, devoted full attention and maximum effort to the upbringing of his young boy, coincidentally, and to many people's surprise, giving him freedom to choose throughout his learning career. Alexander was trained in physical combat, warfare and strategic thinking by the best athletes and soldiers of his day; in culture and the arts he was schooled by the leading artists and musicians; and in philosophy and science he chose, as his personal tutor, the immortal Aristotle, who considered Alexander a model and brilliant student.

The result of this training was not, as many had predicted, an ego-maniacal power-hungry plunderer and murderer, but a leader renowned for his vigour, enthusiasm, compassion, understanding of his people's needs, vast knowledge and vision. He alone was responsible for the establishing of over one hundred major universities devoted to the arts, sciences and physical culture at all extremes of the largest empire the world had known to that date.

THINGS FOR YOU TO DO

 The child's brain can only learn from the environment that surrounds it. Ensure that that environment includes a Mastermind Group selected from the menu provided, and you will have provided your baby with a 'formula' far more significant than that received from any can of baby food or Ferrari!

part five

the senses

chapter 1

the happy homunculus

☆

In the latter half of the twentieth century, a Canadian scientist by the name of Dr Wilder Penfield made an amazing discovery.

☆

Dr Penfield was probing, with tiny electrodes, the open brains of people suffering from epileptic fits. The purpose of his probing was to trigger individual cells, or tiny groups of cells, in order to locate that small area of the patient's brain that was giving rise to the fits.

As is so often with great discoveries, what Penfield discovered in his probings was even more significant than the extremely important goal he had set himself.

As he toured the surface of the brain, he found that when he probed certain areas of it, different parts of the body responded.

By continuing his probings, Penfield was able to 'map' the entire surface of the cortex, noting as he went which part of the cortex was devoted to which part of the body.

Dr Penfield then calculated the percentage of the brain that was devoted to each part of the body.

He then 'redesigned' the human body, creating a 'Sensory Man' based on

193

The Happy Homunculus

brain child

the importance of the parts of the body as judged by the brain and the amount of the brain devoted to that part.

The resulting figure is the Happy Homunculus.

At an instant you can see that by *far* the most important parts of our body, from the brain's point of view, are the hands (easily in position number one), then the feet, followed closely by the mouth. The remaining senses follow these gold, silver and bronze medallists, with the remaining limbs, torso and sex organs trailing behind.

Why *should* the brain organize its bodily priorities in this way?

The minute you realize that this is the case, the reasons do become glaringly obvious:

1. The hands are the brain's prime, unbelievably complex, astoundingly sensitive tools, protectors and providers.
2. The feet are the body's 'second hands'. They provide the body with all the sensory information about the surface of the planet as well as maintaining balance and poise.
3. The mouth is a multi-layered defence system against a million million potential biochemical and chemical invaders, and is an astoundingly precise and strong cutting and grinding machine. It is the world's (if not the Universe's) ultimate chemical laboratory. It is the main entrance to your baby's internal physical Universe.

───────────── ☆ ─────────────

The Happy Homunculus can thus act as a marvellous and constantly beckoning guide for the caring and loving parent wishing to know what emphases should be placed in the caring for and development of the baby's brain and body.

───────────── ☆ ─────────────

Each of the following chapters is devoted to an exploration of the individual senses, and to an explanation, in more detail, of why the Happy Homunculus has been given, by the brain, his extraordinary shape.

THINGS FOR YOU TO DO

Read the following chapters always bearing in mind the Happy Homunculus and the brain's apportioning of priorities to the baby's senses.

Observe that your baby's biggest sensory organ, the skin, is involved in virtually every aspect of your baby's developing brain. The skin is the communicator between the outside Universe and your baby's developing brain. Keep your baby's skin healthy by ensuring that his diet is good (see page 316) and that you are rigorous about basic skin hygiene. One bath a day, before bed, is enough, but ensure that your child washes his face, hands and upper body in the mornings. A good way to avoid nappy rash is to let your baby go without a nappy for a part of every day. If you are at all worried about more serious skin problems such as eczema, consult your health visitor or general practitioner (who will be one of the members of your child's Mastermind Group).

Buy the Happy Homunculus toy, as a constant reminder to both yourself and your child of the brain's priorities. Alternatively, you could copy his picture and post it in a place where you will see it frequently.

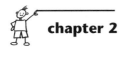

chapter 2

eyes — sight

---☆---

Each of your baby's miraculous eyes contains one hundred and thirty million (130,000,000) light receivers. Each of these light receivers is capable of taking in five photons (bundles of light energy and information) every one-hundredth of a second!

To make just one human eye like your baby's would require modern technology's most sophisticated computer, microscope and telescope systems, a building the size of a large house, and a budget of £100,000,000.

---☆---

Your baby is valuable and *priceless!*

Like a camera the baby's eye sees everything upside down, but magically turns it right side up at the back of the brain, where everything she sees is sorted out, related, made sense of, recorded and filed for lifetime memory and linked to the sounds, smells, sensations, tastes, and touch at the time the picture happened.

Your baby's eyes, with their back-up nervous system, are in fact like a television studio – but what a studio! Only two television cameras, but several *million million* miles of video and sound tape. A fantastic recorder, which records sound, smell, touch, taste, and archives of taped scenes that would cram several Albert Halls right up to their ceilings, and above all, a work-force the size of London's total population: writers, artists, film directors, thinkers, mathematicians, scene shifters, workers somehow jammed into the studio, all working and talking at the same time.

In addition, your baby owns and runs her own projection theatre, where she recaps on the day's events about herself. Her dreams are very important. No one yet knows how a dream is screened in her brain and every other child's.

THINGS FOR YOU TO DO

Make sure that your baby has regular opportunity to see short-, medium- and long-term perspectives — this keeps the eye 'muscularly fit'. When you are out, don't limit your baby's viewing range by hanging toys right in front of her face in her baby buggy. She'll get sick of seeing that silly toy bouncing about and she'll be far more intrigued by clouds, trees and cars in the distance.

If you are at all worried about your baby's eyes in between routine checks, ask your health visitor or general practitioner (who will be part of your Mastermind Group).

ears — hearing

---☆---

Each of your baby's ears contains 24,000 fibres and many intricate parts that make it by far the most sophisticated musical instrument in the known Universe. These fibres are able to detect enormous ranges and subtle distinctions in the tiniest molecular vibrations of the air. As with the eye, the central system classifies, relates, explains, records, files and cross-references all the sounds heard in a lifetime.

---☆---

Your child's ear will be able to record and replay perfectly every birds' song, every whispered word of love, and every symphony he ever hears, perfectly.

It had been assumed until very recently that the new-born baby was primarily an insensate, moronic, slow-learning, dribbling human blob that had needed little mental stimulation and that his main requirements were food and cleaning until he reached the more active and alert age of between six months and a year.

We know that exactly the opposite is true.

A new-born baby is a Leonardo-in-the-making, with incredible strengths; extraordinary co-ordination (remember, he can swim competently at birth);

with senses that are already honing in on his new world with incredible speed, precision, capacity and accuracy; and with memory banks that have been gorging themselves on information for most of his nine-month life to date.

An interesting modern experiment, which has now been repeated thousands of times, has confirmed aspects of this:

Once the new-born baby has suckled and is resting on his mother's breast, the team of doctors, nurses, midwives, spouses and friends stand in a circle or semi-circle equidistant from the baby. One by one they take turns saying the baby's name. In nearly all those cases where the father has spoken to the child in the womb, an intriguing result is observed: as each person intones the baby's name, there is basically no reaction until the father speaks. The second he does, no matter where in the circle and no matter which 'number' he is, the baby directs his attention towards him, proving that while in the womb he has both heard the father's voice and learnt to recognize and distinguish it from other noises and sounds.

IVAN AND LARISA'S STORY

Ivan and Larisa, the young Mexican couple (see page 47), confirmed these experiments from their own experience, which is now told in Larisa's words:

'Daddy's Voice'

With my first baby I had to have a caesarian because he hadn't turned. When the doctor took him out he cried a lot and held up his hands in front of his face to try and shield himself from the bright lights. He just cried and cried.

When they had finished cleaning him he was still crying. My husband, who was beside me all the time, approached our baby and started to sing one of the songs he used to sing every single night during my pregnancy. He stopped crying immediately.

brain child

THINGS FOR YOU TO DO

 See Things For You To Do – Music, page 252.

Encourage your baby/child to listen to natural sounds. Birdsong, rustling leaves, rushing water, crashing waves, the sound of undertow running over beach pebbles. In the home, play different types of music and encourage your child to experiment with sounds by 'testing', for example, the different tones that a row of partly filled glasses make when struck.

If you are at all worried about your child's hearing in between routine checks, ask your health visitor or general practitioner (who will be part of your Mastermind Group).

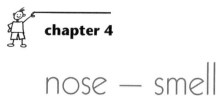

chapter 4

nose — smell

☆

A baby can distinguish an individual smell when there is only one molecule per million million million.

☆

Smell will become a major part of your child's memory bank because smells act as triggers for the memory. Have you ever had the experience of briefly smelling a smell, such as someone's perfume, for it to immediately remind you of a person you knew ten years ago? This is the extraordinary power of the sense of smell. Remember that smell and taste are very closely connected.

THINGS FOR YOU TO DO

 Make sure that your baby is constantly stimulated by different smells (nature and especially flowers are paramount here). Who can ever forget the smell of a rose or a favourite flower, once experienced as a small child?

Play discrimination games with different fragrances. Oils, perfumes and fruit essences make good laboratories. You can try playing a blindfolded guessing game – the more children who play, the more fun you will have. Gather together a number of the following, plus anything else you can think of: a segment of orange, a rose, a chunk of freshly baked bread, a lavender sachet, a moth ball, etc. Blindfold all participants and ask them to sit in a circle. Pass round each item and sniff deeply. See who can guess what everything is. For older children, make the game more challenging by getting each person to remember the sequence of smells and then jot them down afterwards.

See how your baby reacts to different smells. If you are at all worried about her sense of smell, ask your health visitor or general practitioner (who will be part of your Mastermind Group) for a thorough check—up.

chapter 5

mouth — taste

☆

Your baby's mouth is like the ultimate chemical laboratory. It is capable of distinguishing a million million different tastes and textures, and can instantaneously detect any form of danger, be it a molecule of poison or rotten food or the tiniest sliver of hair or splinter of bone.

☆

Your baby's mouth is a giant portal to the interior of your baby's body, and as such, like a space station, is equipped with all forms of defences and early warning systems.

As you will see from the homunculus (see page 199), the brain gives enormous importance and precedence to the mouth/taste system, devoting nearly 10 per cent of its 'power' to this area. (See Food and Play, page 206.)

THINGS FOR YOU TO DO

Stimulate your baby's sense of taste by allowing him a wide variety of tastes and textures. As your baby moves on from milk to 'solids' let him try out a variety of different tastes, as it is a great temptation to stick to tried-and-tested foods that you know he likes. When your toddler starts to get picky about likes and dislikes (which they all do), again, don't take the easy way out and only give him what he prefers. Carry on offering a wide variety of different foods and take the approach that he should try out and explore new foods. Encourage him to chew tough or chewy foods (though watch out for choking).

Allow your baby (child) to experiment! Many parents worry too much about their planet-exploring babies eating dirt and insects, etc. Don't be so worried. As with all things, your baby needs to explore, in order to toughen and strengthen the immune system, and to learn 'good' from 'bad'. If the baby is not allowed to experiment, he will never learn and will remain immunologically weak. In addition, the body has a wonderful back-up system, and should harmful materials get past the guardian lips, teeth, tongue and salivary acid baths, the throat and stomach muscles are waiting eagerly to expel the intruder!

See how your baby reacts to different foods and varying tastes. If you are at all worried about his mouth, sense of taste, approach to food or any aspect relating to diet and food, consult your health visitor or your general practitioner (who will be part of your Mastermind Group) and ask for a thorough check-up.

mouth — taste

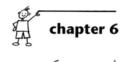

chapter 6

food and play

'STOP PLAYING WITH YOUR FOOD!'

This unfortunate tirade has been the death-knell for millions of aspiring chefs, and has been a contributing cause to weak gums, chapped hands, dry lips and skin and stiff necks.

It is natural, enjoyable and beneficial to eat food with the hands (that is why barbecued foods, hamburgers, nachos, and sandwiches are so globally popular, and why many people at home surreptitiously eat much of their own food with their hands) and it is therefore beneficial to *encourage* your baby to 'play with her food'.

The hands are an exquisitely tuned instrument that send highly sophisticated (see The Happy Homunculous, page 199) 'early warning' messages to the brain and stomach concerning the texture, nature, temperature, consistency, and digestibility of the food about to be consumed (or rejected). In conjunction with the eyes and nose they allow the entire digestive system to prepare for what is coming before it even reaches the mouth. The foods, which will inevitably contain vegetable or animal oils, will naturally oil the skin of the lips, face, hands and forearms.

The finely tuned muscles of the fingers increasingly allow a more delicate and appropriate placing of the food into the mouth.

If the food is in any way tough, the hand, teeth, gums and neck muscles act in harmony, the pulling and biting combination strengthening arms, gums and the neck, which is also massaged by the fine-muscle rotation involved in this activity.

Using eating implements at an early stage is not recommended. The baby's hand, holding a metal spoon, sends a bodily message to the digestive system explaining that this is metal and should not be eaten. Similarly when the spoon approaches the mouth, there is a natural tendency for the muscles of the neck and mouth to slightly tighten in view of the imminent metal invasion. This causes an increasingly permanent 'freezing' of the muscle systems of the neck and jaw, which can in turn lead to tension, strain, headaches and stress.

Eating food with the hands is natural, beneficial in many ways, and to be encouraged. Indeed it is quite natural in many countries all over the planet, where the hands are used instead of chopsticks, knives, forks and spoons.

Food is also an item for gift-giving, a wonderful opportunity for games, and an expression of affection and love, as the following story of my 'romance' with a three-and-a-half-year-old Swedish girl unveils:

LEILA'S STORY

On a snowy Christmas-season evening in Stockholm, I had been invited to dine, overlooking a Stockholm harbour, by five Swedish friends. One of the couples had brought along their three-and-a-half-year-old daughter, Leila, and we all sat down in festive and playful mood at a large rectangular feasting table. I sat in the middle of one side, with little Leila sitting 'kitty corner' across from me at the end of the opposite side.

The table was festooned with glistening drinking glasses for all manner of libations, and soon our celebrations and enjoyment were well under way.

Leila was quite understandably a little overawed at the beginning of the evening, but as soon as the food arrived began to tuck in enthusiastically. I had also ordered chips with my meal and then, as they say, the games began!

Leila picked up a chip, caught my eye, began very slowly to move the chip towards me and the nearest glasses on her side and then quickly pulled it back, paused, and then took a good chomp out of it.

In response I did exactly the same.

The game progressed apace, with each successive chip being moved closer and closer to the intended receiver, snaking their way through the forest of glasses and then, just as it was about to be taken, being whisked back with increasing glee, and eaten with great joy and a total fixation on the other's eyes.

By this time Leila had begun to intersperse the chip offering and retraction with the odd tiny fistful of peas. Her parents were at first reluctant to let Leila eat with her hands in public, but on my insistence allowed the games to continue.

Finally Leila allowed me to take one of her chips, and then a most extraordinary thing happened: Leila picked up a large fistful of her petit-pois, and stuffed her mouth with them. She then picked up another fistful, wriggled down from her chair, ran around the table, and climbed on to my lap. Like a little Statue of Liberty she was holding her clenched petit-pois-filled hand up to my face. As she did so she began to chew her own mouthful of peas very deliberately and with a wide-open and then closing mouth. She was showing me, in slow motion, the entire mechanics of eating, in conjunction with the obvious assurance that this was both safe and good food. Mesmerized by this astonishingly open display, which was a mixture of communication, objective science, biology, and affection, I watched in awe, and saw for the first time, a human mouth perform its unimaginably complex yet nevertheless eerily beautiful function.

brain child

When the peas were well on their way to the kingdom of soup, Leila suddenly opened her little hand half-way, and gently offered me the peas in it.

It was one of the most considerate, beautiful and complete gifts I have ever been offered. I ate the lot!

Leila had taught me a lesson about communication, the joy of food, the bio-mechanics of eating, and the nature of food as an expression of affection and love that I will remember forever. All babies around the world are waiting to teach all parents the same marvellous lesson!

THINGS FOR YOU TO DO

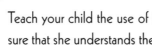 Allow your baby to play with her food for as long into her childhood as possible. That childhood will hopefully end past her 100th year! Learning to enjoy food is an important life skill. So many people have been brought up to fear food by having to 'eat everything on the plate', while many others have become fussy eaters through not being taught to experiment with food with gusto. This can store up food-related problems for adult life, possibly even contributing to anorexia and bulimia. If you are worried about your baby throwing food around and making a mess, acquire a large plastic sheet and spread it under her chair. Deck her out in a large plastic overall and bib and let play commence!

Teach your child the use of implements as an extension of social etiquette and make sure that she understands the different environments in which different 'languages' are appropriate. If you explain this clearly very few infractions will occur.

 Study the posture and facial and neck tensions of people using knives and forks or other sharp eating implements.

Similarly study the 'body language' in terms of enjoyment and muscular activity of those eating foods with their hands.

Especially explore cultures in which eating with the hands is still considered proper etiquette (you'll be surprised at how many there are) and ideally incorporate their foods and practices into your child's growing awareness. She will find it useful, later in life, if she is already aware that eating with the left hand is not acceptable in some cultures.

brain child

touch

---☆---

Your baby's skin is its largest organ. This organ is almost mystical in its powers, being able to distinguish an infinite number of textures; to distinguish temperature differences of a fraction of a degree; to 'predict' the taste of a food; to determine whether something is animal, vegetable or mineral; and in conjunction with the brain being able to 'see' in much the same way as the eye.

To protect your baby from harm in an environment which can often be damaging, your baby's skin possesses 4,000,000 pain-sensitive structures. In addition to these four million pain-sensitive structures, your baby also possesses 500,000 touch detectors.

In addition to the pain-sensitive and touch-sensitive structures, your baby's skin also possesses 200,000 temperature detectors.

---☆---

If all this were not so, and one special individual possessed even a fraction of this ability, we would call it Supernatural!

THINGS FOR YOU TO DO

Allow your baby's skin to breathe by not keeping it permanently covered up (see Clothing page 216). In warm weather, let him roam around in just a nappy — especially in the garden. Let him feel the sun on his body. In cool weather — if your home is warm enough — let him do the same indoors.

Give your baby as much variation in tactile experience as possible by encouraging him to touch, feel and stroke a whole variety of differently textured materials. Explore with him the differences between satin and steel or between sheepskin and potato skin.

Make sure that your baby's skin gets as excellent a supply of oxygen as possible. This is primarily done by making sure that the baby's heart is aerobically fit, and is pumping strongly enough to create the tiny capillaries that supply the skin with nourishment and cleanse it of impurities. This can also be done by allowing your baby to become acclimatized to cooler temperature. There is always great anxiety about whether the baby is warm enough. Don't be tempted to bundle him up in unnecessary clothing if he doesn't really need it, though it is important that he wears a hat out of doors.

Cuddle and massage your baby constantly — skin is made to be touched and caressed.

Keep an eye on your baby's skin. If he develops rashes or skin complaints of any kind, consult your health visitor or general practitioner (who will be part of your Mastermind Group) and ask for a thorough check-up.

chapter 8

feet

---☆---

UNSHOD! UNSHOD! UNSHOD!

---☆---

Your baby's feet (and your own) have the singular disadvantage of being called feet, thus making us think of them as very different from 'hands', when in fact that is precisely what they are. They should be called the 'third and fourth hands'.

As you can see on the homunculus (see page 199), a gigantic proportion of the brain is devoted to these incredibly sensitive parts of our anatomy.

The reason for this is that the baby's feet perform 'Feet Feats' that are both remarkable in their variety and sophistication, and without which the baby would rapidly die.

These 'Feet Feats' include the following:

1.   Your baby's feet provide its brain with constant information, through millions and millions of tiny sensors, about the infinitely varied surfaces with which they are in contact. They provide essential knowledge on: temperature; texture; solidity/ liquidity; sharpness; and substance. Remarkably, your feet, like your hands, can

identify instantaneously the difference between animal, vegetable and mineral, and can even give you a pretty good idea of whether or not something is edible.

2.	The feet of a baby are the prime and driving mechanism by which the baby's body completely integrates its muscular system.

When the baby is standing, the sole of her foot is doing hundreds of millions of mathematical and geometric calculations, making sure that every angle of the ground underneath it (think of what the foot has to do when it is standing on small stones) is compensated for, that all these messages are instantaneously transmitted to the brain, and that every single muscle in its body is minutely and delicately rearranged in order that the baby may remain upright and poised. This upright posture allows the freer and better function of all the baby's internal organs, better circulation and the more free and appropriate use of the limbs.

To accomplish these astoundingly complex 'Feet Feats', each foot is endowed with an incredibly complex architecture of delicate but extremely resilient bones that in number are approximately 30 per cent of every bone in your body! You can see instantly that the foot has been designed by evolution to be by far the most complex flesh-and-bone structure in your body. It must be allowed freedom to develop its multiple and multi-sensory skills.

THINGS FOR YOU TO DO

Go swimming with very clear goggles. Ideally find a multi-surfaced beach, river, or pool surface on which you can walk under water while watching what your foot actually does. You will be amazed. Your babies' feet need to be free to do the same.

For one hour wear a pair of shoes on the first two of your four hands. Draw your own conclusions!

brain child

Watch a baby's feet. You'll be stunned by what you see and what they can do. And don't worry, as many parents tend unnecessarily to do, about the feet getting damaged or cold. Cute and fragile as those sweet little implements may look, they are incredibly tough and remarkably resilient. Even in quite cold weather, when adults are feeling chilly, a baby's feet are as warm as toast. In some traditional Japanese martial arts, to attain your Black Belt status, one of the tests is to sit, naked in the snow all night, controlling your temperature. When the dawn breaks you must have controlled your body functions and temperature to such an extent that there is a dry patch of ground around you! We lose this natural ability to adjust by wearing too much and inappropriate clothing. Your Brain Child is a natural Black Belt in these arts!

Observe the stilted, jerky, mal-coordinated walking of toddlers with shoes on.

Wherever and whenever you can and it is appropriate, go, like your baby, unshod. Resist the temptation to buy your baby those cute little shoes that you see in every shoe shop. Until your baby is walking unaided out of doors, there is no need to cram her soft, growing feet into hard leather, or even into soft leather. If you do need to cover your baby's feet while she is out of doors, use soft fabric slippers with non-slip soles and loosely fitting socks. When the time is right for proper shoes, go to a specialist shoe-fitter for her to be measured and fitted properly (and watch for rapidly growing feet). But even afterwards, encourage her to go bare-footed whenever possible. The baby's foot is literally its contact with planet earth. Make sure that contact is maintained.

feet

chapter 9

clothing

---☆---

Your baby is born a nudist. He should remain so for as much of each day as possible.

---☆---

Your baby's skin is by far the largest organ of his body, intricately muscled, able to detect the most incredibly small changes of every aspect of the environment, and in need of constant stimulation and feedback. It is, indeed, one of the main methods for the baby to establish his location in the world, and to know, physically and in the finest detail, 'where he is'. The skin is also extremely tough and astoundingly resilient. It will, can, and should be allowed to adjust to quite extreme changes, and especially in temperature. When the baby is in a slightly cool room, his skin will send messages to his brain that more blood is required near the surface of the body, and will thus encourage the heart to beat slightly more strongly. The fine blood-transporting-capillaries that feed the skin will become larger, and more 'muscular', thus allowing the entire system to become more resilient and healthy.

It is interesting to note that in the martial arts, adults, who have lost the childhood ability of their skin to adapt to a wide range of temperatures, are retrained 'back to childhood'. They are trained to go barefoot in increasingly cold climes, and eventually to walk barefoot in sub-zero temperatures. Their feet remain warmer than had they been shod. In the more advanced and extreme training, this process is applied to the entire body, with similar results. It is important that adults don't place their own trained restrictions and fears on their far more flexible and resilient offspring.

Clothes not only diminish this necessary learning and growing by/of the skin; they tend to restrict physical movement and to retard the development of skeleto-muscular co-ordination.

THINGS FOR YOU TO DO

Fasten nappies as loosely as is practical and let your baby go without anything on his lower half for at least some of the day, all year round. Tightly fastened nappies can constrict the hips too much, forcing the legs into a permanently bowed position. Soft towelling nappies are preferable to stiff, plastic disposable ones. An added bonus is that he may also start taking an interest in using a potty.

Watch, like a scientist, the difference in the movements of your baby when he is unclothed and clothed.

Observe the same in yourself!

Acquire baby clothes that allow maximum movement, freedom and sensual awareness. This is an economical thing to do, as bigger clothes will last your baby longer. Don't be tempted to buy any clothing that constricts. (See also Feet, page 213.)

learning

curiosity

☆

Leonardo da Vinci claimed that curiosity was one of the seven main principles that helped him to develop his own genius and that it should be
developed in everyone. It was once said of him that he was so curious that
he wouldn't even accept 'yes!' for an answer.

And it is so for your baby's brain.

☆

Question marks that punctuate children's probings can be likened to multiple
grappling hooks that help the child ascend the Himalayas of Knowledge. It is
essential that this habit and skill be strengthened and trained. It must be done
with considerable skill, however, for most young children rapidly come to
learn that questions can become an infinitely irritating weapon. If they are
accurately placed there is no end to them and they will always lead the parent
to the edge of the precipice of ignorance, not to mention frustration and
embarrassment. It is important for the child's development that parents admit
when they don't know. In this way the child learns that ignorance, in its purest
form, is the launching pad for questions, the entire nature of science, and the
acquisition of all the knowledge they will ever learn.

For example, even Einstein's child could have led him into the realm of ignorance with a very few well-placed questions:

Child: 'What's a rainbow?'

Einstein: 'Well, my child, it is when light is bent inside a raindrop and sprays out into red, orange, yellow, green, blue, indigo, violet, the main colours in the prism.'

Child: 'What's light Daddy?'

Einstein: 'Well, light is something that we think is made up of little bundles that travel at an incredibly fast speed.'

Child: 'How fast Daddy?'

Einstein: '186,000 miles a second, dear'

Child: 'Can it go faster?'

Einstein: 'No, we don't think so.'

Child: 'Why not Daddy?'

Einstein: 'Either (a) shut up and eat your breakfast; or (b) when I know the answer to that, my child, I'll get yet another Nobel Prize for Physics ...'

The miniature mental warrior can also use questions to bombard you into a state of numbness.

Questions should therefore be answered in the context of the realization that there can be no stupid questions, that all questions should be answered where reasonable and possible, and that *the answers should not be the end of the process*. The question should not be answered with the finality of a quick response (thus ending the process and leaving the child increasingly dependent upon you for all knowledge) but should end with a further question that the child is instructed to pursue.

If, for example, the child asks how trees grow, you could explain that trees drink water and food from the ground and that the sun gives them more energy. The answer can be ended by saying 'so how do you think the tree "eats" sunlight? And why do you think most of the leaves are green?'

NOORA'S STORY

A charming curiosity story involved Noora, the three-year-old daughter of a massively knowledgeable and very articulate Arabian Sheikh. She asked him one day, he having been able to answer a fusillade of questions that she had been asking, 'Daddy, do you know everything?' Amused he responded 'Yes, my dear, perhaps I do!'

'Daddy,' she immediately shot back, 'will you tell me the name of the person who invented the first cup of tea?' The father collapsed with laughter, admitted that he didn't really know everything, and praised her profusely for such a very clever question.

Children will ask interminable (read 'from an infinite supply'!) questions, simply because they *need* to in order to survive and because their brains are designed to explore the world and Universe around them. Common child's questions such as:

Why doesn't the moon fall down?
What makes a rainbow?
Why is water wet?
Why does $1 + 1 = 2$?
Where does the sun go at night?
Why don't people on the other side of the earth fall off?
If animals can't talk how do they understand each other?
Where does the Universe end?

are the natural questions of science. *Every child is a scientist by birthright* and will only ever come to dislike science if the questions and curiosity are taken away and only the carcass of arid procedure left.

THINGS FOR YOU TO DO

Acquire or borrow a beautifully illustrated children's encyclopaedia where many answers to children's questions can be found. This is just the sort of present that loving grandparents like to give — so drop a few gentle hints if the subject comes up.

Remain, throughout your life, as curious as your child. Don't assume that you can stop learning, now that you have become an adult. Keep an open, questioning mind and aim to expand your boundaries in as many different directions as possible.

Explain to your child that not knowing things is a natural state, and that the history of the human race and the development of all knowledge, especially science, has been simply to find the answer to the next question and then to find the next exciting question, and so on ad infinitum.

Encourage your child, on a daily basis, to find fascinating questions, and reward her, appropriately, for finding them.

When you are rewarding your child for extra-special questions, give some superb reward or encouragement if a question is found to which no one at the moment knows the answer. It is often the pursuit of such answers that leads a child to great achievements in later life.

brain child

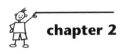

chapter 2

concentration

☆

Concentration goes hand-in-hand/brain-cell-in-brain-cell with curiosity, and unfortunately the all-pervading presence of the latter is misinterpreted as a lack of the former!

☆

The fact that the child is interested in *everything* we mistake for a lack of ability to concentrate. It sometimes seems as though the child is skipping restlessly from one thought to another, from one subject area to another, without giving any one thing its due attention. In fact, what the child is demonstrating is a virtually ceaseless desire and ability to concentrate on the multitudinous subjects the world offers his insatiable appetite.

The baby's brain is so fast, so precise, so thorough and so immaculate in its rapid-fire investigation of the next object of focus that we assume he has been only cursory in that investigation. In fact the baby's brain is like a speeded-up super-detective or scientist, running through a full and comprehensive analysis in a surprisingly short time.

Watch, for example, your three-month-old baby when you have just given him a sheet of paper.

Even a piece of paper will be minutely investigated

You know that that piece of paper is not going to last very long!

Does your baby simply stare blank-eyed into a distance and casually tear the paper in half?

No!

Your baby looks at the paper intently as he crumples it, drawing it close to his eyes. He then bangs it repeatedly on the nearest available surface.

After this he will show it to whatever other brains are around, and will then yank the paper backwards and forwards with his hands, probably tearing it again, before putting it into his mouth, chewing briefly, spitting it out, banging it on the surface, and then throwing it away.

What you have just witnessed is *not* a senseless little brain performing random actions with an irrelevant object. What you have seen is a complete little Madame Curie or Isaac Newton applying the complete Scientific Method immaculately!

The initial banging was an investigation to see what kind of musical instrument could be made from the material.

The showing it to other brains around was a psychological, sociological

brain child

and economic exploration: 'Does anybody want some of this stuff – does it have any interpersonal or economic value?'

The yanking about of the paper was an engineering investigation into the tensile, mechanical strength of the material.

The final investigation was placing it in the million million-faceted chemical laboratory known as the mouth to make an immediate and final check on its edibility.

Banging the paper once again was a review of the initial musical instrument experiment to confirm, after the other investigations, whether there was still any musical value to the paper.

And then what?

On to the next experiment in an infinitely fascinating and infinitely interconnected Universe, using the combined laser beams of his curiosity and concentration, and carrying out the investigations with every available channel to his omnipotent, omnipresent and all-seeing single eye brain, his five senses.

Our probability of misinterpreting the baby's ability to concentrate is enhanced by our own unfortunate choice of baby toys. We provide our young geniuses with rattles, models, cars and other objects that are often dull in colour, tasteless, often soundless or producing only one monotonous sound, made of plastic, and therefore boring to the sense of touch, odourless, and composed of only one, two or a few working parts.

The gargantuan baby's brain observes this uncomprehendingly dull and uninteresting object, more or less instantaneously determines its utter lack of use, interest or relevance to its life, and discards it rapidly in order to move on to something more absorbing and relevant.

We adults have often unfortunately had our curiosity bludgeoned out of us or severely stunted. We may have been trained to concentrate for long periods on the relatively mundane, and we woefully misinterpret the baby's absolute commitment to relevance, learning and the most rapid accomplishment of this. We feel it to be a mental inadequacy, about which we fret needlessly and arrogantly.

Your baby is, in a very real sense, the ultimate hunter, whose eye is invariably on target, and whose aim is so immaculate that the bull's eye is the norm. The infinite prey your baby stalks with such absolute concentration is Knowledge.

THINGS FOR YOU TO DO

Concentrate on your child's real ability to concentrate! Watch him to see how long he concentrates for and aim at increasing this time. The things he chooses to concentrate on are meaningful and valid. Beware of trying to get him to concentrate on things you believe are meaningful and valid. You can encourage this by leaving him to manage his own play, by giving him lots of free time, and by not breaking his concentrating with requests to do other things (except, of course, things like eating). We now live in a restless society of soundbites. People have short attention spans and adults are rapidly losing the ability to concentrate. Let your child's legacy be something more meaningful.

Keep a record, for a single day, of all the different things on which your baby concentrates, and the methods of his investigations.

Watch your Brain Child crouched over an ant's nest. These tiny insectoid and immaculate intelligences can keep your Brain Child entertained and transfixed for hours.

Similarly, watch your Brain Child and observe his different forms of concentration:

broad/narrow; surface/deep; returning to the original activity with what regularity; short/long; positive/negative; and active/passive.

Teach your child Mind Sports (see page 278); they massively hone the powers of concentration.

Make sure your child is aerobically fit. A fresh supply of good oxygen to your child's brain enhances the powers of concentration and increases stamina, both mental and physical. Ensure that he goes outside to play and run around at least once a day, rain or shine, away from car-filled streets. When indoors, keep air circulating by leaving a window open, including in the child's bedroom at night. Even if you live in the middle of a big city and the air is polluted, you can take steps to improve your child's air quality. Do not smoke, and if you cannot break your habit, only smoke outside the home. Never smoke near your baby.

Make your home and the child's environment vastly stimulating and entertaining, and worthy of his concentration. Keep a good range of toys and activity props, but don't have them all out on view at once. The average child owns a great many toys. Just have a few out at a time. Keep the rest put away, though within easy reach, so that your child doesn't get tired of them. In addition, keep sets of things, such as Brio and Lego, in separate boxes, not all mixed up together. Enlist your child's help, every day, in clearing up and putting away toys and activities so that he learns how important it is to care for his possessions.

Make sure that your child is regularly 'in paradise' (see page 159).

When selecting a school for your child, choose one that stimulates all the senses, provides a large range of varying mental and physical activities, engages all the cortical skills, and celebrates your child's lust for learning (see page 311).

concentration

chapter 3

logic

---☆---

It has been the received wisdom for the last century, largely due to the researches and publications of Piaget and the 'I'm OK, you're OK' school of thought, that your baby's brain does not develop logical thinking until she reaches roughly the age of six.

---☆---

This gross and often tragic misapprehension has led many babies to live their early lives comprehensively misunderstood, massively frustrated, justifiably resentful, and with a major intellectual tool underdeveloped and stunted. Three charming stories illustrate the point.

THE LIECHTENSTEIN STORY

The four-year-old son of HSH Prince Alois von und zu Liechtenstein had been accustomed to being taken upstairs to bed every night in his father's arms. One night, Prince Alois, who is trained in physical skills, law and finance, was feeling tired, and cunningly developed the following ruse.

He explained that tonight the little boy would have to walk upstairs himself, as his three big toys would require Daddy to carry two, while the boy carried the one other. The Prince would then tuck him in for the night.

The little super-sleuth, of whom Socrates would have been proud, immediately shot back with the following devastating reposte: 'Daddy, you have to come upstairs to put me to bed anyway, so you can carry me and one of the toys. When you have put me to bed you have to go back downstairs to Mummy. When your evening with Mummy is finished you have to come upstairs with Mummy again, so you can bring the other two toys with you then.'

Stunned and delighted by the immaculate and complicated logic of his offspring, the Prince admitted his son's masterful victory and did as logic dictated!

Prince Liechtenstein is cornered by his son's immaculate logic

logic

NICK AND CHRIS'S STORY

In the second story, the three-and-a-half-year-old nephew of Nick and Chris, a ship's Captain and Mate, came into his father's presence holding a rolled condom.

Holding his mental breath, and hoping the incident would pass as they sometimes (but rarely!) do, the father waited.

And then came the inevitable question: 'Daddy, what's this for?'
Daddy: 'It's for stopping babies.'
Son: 'Do you put it on your willie Daddy?' (no-one to this day knows how he came to this conclusion!)
Daddy: 'Yes you do.'
Son: 'That's silly Daddy. Men don't have babies!'

The last three short stories come from the same little Arabian girl, Noora, who asked her daddy about the invention of tea (see page 223).

NOORA'S FIRST STORY

In this instance the father, about to go to work and aware that his five-year-old daughter was going to have an x-ray that day, tried to make the whole situation feel much more 'safe' by telling her that she was going to hospital to have her photograph taken.

He returned later that day to find his three-year-old daughter confronting him in the door way, hands on hips, and face afrown.

He asked her: 'What's wrong, my dear?'
Daughter: 'Daddy you lied to me.'

Father: '*I don't believe I did.*'

Daughter: '*Yes you did.*'

Father: '*What did I say?*'

Daughter: '*You said I was going to the hospital to have my photograph taken. They didn't take my photograph Daddy, they took a picture of my skeleton instead.*'

A few months later, when Noora was still in her fifth year, her teacher phoned the father, and recounted an extraordinary tale:

NOORA'S SECOND STORY

During one of the playtimes Noora had approached the teacher with a well-thought-out and somewhat extraordinary offer. Noora explained in some detail to her teacher that it was quite apparent that she was the only adult in a class that otherwise consisted entirely of five-year-old children. Noora straightforwardly explained that it was obvious that the teacher could not be expected to understand the language of five-year-olds, and that as she, Noora, had extensive experience with the adult world, she hereby volunteered herself as translator and intermediary for the children to the teacher and for the teacher to the children!

NOORA'S THIRD STORY

A few months later, Noora came home from school and announced to her father, with complete conviction, that she no longer needed to do her homework, and that in fact, she no longer needed to attend school.

logic

'How did you come to that conclusion, my dear?' asked her somewhat non-plussed father.

'Well, Daddy,' said Noora, 'I asked my older sisters if they had remembered what they had learnt in school when they were six. They both said no. If I'm not going to remember any of it then I don't need to do any homework and I don't need to go to school any more to learn it!' stated the immaculate little logician.

These stories, and my own story at the age of four concerning sex (see page 287), illustrate as clearly as the child's immaculate logic itself, that the baby's brain thinks logically virtually from the moment of birth, and develops its logical and thinking skills at a staggering rate.

THINGS FOR YOU TO DO

Look for all manifestations of logical behaviour in your developing child. When you notice them, don't be tempted to squash them with an 'adult-logic' comment. Just observe and reward.

Reward, as the Prince did, excellent logical thinking by letting the child see that you have understood her thinking and congratulating her on it.

Study logic, be logical yourself, and extend your child's logical thinking abilities. Try not to let other people, who may not understand your child's logical thinking as well as you do (friends, family, teachers) crush this kind of thinking. Many people have low tolerance of children and their thinking. Not everyone is as fortunate as Noora was to have inspired and intelligent teachers.

chapter 4

mathematics

---☆---

One of the great tragedies of modern times is that an entire planet of mathematics and number-loving babies and children have grown into adults who are convinced that they are incompetent in mathematics, don't like it, and harbour deep fears about it. In field surveys I have carried out around the globe, similar to those concerning music and art, 75 per cent or more of those surveyed felt that they had some fundamental genetic incapacity in the field and were reluctant to get involved in activities that required calculation and the manipulation of numbers.

---☆---

The tragedy lies in the fact that babies and children love the magic and mystery of numbers and playing and juggling with them. Not only that, but they perform, on a daily basis, post-doctoral-level mathematical acts, at which, when we are fully aware of what those acts really mean, we can only marvel.

Apart from the delight that all children express when they begin to grasp the fundamentals of numbers and their meaning, consider the normal playtime activity of a three-year-old child from the mathematical/geometric point of view. The toddler's mighty mathematical brain takes an astoundingly complex series of interwoven levers and pulleys (its millions upon millions of muscle fibres and its 500-plus delicately architectured bones) and negotiates them through three-dimensional space at lightning speed, accurately estimating microsecond by microsecond the constantly changing position in which the child wishes to be.

Concurrently with these calculations, the child's brain is simultaneously observing the current positions of many other such lever-and-pulley systems (other children), predicting where, in time, their multiple trajectories will lead them, and constantly adapting its own system in order to bring it, as desired, nearer or further away from those systems.

The sophistication, complexity and magnitude of your child's mathematical calculations goes far, far beyond the capacity of the world's greatest number-crunching super-computers. What your child accomplishes in one hour of playtime with consummate ease and no stress would take those same super-computers *thousands of years* to calculate.

So how is it that such a super-mathematical device as the human brain can ever come to believe that it is incompetent in the field, while simultaneously disliking it and being increasingly afraid of it?

Four stories will shed some light:

OLIVER'S STORY

Gerard Benson, the mathematician, musician, code-breaker and poet, who was the father of persistent Olivia (see page 117) had brought up his five-year-old son Oliver to adore mathematics. They constantly played mathematical games together, and young Oliver was learning to speak 'mathematise' with a facility that was approaching his level of competence in English.

I had the good (though disturbing) fortune to be visiting their home when Oliver returned from his first day at school. His face was not a happy one, and Gerard very gently and concernedly holding back on the real question he wanted to ask, enquired about the day in general, the school, the teacher and other odds and ends. Oliver answered perfunctorily, giving little information, and obviously reluctant to communicate.

Finally, unable to bear the suspense any longer, Gerard posed the prime question:

Gerard: 'Did you do mathematics?'

Oliver: 'Yes,' surly.

Gerard: 'And ...' expectantly.

Oliver: 'I don't like maths.'

The shock registered in every fibre of Gerard's body, but being alert and not wanting to in any way alarm or upset Oliver, he asked very 'casually', 'why don't you like maths?'

Oliver thought for a moment and then replied: 'because of work'.

We were both intrigued by this answer, and Gerard, one of the world's great decoders, asked the next probing and appropriate question: 'what's work, then?'

At this, Oliver frowned deeply, thought for a considerable time and finally said: 'work is doing what you want to do when you don't want to do it'.

Both Gerard and I were stunned by the profundity of this definition. It turned out that the teacher had forbidden Oliver to do mathematics in the morning when he had wanted to, and had forced him to do mathematics at, for him, a boringly simple level in the afternoon when he did not wish to. From the mouths of babes ...

MOON NUMBERS

In Liverpool, England, a father told the members of one of my seminars a story that was inspirational, moving and sad at the same time.

His young son, like Oliver, had gone to school loving numbers. He had been a fairly quiet child, and had always done superbly in mathematics. However, as the complexity of the problems presented to the children increased (it was an accelerated mathematics

Billy intuitively discovering 'Moon Numbers'

class) the young boy began to irritate the teacher by constantly blurting out the answers to problems that were being written on the board, comfortably before the writing of the problem had been completed!

As the frequency of these 'interruptions' increased, the teacher became increasingly frustrated and annoyed, initially thinking that the boy was somehow cheating, but then realizing that he could not be, and that something else was going on. He asked Billy how he was coming up with the answers, to be surprised by the reply 'Moon Numbers'. At this everybody else in the class laughed, and unfortunately the teacher mocked Billy.

From that day on Billy, having been rejected, rejected mathematics.

Only some time later did Billy's father discover what had happened, and when asking the child what 'Moon Numbers' were, was told that they were special numbers he had discovered that were not anything that was taught in school and therefore could not have come from the earth. Billy had decided that they therefore must have come from somewhere else, and the moon seemed to him the obvious place. He had unfortunately stopped using them and thinking about them, but the father's discussions with mathematicians subsequently revealed that somehow the boy had intuited power and logarithmic relationships in numbers, and had used these in his mental calculations.

Unfortunately he never returned to them, and Moon Numbers were never revisited by the astronauts of the child's imagination.

brain child

JOANNA'S STORY

Joanna was a six-year-old girl from Johannesburg, South Africa, who, like Billy, constantly interrupted her teacher with answers to the questions that were being written out on the blackboard.

As was the case with Billy, her teacher became increasingly frustrated and angry, eventually asking her, in an accusing manner, how she did it. Frightened by the aggression of the teacher, Joanna retreated into a shell of silence and was accused of bad behaviour. She was told that even if she got the right answer, if she did not show the 'proper' workings by which she arrived at it, she would be failed.

Which she was.

In later years she explained, with a mixture of enthusiasm and perplexity, that as she listened to numbers being spoken and saw them being written, geometric shapes in different colours appeared on a vast landscape in her mind. As the mathematical problem progressed, the shapes performed a fantastic and ethereal dance, joining and separating, leaving, by the end of the stated problem, a single shape that immediately translated into a number. She still had no idea how this happened, but knew only that the number derived from the final shape was always the correct answer.

LORRAINE'S STORY

Lorraine was a little Australian girl of seven who had already demonstrated a precocious ability with art, and who was already becoming known for her ability to see and record in minute detail. Her mathematics teacher took an irrational dislike to her, and increasingly, and with more intellectual violence, made her his 'whipping girl'.

One day, in particularly vicious mood, he strode down the child's aisle, planted himself, towering over her, took out a ten-cent coin, thrust it within five centimetres (two inches) of her artist-seeing eyes, bent down, and with his mouth virtually touching her ear, bellowed at the top of his voice: 'You stupid little girl! You can't even tell me what number is on this coin, can you?! Can you?!'

The coin was etched, like a branding iron into her visual cortex. Her fear and loathing of anything to do with numbers or money was a new mental absolute, and in later years the mere mention of even the most simple financial transaction made her palpably tremble.

Many such stories are told. The approach of parents and teachers to such children must be to explore the 'new mathematics', which many children spontaneously invent.

The world is filled with children who 'can't do maths' and who 'don't like maths'. The order of these two thoughts is significant.

As I have said before and will repeat for emphasis, every child *loves mathematics*. Even adults who think they don't, do! Everyone loves to be told: 'you are the one, you have just won **£100,000**', 'you are two times better than you were before', 'we've discounted 60 per cent from your bill', 'I love you in more ways than the number of stars in the galaxy', 'your probability of success in this endeavour is over 90 per cent', 'your mark in this exam makes you one out of a million', 'your favourite sports team is top of the league by a staggering 10 points', 'you can have the biggest piece of your favourite pie'.

What transforms these maths lovers into maths haters is very similar to what you will discover goes wrong in the fields of art and music (see pages 244 and 248). At an early stage in learning, events such as those described occur, a simple question remains unanswered, or a few basic errors lead to the false conclusion that 'my brain can't do this'. Many children fall at the first hurdle of 1 + 1 = 2, when they ask the deeply significant question 'why', do not get a satisfactory answer, conclude that they can't understand, and reject the entire field. Others, while being taught some fundamental mathematical procedure, happened to have been spending those few moments daydreaming about something that at the time seemed

brain child

In teaching mathematics to very young children we must be constantly aware of the *rationale* and *processes* by which they reach their numerical conclusions. Very often they are far more imaginative, creative, and deeply reflective of the true nature, magic and mystery of the mathematical Universe than the simple procedures we try to instil in them. **Failure!!**

In conclusion, it transpires that the millions of people who 'don't like maths' *do* like maths. What they *don't* like is something else entirely: they *don't* like the pain of *thinking* that they 'can't do maths'. Unfortunately they confuse this dislike of failure with a dislike of the subject itself. This leads to a negative synergetic spiral in which the dislike of failure feeds the false thought of the dislike of mathematics, which again increases the fear of failure, which increases the avoidance of the subject and so on, spiralling ever downwards. The simple understanding and application of the TEFCAS principle on page 105 (those first failures were simply interesting Events) will realign the mind with mathematics.

THINGS FOR YOU TO DO

Make numbers and mathematics another natural language in your home environment. You can introduce your baby to numbers from a very early age. Babies love counting songs such as 'One, two, three, four, five, once I caught a fish alive. Six, seven, eight, nine, ten, then I let it go again.' Toddlers can count out apples or oranges when they are helping with the shopping, and older children can be sent on independent shopping errands so that they are in charge of money and change.

Love numbers yourself, and your child will mimic that love. Make any encounter you have with numbers a fun activity for yourself and you will soon transmit this feeling to your child.

Play number games and encourage your child if he shows the tendency as many do, to see numbers as colours, shapes or characters. Many great mathematicians did. For children of about four or five, make a series of 'number-picture' cards and post them up where the family can all make use of them. For the number one card, choose with your child a bright colour and make a single spot in the centre of the card. For number two choose another colour and arrange two spots side by side. For three, place three spots in a triangular arrangement, for four have them in a square shape. And so on. The spots will become part of the child's visual memory and will help with number play.

Teach your child to estimate. Again virtually all those who have excelled in mathematics have stated that estimation was a prime skill, and that it gave them both confidence and an 'area' or 'target' into which they could aim their precise answer, instantaneously knowing whether it was 'in the ball park' and therefore giving them some idea of the probability of the correctness of their answer. Ask your child to guess, very roughly, how many peas he thinks are in the bag, or marbles in the pot. Then ask him to count them out by way of checking his own guesswork. Let him know that there is nothing 'wrong' about making a guess and making an inaccurate guess, and that it is not always possible to know exact quantities. Encourage him to learn how to trust his own guesswork. Practice with guesswork will make it more accurate as time goes by. Be playful when you are engaged in guesswork. Make estimating a valid activity.

Teach your child mental calculations, emphasizing 'working it out in the head' before working it out on paper or with a calculator. You can start this in a simple way when teaching the child how to handle money.

When your child graduates to the use of calculators and computers, encourage a positive competitive spirit. Wherever basic calculations or estimations are involved, have the child use the calculating machine as a stimulus, competitor, trainer, friend and guide. Not as a crutch!

and your hand's untrained ability to do anything about transferring that perfect image onto your paper.

You finished your little aeroplane, and then you were allowed to look around. What did you see? Better aeroplanes!

Nearly every child sees 'better aeroplanes', because by that time they are already trained that they must not fail, and that they must not copy – two of the most devastating destroyers of learning and creativity imaginable. So each child registers the worst part of his own painting and the best of the others, and thus unwittingly and incorrectly demotes himself in the hierarchy.

The other children are also likely to assist you in the realization of the relative lack of merit of your artwork, and this will be reinforced by the teacher who will come up, arms folded and say something like: 'That's not very good, is it, child? You could have put *wings* on it!!'

And then the agony is compounded. For on the wall of your little classroom is either *not* your little aeroplane (condemnation by absence) or even more horrifying *is* your little aeroplane and you have to look at the blasted thing for the next three weeks!

When the teacher next comes in and announces that you are going to do art again, your little brain will immediately say: 'Noooo *way*! I'm going to be talking to my friends or looking out the window or daydreaming, but I'm not going to be doing art because I *can't*.'

And in such a manner, simply for the want of being allowed to copy, did many and most aspiring artists fall at the first hurdle.

Knowing the Mimicking Brain Principle, the teacher would respond very differently to that aeroplane. Instead of mocking or condemning it, the teacher would say something in the order of: 'That's an interesting little aeroplane! Would you like the next one to have wings on? What I suggest is that you do two little lines here and two little lines here like this, and that you go over and see Sally, who does really good aeroplanes and ask her to show you how she does them. Then come back to me and we can continue to make your aeroplanes better and better and better and you'll be a *really* good artist.'

If such a course had been followed, similar in art to that of Suzuki in music, Doman in reading and Tractenburg and others in mathematics, our modern world would be filled with artists, painters and sculptors, and the Global Renaissance, which is only just beginning to burgeon, would have been with us for centuries.

THINGS FOR YOU TO DO

Learn to draw yourself, and allow your child to mimic. A good way to start this is to use Conni Gordon's introductory method of instantaneously proving to you that you can be an artist (see page 327). Do the following Conni Gordon exercise, realizing that it can be varied many times, simply by changing the shape of the mountains, changing the height of the lake's horizon, and by changing the shape and number of branches and leaves of the tree, etc. When you have mastered this introduce it to your baby before the age of one year. When the baby is ready to mimic you, she will, and drawing and the recreating of images will be as natural to your child as it is to the children of the aboriginals.

Supply your child's bedroom, study or den with coloured pens, crayons, blank drawing and art paper of all sizes, paintbrushes, little easels, introductory books on art and drawing and beautifully illustrated books of the great artists. One enlightened family allocated a whole blank white wall of their playroom to the children's artistic creativity. The children were told that they could draw and paint all over this wall in whatever way they saw fit. No holds barred. If you don't have this luxury of space, allocate a corner of your family room to art. Spread a large plastic sheet on the floor and place an easel in the centre. Pin finished artworks on the wall for everyone to admire.

now, your own baby brain would have absorbed that language as rapidly and fluidly as you now speak your own main tongue. And not only would you have learnt the language of that country, you would have learnt the specific language of the special area of that country in which you had been born. In future you can describe your accent in the following manner:

The way in which I speak is a result of my perfect ability to randomly select any one of the million million million languages and copy it so perfectly and with such fine-tuning of rhythm, tone, pitch and melody that anyone from any other village in the Universe would be able to recognize me by the perfect way in which I had copied from the original!

If you, for example, were a Caucasian baby and had been born in Beijing, you wouldn't have looked up with your little baby eyes and exclaimed 'Oh, Chinese. Far too complex for me! Think I'll stay silent for the rest of my life!'

What Suzuki had discovered was that the voice/ear/brain system was a virtually perfect copying machine, with an almost infinite capacity to learn the music (songs) of an infinite number of languages.

And it didn't matter whether the language was Chinese, Portuguese, Music-ese, Maths-ese, Art-ese, Burmese, or Japanese. So long as the baby was given the right learning environment and proper encouragement, he could learn *anything*!

Suzuki's third revelation was the last piece in his paradigm-shifting jig-saw puzzle.

In the middle of his musings on the little chicks' brains and the amazing baby's brain, a friend asked Suzuki if he would teach the friend's four-year-old son to play the violin. Thinking very little about it, Suzuki apologized, saying that it was impossible to do so because the child was too young, and in any case would never be able to handle a violin, which in proportion to the child's size would have been like asking a normal human to play a double base in the position of the violin.

A short while after he had parted from his friend, Suzuki was thunder-struck by his own narrowness of thinking. He had said that the child was too young to learn, when by his own admission all babies everywhere are learning music and becoming master musicians by the time they are three. Secondly he had said that the violin was too big. Why not, he therefore thought, make a violin that was an appropriate size for the young child.

Utterly inspired, Suzuki set about making a number of little violins. But how then to teach it? Suzuki realized that the answer must be to copy what the little chicks had done: i.e. to COPY. 'That's why', Suzuki thought more than 95 per cent of us never learn to sing properly or enjoy playing musical instruments or draw – because we are told never to copy. The prime learning tool, mimicking (see Mimicking, page 95) is taken away from us. To make it even worse we are told that copying is cheating and cheating is bad, wicked and wrong, and that we are never to do it.

Armed now with his child-sized violins, his revelations, and his clear understanding of how proper education must be structured, Suzuki approached friends who had young children, and asked them if they would like their children to learn to play the violin.

In his first classes, Suzuki scattered violins and bows around the room, and invited the toddlers to come and play with whatever they wanted, including other toys that were around the room. Suzuki, squatting cross-legged on the floor, simply picked up one violin, picked up one bow and played one note. As he had expected, one by one the children copied what he was doing, at which point he began to play two notes. Exactly as the little chicks had learned the Master Singer's song by listening and practising themselves, the children, at their own paces, learnt the violin with as much ease and grace as they had learned their native language.

chapter 7

reading

Should you teach your baby to read?
Yes!

Despite much misinformed negative debate that surrounds this issue, the real issue, at the base, remains simple, and very much as Glenn Doman, the founder of this 'Gentle Revolution', as he calls it, originally stated:

1. Tiny children can learn to read.
2. Tiny children want to learn to read.
3. Tiny children are learning to read.
4. Tiny children should learn to read.

The story of how Dr Doman made his discoveries and developed his, at the time, revolutionary theories concerning reading, is one well worth the telling.

DR DOMAN'S STORY

The story began in the late 1940s, when Dr Doman started to work with a small team of medical specialists including a brain surgeon, a physiatrist (an MD who specializes in physical medicine and rehabilitation), a physical therapist, a speech therapist, a psychologist, an educator and a nurse.

The team had been formed because each one of the members was individually charged with some phase of the treatment of severely brain-injured children. They individually and collectively were aware of the horrifying fact that none of them had ever seen or heard of a single brain-injured child who had been comprehensively cured.

The team realized that they had been focusing on such relatively unimportant matters as the cause of the injury or damage, and not enough on the vital issues of how badly the child's brain was hurt, which part or parts were damaged, and what could be done about that.

The team realized that both they and other individuals and teams in the field had been desperately attempting to help by treating the symptoms that existed in a full gamut of physical locations, including all the senses, all the joints, and indeed all the major functioning bodily parts.

Dr Doman and his team decided that the only way forward was to begin to attack the central problem itself — the child's injured brain.

After a few years of experimenting, the team came to the realization that even more important than dealing with the hurt brain itself, was to 'go back' to the brain's formative years, and allow it once again to go through the normal formative developmental stages of activities such as creeping and crawling — activities that are essential to the brain's growth and integration, and which in the brain-damaged child needed to be revisited.

Concurrently with these awarenesses and increasing practices, the growing team had gathered to itself a sub-team of neuro-surgical specialists who began to devise ground-breaking procedures for assisting the injured brain. These included surgically removing sometimes giant areas of one hemisphere that were wildly misfiring like an

making about Tommy's ability to read. For Mr and Mrs Lunski had decided, on their own accord, to stimulate him with letters, words and 'baby books'.

When Tommy was four years of age, Mr Lunski reported that Tommy could read all the words in his simple alphabet book more easily than he could understand and recognize the letters.

When Tommy was four years and two months old, Mr Lunski said that he was able to read the whole of the Dr Zeus' Green Eggs and Ham.

By the time Tommy was four years and six months old Mr Lunski announced that Tommy could read, and had read, the entire oeuvre of Dr Zeus!

When Tommy had just turned five, he arrived with his parents for his eleventh visit to the team, and Mr Lunski announced that before his fifth birthday Tommy had been able to read almost anything, including the Reader's Digest, and that his understanding of what he read was excellent.

Once again Dr Doman and the team casually noted this, attributing it in part to Mr Lunski's over-enthusiasm as a 'proud parent', and continued to focus on Tommy's remarkable development physically and linguistically.

This time Mr Lunski was not to be denied.

In front of the team, he wrote down complex sentences describing what the team had been doing, and gave them to Tommy. Tommy read them at high speed, and responded with seriousness or laughter, as appropriate.

Everyone was stunned.

With the help of Mr and Mrs Lunski and Tommy, the rehabilitation, re-education and education of brain-damaged children had leapt from the physical and verbal to the reading and conceptual domains.

If a 'vegetable' child could learn to read so skilfully before the age of five, what was the potential for learning to read for a child with an undamaged brain?

The team continued to be influenced and inspired by Tommy, who, by the time he was six years old was already able to walk. His reading had advanced to the level of an 11–12-year-old!

How to Teach Your Baby to Read

On the basis of his medical and neurological researches, and as a result of the paradigm-shifting experiences with Tommy, Dr Doman developed his revolutionary method of teaching babies how to read.

The fundamental premise of the method lies in the observation that babies and very young children find it difficult to distinguish small print, though easy to recognize large print. This is exemplified by the fact that many children between the ages of one and two can already 'read' television advertisements, the large capital letters on food packages, the screaming words on billboards and many company logos.

To introduce your baby to the wonderful world of reading, construct large 'word cards' between 30 and 60 centimetres (one and two feet) long and 5 to 13 centimetres (two to five inches) high. Print them clearly and evenly, and ideally for the first few months in red, as this colour is the most easy for the fledgling eye to perceive.

The initial 50–100 words should be nouns, as these are easy to identify, and have an obvious physical association.

It is significant to note that Dr Doman's method is in complete harmony with the memory principle of Association, and with the development of vocabulary. With vocabulary development, the child *hears* the sound and associates it with the appropriate object. In reading the process is identical. The child *sees* the word (and to the baby's brain it matters not whether it receives the associative information as a sound wave or a light wave) and similarly *associates* it with the appropriate object.

In compiling your child's list of key words, it is advisable to start with such 'standards' as 'mummy' and 'daddy' and then to add words of objects in which the baby has shown particular interest, including its pets, favourite toys, favourite animals, household objects and names of friends and relations.

I asked him if he wanted to play the word game and he immediately responded 'yes'! I showed him each card, responding enthusiastically to every correct answer, and found, like John, that he was getting roughly 75 per cent correct. As per all the advice contained in Brain Child, I kept the 25 per cent 'errors' aside, and after we had gone through the full 100 showed him them again, giving him special associations and mental images to help him remember them more accurately next time through. 'Next time through' OJ could not wait to do!

We went joyously through the 100 words again, but to my amazement and mounting concern, OJ kept making mistakes, often getting words wrong that he had recognized correctly before, sometimes immediately recognizing words on which he had previously made mistakes, and sometimes appearing confused and then making a mistake.

Once again I went through the 'error words' giving him even more emphatic and imagistic methods for remembering them correctly next time through.

Did OJ want to go 'next time through'?

Emphatically! Once again and once again joyously, we went through the same 100 words. To my amazement, growing concern (and I must admit, growing frustration) OJ repeated his previous performance, once again making mistakes on words he had previously done correctly, regularly but not always remembering the words I had helped him to remember, and occasionally appearing confused.

Did he want to do it again?

Yes he did! I went even more carefully through the 'error words' and off we went. And off we went on exactly the same routine. As we approached the end, and as OJ's performance once again approached, virtually identically, all his previous performances, a thought of embarrassing significance struck me: had I been playing Watson to OJ's Holmes?!

Did he want to play it again?

Yes! (With even greater enthusiasm!)

As we went through the next time, whenever OJ gave the correct response I said 'correct!' with singular enthusiasm. Whenever he gave the incorrect response, I responded 'correct!' with even more singular enthusiasm. When we had completed the 100, I proclaimed, with both fists pumping the air, 'Well done OJ! 100 per cent! Perfect!'

OJ immediately wanted to play the game again.

And so we did.

Once again, whenever OJ gave a correct response I responded enthusiastically, and whenever he gave an incorrect response I similarly responded that he was correct.

After about 80 words, when I had shown him 'dog' and he had responded 'cat', and I had responded with enthusiasm 'correct again!' OJ suddenly pounded the floor with his little fists and said 'it's wrong, it's wrong, it's wrong, it's WRONG!' It was then that we adults realized that we had been privileged to witness a majestic and Olympian mental event: young OJ, at the 'mere' age of two years, four months, had become so bored with limited perfection, that in order to make the word game more interesting, he had had to remember not only the 100 perfectly, but which 25 he had purposefully got wrong, and to 'spread them out' in his next set of responses so that some were correct and some incorrect next time through. In addition to this he had had to adjust his emotional, facial and enthusiasm responses, pretending that in some instances he was confident, some not, and some confused.

In doing this, and again I emphasize that this was before the age of two-and-a-half, he had totally outwitted the combined forces of multiple university degrees, a karate master, a teacher, a psychologist, an author on the brain and learning, a musician and many others.

When your child is beginning to approach OJ's 'initial perfection' stage, the reading games can be happily expanded and extended to include large Mind Maps that show the multiple and multi-ordinant relationships between the words the child is learning. This has the added advantage of repeating the key words, showing their associations, and thus improving

As you now know from the chapters on memory, the multi-ordinant nature of words, music, art, Mind Mapping and reading, your baby's brain is a gigantic Association and Mimicking machine.

To language learning your baby applies these two prime tools in pursuit of a goal that is far more complex, difficult and demanding than the achievement of a PhD.

Again put yourself in the position of this newly landed cosmonaut from the womb to see just how difficult the task actually is. Having never spoken a language in your life, other than that of bio-molecular exchange, you land on a planet where giant creatures are babbling strange sounds, none of which you have ever heard before, and none of which is distinct from the others. These giant beings look at you and hold you while uttering such complete gibberish as the following:

'coocheycoocheycooisn'tshealovelylittledarlingthenoohlookatherbeautifuleyesshe's goingtobesuchalovelylittlegirllookatthewayshe'slookingatmeandholdingmyhand andisn'tsheamazing?'

Only by the most intense concentration and application to the decoding of this constant stream of Sound-Rosetta-Stones, can language be learnt. Yet every normal baby, and even many with considerable brain damage, learns to speak fluently whichever one of the world's 6,000 languages and infinitely varied accents into which it is randomly born. But this is not all: in addition to deciphering and decoding this constant hail of random sounds, our baby astronaut has, simultaneously, to work out the mechanics of, and how to 'play', a musical instrument of such complexity and sophistication, and with so many millions of working parts, that it makes the grand piano, with its less than 100 working parts, seem like a beginner's toy by comparison.

I refer, of course, to the human voice which modern science and technology has shown us is capable of an infinite variety of sounds.

Knowing that these two processes occur simultaneously helps us with the realization that the baby *understands* language *long* before he is able to *speak* it, and that we have misguided ourselves and grossly underestimated the baby brain's ability and speed in language acquisition; we have assumed that it is only when the baby begins to speak that he has begun to learn the language. In fact he began to learn it from before the day he was born and probably understood most of the important key words in the language before he was six months old. Remember that your baby sees and hears in exactly the same way as you do – the perceptual processes and images are identical – it is only the accrued database that is different.

As you watch your baby go through the magical process of language acquisition, you will observe him making fundamental associations between objects and the sounds that describe them, followed by more complex associational relationships and networks; you are seeing millions of Mini Mind Maps being created, which, as the child's databases expand, inter-link with each other and become the giant Meta Mind Map of a complete language.

Note, significantly, that sentences are often and usually the last feature of the spoken language to be mastered and used.

Baby Talk or Adult-Speak?

As with so many other areas concerning the baby, this discussion has languished in the either/or Dyadic Dilemma. And as usual, the most productive answer is 'both'.

If you think what the parent naturally does when speaking to its child in baby talk you will realize that that parent is naturally using the brain's fundamental operating principles of Association, Mimicry, Outstandingness, Location and Repetition.

Baby talk does appear to be the Language of Love.

Slow Learners

Although many children are quite advanced in language learning and speaking by the time they are one year old, many do not start until well after two. Although the parents should be alert, there is usually no cause for undue alarm. I, who spend the bulk of my time both speaking and writing, did not learn to speak until well after my second birthday, and many other people I know are the same. If you were also one of these, we can all take solace from the fact that Albert Einstein is reported to have begun to speak only after the age of three!

The explanation for the 'slow learning' is that it is in fact a very conscious and specifically designed *non*-learning. 'What is the point', the one-and-a-half-year-old genius asks herself, 'in spending all my time learning how to play this incredibly complex instrument, when I have already learnt and understood the language they are trying to make me say, and when instead of having to say incredibly complex things like "please Mummy will you go over to the table and get me a glass of water because I am thirsty, thank you very much" all I have to do is point and look at that glass of water, and my giant slave will always and faithfully bring it to me with gurgling and appreciative sounds about the excellence of my intelligence?!'

Child Versus Adult

There is an increasing amount of 'evidence' that the child is the super-language learner, and that as the adult progresses through life new language learning becomes increasingly difficult and eventually impossible. A case in point concerns a 40-year-old oil executive, who on hearing that he was being posted overseas, went to a language-learning laboratory in order to study and learn the new language. He was summarily dismissed by the teacher-in-charge who said: 'I'm sorry sir, but you're over 40; the ability to learn a new language is one which I'm afraid you've now lost because of your age.'

Sadly, studies on language learning do accurately record the fact that most adults do have great difficulty with new language acquisition. These studies, however, make two egregious fundamental errors: firstly they assume that what is 'normal' is 'natural'; secondly their studies record the equivalent of measuring the walking efficiency of people who, with every step, add another 230-g (half-pound) weight to their shoulders.

How is this? Adults who come to learn languages have already been taught that they 'must not fail', that mimicking is copying, that copying is cheating, and that cheating is bad, and that to be understood in a foreign language you must speak as near to grammatical perfection as you can. Thus, restricted by fear, unwilling to use their prime learning tool of mimicry, and learning grammar, sentences and phrases first, they do *exactly* the opposite of what the super-genius language learning baby does, and *exactly* the opposite of what their brains need in order to acquire a new language. The studies study them, and erroneously conclude that the adult brain cannot learn a new language.

It can. As long as it learns, the Brain Child learns.

chapter 9

hot housing

Quite simply, NO!

Hot Housing refers to 'force feeding' children information, usually against their will, in order to make them into little geniuses. This attempt to produce 'brain *foie gras*' is against the spirit of everything contained in *Brain Child*, and can have serious negative repercussions such as that experienced by little Oliver when force-fed maths (see page 236).

Your baby is born to learn, and will naturally siphon up information without having it stuffed down her intellectual throat.

It has been said by many that approaches such as Suzuki's and Glenn Doman's are Hot Housing techniques. They are not. Critics are missing the very subtle point that these approaches are exactly the opposite; they involve making learning into a game and delight that the child seeks and constantly pursues and which involves no parental pressure.

Hot Housing can be likened to attempting to force water uphill, which is possible but involves an enormous amount of unnecessary energy. The approaches advocated in *Brain Child* are like allowing the water to flow downhill, directing its energy where appropriate.

THINGS FOR YOU TO DO

Develop, both individually and with your Mastermind Group, ways of 'allowing the water to flow' in appropriate directions. Be led by the child herself. Don't force her in directions she doesn't want to go. Let all learning be a joy and a pleasure. Encourage her in all her interests and abilities and be prepared to facilitate her learning at all times. For example, if your four-year-old develops a near-obsession about dinosaurs and wants to read her dinosaur book at every available moment, learning all the complicated names and talking about dinosaurs to anyone who is prepared to listen, don't become impatient and try to get her to move on to another subject. You may be bored, but she is pursuing her interest with genius-like passion. Be enthusiastic and encouraging, for dinosaurs will lead her to history, geography, geology, biology, zoology and, indeed every other subject there is! Ask sensible dinosaur questions and see that this kind of learning is developing her memorizing ability and learning skills for all her future learning. You may even learn something yourself!

Be aware that gentle and firm pressure is sometimes entirely in keeping with your child's learning needs, being alert to any signs that such pressure is causing unnecessary stress. Bear in mind in these situations the many, many examples of adults who regret that their parents were not a little more assertive in having them continue their music or other lessons.

THINGS FOR YOU **NOT** TO DO

Hot House, in its commonly misunderstood form.

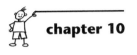

chapter 10

information technology

---☆---

Television. Videos. Computers. Computer games. Walkman. The Internet.
The Web.

---☆---

Are they good? Or are they bad? Will they allow your child's brain to 'go
to where no one has gone before'? Or will they leave a 'fried' and burnt-
out wreck of a brain?!

Whichever you wish!

The questions posed above are yet another example of the limited
twentieth-century dyadic approach to questions: the either or; black or
white; yes or no; good or bad approach.

It is the same as asking whether the human hand is good or bad. It can be
'good' when it gives, caresses, holds, builds, plays, paints and provides. It can
be 'bad' when it hits, takes, steals, damages, kills, plunders and destroys.

It is the use, motive and application that determines the 'goodness' or
'badness'.

It is identical with the metallic and silicon worlds.

IT can provide your child with life-enhancing information and skills or
it can fill his mind with rubbish and help undermine him physically.

The best approach to all forms of IT is to use them as simple but willing friends, companions and servants, who are always willing to help if they can, and who are unusually willing to be at your beck and call all hours of the day and night. It is also important to bear in mind constantly the comparison between silicon intelligences and the vastly superior intelligence of your baby.

One of the advantages, especially of computers, is that they teach and enhance a number of your child's essential skills:

1. Manual dexterity and speed
2. Visual dexterity and speed
3. Imagination
4. 'Global picture' perception.

The recommended approach to this growing other world of 'intelligence' which will increasingly accompany your child throughout his childhood and adult years, is summarized in the following Things For You To Do.

THINGS FOR YOU TO DO

Select video and television programmes for your child as if you were the Dean of a University designing the most desirable and entertaining course. Make the programme varied. Allow, where appropriate, your child to be a member of the selection panel, and leave opportunity for pure frivolity and escapism. Limit your child to an average of one hour of viewing (or screen-time) per day (whether TV, video or computer use). Don't be tempted or coerced into letting your child have a TV in his bedroom. You cannot be part of the TV programme-selection process

brain child

and he will watch more than he is supposed to, at least initially, possibly even going without sleep to do so.

Select video games that are positive in content, and that emphasize analytical, strategic and creative thinking, rather than the currently dominant negative games based on shooting, bombing, maiming and destruction.

Become skilled with computers and the use of the Internet and Web so that you may become a 'games partner' with your child, rather than, in their eyes, an alienated, antiquated illiterate!

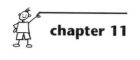

chapter 11

mind sports

─────────────── ☆ ───────────────

Mind Sports are gymnasiums for your child's developing brain. Goethe, the giant German genius and polymath regularly ranked in the top 10 great brains of all time, went so far as to call chess and Mind Sports 'the touch-stone of the intellect'.

─────────────── ☆ ───────────────

Mind Sports are categorized in four main divisions:

1. Board Games
Ranging from the more simple, like Monopoly, through the medium range, such as Draughts/Checkers, to the King and Emperor of games: Chess and the Chinese/Japanese game of Go.

2. Card games
These range from the simple Snap and Solitaire through the medium range including games like Canasta, Whist and Poker, to the considerably more complex Bridge.

3. Mental Skills Games

These include: Memory; Creative Thinking; Speed Reading; Mind Mapping; Intelligence Testing; and Mental Calculations.

4. Computer Games

The full gamut!

All games are useful training grounds for your child's developing brain. As mental skills and computer games have been dealt with elsewhere in *Brain Child*, I shall focus here on board games, as they appeal to the senses of sight, touch and hearing, and in their more advanced forms train and develop the multiplicity of thinking and social skills.

Draughts and Chess, for example, involve and develop the following:

1. Analytical Thinking
2. Strategic (long-term) Thinking
3. Creative Thinking (you have to think of new and original ways to escape from difficult and previously unexperienced situations and positions)
4. Global Thinking — in all board games you must consistently see the 'forest' while at the same time seeing each individual tree
5. Concentration
6. Learning how to lose and lose well
7. Learning how to win!
8. Personal independence
9. Inter-dependence
10. Self-reliance
11. Memory
12. Inter-personal and interactive skills.

This last point is of increasing significance, as latest estimates indicate that there are over two *million million* (2,000,000,000,000) Mind Sports players in the world at the moment. It should be pointed out here that Mind Sports also include such games as crossword puzzles, brain-teasers, word puzzles, and the multiplicity of 'Brain Games' found in most newspapers and magazines.

Mind Sports have unfortunately been considered by many to be 'male territory', perpetuating the false belief that male is 'left brain dominant' and that female is 'right brain dominant'. Nothing could be further from the truth, as the following story will tell:

THE POLGAR SISTERS' (AND FATHER'S!) STORY

The Polgar sisters in action

brain child

In the late 1970s, Laszlo Polgar, a brilliant mathematician and powerful chess player, had just celebrated with his wife the birth of their third daughter Judit. They had no sons. This imbalance was pointed out sympathetically by many of Laszlo's male friends, who commiserated with him on the fact that his brilliant mathematical and chess-playing mind had entered a genetic cul-de-sac with the unfortunate birth of three daughters who would obviously not be able to continue his 'line' in his chosen fields.

Infuriated by the small-mindedness, prejudice and arrogance of their assumptions, Laszlo decided to put the popular prejudices concerning the girl-child's brain to the test. He asked his little daughters if they would like to learn to play chess, and made the invitation more appealing by couching it (context!) in warm, loving and family-activity-oriented terms. The little girls, as one would expect, leapt at the opportunity of playing games with Daddy, and all of the friendship and happiness that would be associated with it.

As time progressed the family became an increasingly tight-knit, loving and playful group, and the girls' chess progressed remarkably.

As you might deduce from everything you have read in Brain Child so far, the two younger children fared most well, and Judit the best of all, simply because she had more 'seniors' to mimic and from whom she could learn.

As time progressed, so did the family bonds and so, in parallel, did the three girls' progress in chess.

Zsuzsa, the eldest, became an international chess master and won many chess tournaments, defeating, along the way, a number of international Grandmasters.

Zsofia rapidly became a women's international Grandmaster, and became International Chess Federation Women's World Champion.

Could Judit surpass the incredible accomplishments of her two sisters?

Indeed she could!

Like Zsofia, Judit rapidly ascended to the rank of International Women's Grandmaster. Shortly after this she acquired the rank of International Grandmaster, and became, by far, the highest-rated female chess player in history, with a ranking of 2680, entered the elite 'Top 10' of the world's Super Grandmasters, which include the greatest player of all time, Garry Kasparov, and had reached the quarter-finals of the 1999 International Chess Federation World Championship. Apart from being a great chess player, Judit is married and leads a very full life. Persistence and consistently going beyond perceived limits have led her to success.

The three sisters are models of the well-rounded child, being known for their playfulness, wit, cheerfulness and inter-personal skills. Laszlo and his wife Klara exult in their daughters' successes, and in their family's demolition of the wide-spread prejudices about girl-children and Mind Sports.

Mind Sports and Academic and Other Success

With the rise and rise of Mind Sports, so have there been an increasing number of studies investigating the effect that playing Mind Sports has on academic and other areas of endeavour. As with the relationship of play and other areas (see Play, page 148) the correlations have been extremely positive.

The Mind Sports Player – the Image

The popular image of the Mind Sports Player rampant in the twentieth century is being transformed at the beginning of the twenty-first.

And what was that image?

The image of the nerd: thick-bespectacled; pallid of complexion; smaller than average; stooped in posture; physically weak; lacking in physical skills; lacking in social skills; isolated; friendless. This image of intelligence as nerdish is why many millions of children around the world actively use their intelligences to *disguise* their intelligence, for fear of being labelled a 'geek'.

Fortunately the truth is exactly the opposite of the global misconception. A recent survey of the Mentathletes competing in the third global Mind Sports Olympiad showed that most of the competitors had a wide range of interests, and *over 60 per cent* listed physical sports as their main hobby.

To further ram home this good-news point, the Mental World Champions, including Garry Kasparov, the greatest chess player ever; Dominic O'Brien, the eight-times World Memory Champion; and Ron King, the virtually unbeatable Barbadian World Draughts Champion, are all superb athletes. They involve themselves in physical pursuits including running, swimming, hiking, table-tennis, aerobic training and dancing in order to keep their bodies, and more importantly for them, their minds, in tip-top shape.

Introducing your Brain Child to Mind Sports will help that child become mentally *and* physically fit.

THINGS FOR YOU TO DO

 Introduce your child to a wide range of Mind Sports, including many of the simple and fun Christmas games and reaching upwards to the Royal games of Go and Chess.

Check in on the World Memory Championship website: **www.worldmemorychampionship.com.**
This site introduces you to the world of Memory and Memory Sports. You will find information on the latest techniques and advances in Memory, as well as chat-rooms, news on upcoming competitions, and the latest world rankings. This is a wonderful world for your child to become involved with, and will provide tremendous benefits in his academic, personal and professional life.

mind sports

Enter your family in a national, regional or global Mind Sports event. Such events are run on an all-comers basis, so beginners can play in the same tournament as world champions. The 'Swiss System' on which these competitions are run is much like that of the major physical sports such as Tennis, and has one major advantage over their format. In tennis, if you lose in the first round, you are knocked out of the tournament. In a Mind Sports competition, if you lose in the first round, you advance to the next round and play someone else who has lost in the first round. If you have won, you play someone who has won. This procedure continues as the tournament progresses, so that if you keep losing you continue to play people who have lost as many games as you, and if you keep winning the process is identical. Thus every player in a Mind Sports event finds, as the tournament progresses, his or her appropriate level. Your family may find themselves in the delightful position of that of the family of young David Howell, an eight-year-old chess player in the third Mind Sports Olympiad in London, August 1999. In a Speed Chess Tournament, young David comfortably and brilliantly beat John Nunn, an International Grandmaster, former British Chess Champion, and one of the world's top authors on chess strategy.

dance

---☆---

Your baby begins his 'Dance of Life' at about the beginning of the twelfth week — well before the mother feels the first movements inside her. The baby moves a limb or his head or his spine in regular patterns, some of which are, and some of which are not, repeated. In this way the baby's brain, acting on the orders of master genes, drills the infant body into broad movements that prepare the baby for 'free' movement when he is born.

---☆---

Each movement made creates, in the brain, a rough memory of that movement. After birth, these basic movements are repeated freely hundreds of thousands of times in order to refine the memory, making it both accurate and purposeful. Hundreds of muscles are involved in each movement, each needing its own specific memory and each needing to be co-ordinated with all the others.

For full muscular development and co-ordination at birth, it is important that 'the dance of life' be allowed to continue its symphonic development undisturbed. Only physical or mental trauma can disturb it, and these should obviously be avoided.

Your baby is thus born a dancer, and this natural state and talent needs to be encouraged throughout childhood and life. In countries that have a strong culture of dance, babies and children learn to dance from day one. Dance is a natural response to music and a natural expression of one's body and sensuality. It is very much a part of life itself and of being alive in one's own body. Unfortunately, we are not always exposed to dance in the same way and it is common to see very wooden performances on the dance floor at weddings and parties.

THINGS FOR YOU TO DO

 Incorporate dance into your baby's and your musical activities (see Music, page 248). Have music as a background to your daily life and, from a few weeks old, 'dance' your baby on your knee. Later, have little dance sessions with your toddler. Let him see your lighter side. If your older child remains interested, find a local informal dance group for your child to attend.

Take the time to keep dance alive in your family life, knowing that it is good for you, your self and your body. It will help connect your body and your soul and you will remain fit, healthy and happy, too. These feelings will be naturally transmitted to your baby.

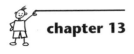

chapter 13

sensuality and sexuality

───────────── ☆ ─────────────

Many parents fret intensely over questions surrounding sensuality and sexuality, worried that they may in some way permanently and deeply scar their child's psyche while revealing the facts of life at the wrong stage.

───────────── ☆ ─────────────

Such fear is totally unfounded, and is the product of a gentle mass hysteria initiated by Freud and his followers.

To the child in a loving, open-minded and open-hearted environment, knowledge of all things is objective data, and if sensitively and clearly presented will in no way harm the child's developing brain.

My own parents, Gordon and Jean, developed what I considered to be an ideal approach, which gave rise to a most entertaining story. My parents had decided that whenever I asked about the 'birds and the bees', they would tell me openly, scientifically, and romantically about the human mating ritual.

One day in Sheperton-on-Thames in England, at the age of just three, I burst into my parents' room, and saw them standing both naked and facing me. Struck by the obvious anatomical differences, I asked why Daddy had a penis and Mummy didn't, and why Mummy had breasts and Daddy didn't.

They spent a good fifteen minutes telling me everything there was to know, and Mum reported to me later in life that within a few minutes of having completed the explanation, she and my father were already very concerned that they had made a fatal mistake in deciding to be so open. Apparently I began to frown as the explanation neared its end, and for two days was very silent and unusually withdrawn.

After those two days I came to my mother very intense and bursting with the following question, which by its very nature shows the deep concerns and profound contemplation that had overtaken me for those two days: 'Mummy, if Daddy had put a vegetable seed into you instead of a little boy seed, could I have been a carrot?'! (See Logic, page 214.)

This story illustrates, as is so often the case, that what is so (see Truth Seeking, page 134) is by definition acceptable and natural to the child. The child's only concerns and fears tend to revolve on perceived consequences, and it is those sometime mistaken thought processes for which the concerned parent should be alert.

THINGS FOR YOU TO DO

 Be natural and open with your bodies in the home family environment. Do not conceal things that do not need to be concealed from your child. When your child asks questions, answer her straightaway as openly and frankly and naturally as you can. Don't try to explain everything all in one go, or go beyond her level of understanding.

Make sure biological information about the human body is available in either book, video or model form. Acquire some good children's books on the senses, sex and the human body and look at them together.

 Copy my Mum and Dad!

brain child

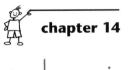

chapter 14

learning difficulties

---☆---

The greatest fear for most parents is that their child will be born 'learning disabled', or in some way brain damaged.

---☆---

Let us deal with learning difficulties first: the two main categories are Dyslexia and ADHD – Attention Deficit Hyperactivity Disorder. The good news in both these areas is that neither is as serious as it sounds and is often made out to be. The real situation is as follows:

Dyslexia and ADHD

DYSLEXIA

If a person has problems identifying letters of the alphabet and therefore reading, they may well be diagnosed dyslexic. In addition, they may get letters reversed, and will probably have untidy handwriting. In some areas, more than 30 per cent of children have this 'learning disability'.

More than 80 per cent of those 'dyslexics' I have met were not actually

It is only too easy to mistake one letter for another

dyslexic. In learning to read, they had mislearned or misunderstood one of the fundamentals of reading at an early stage, and the dyslexic label had stuck.

To understand how easily this can happen, imagine that you are a visitor from outer space, landed on Earth, and someone quickly explains all about these mysterious shapes called 'letters', some of which are very similar to one another, and which are then linked to form words.

(To see the complexity of this, try this following task. Look at the letters in the illustration above and in quick succession identify each of the various shapes, moving as rapidly as you can from one to the other, saying its name. You will find that pretty soon you falter and are unable to identify one of them.)

Meanwhile, in your guise as a visitor from outer space, having been told what all these hieroglyphics are, imagine that you must now write down

brain child

the word 'god'. You think hard, and recall that all three letters contain a circle. You carefully inscribe the three circles, 'OOO', and then sifting through your memory you remember seeing an upward-pointing line and a downward-pointing line somewhere in there. Hazarding a guess, you put an upward line on the right-hand side of the circle and on the last one a downward line, also on the right-hand side. You feel pretty sure that you are almost, if not completely right and hand over your piece of paper. Unfortunately, instead of 'god' you have, in fact, inscribed the word 'dog' and rather than congratulating you on being so so, your examiner declares that you are probably dyslexic or even suffering from a minor form of brain damage.

This statement would probably unsettle you, if not undermine your confidence, and you would be more likely to make further mistakes the next time you try to do the exercise.

This is what happens to the majority of people diagnosed dyslexic, all because, at the outset, they are not given the tools necessary for memory, namely ASSOCIATION and IMAGINATION, which would allow them to remember the names of the letters. Their first mistake coincides with the official definition of dyslexia, so they are falsely labelled and enter a downwards spiral that gets worse as learning goes by.

It often happens that a person labelled dyslexic then tries to read more slowly and carefully so that they can understand better, but this may make the problem even worse.

Most people diagnosed dyslexic are not technically dyslexic, and even if they are, they can solve their reading problems in the same way: by using a guide, gradually building up reading speed, by using Mind Maps as a note-taking and thinking tool. In my experience most people can improve their reading speed and comprehension significantly.

ADHD and Hyperactivity

There is much controversy surrounding Attention Deficit Hyperactivity Disorder. All over the world millions of children are being diagnosed and put on drugs (particularly Ritalin) long-term in order to modify their behaviour. However, there is hope, since leading nutritionists have recently discovered that many brain disorders and behavioural problems can be overcome by adjusting the diet.

The debate continues as to whether the syndrome is a medically definable illness, whether it is a dangerous generalized diagnosis made by ignorant doctors, whether teachers are labelling children ADHD to conceal their own inability to maintain the child's interest, and whether Ritalin is a miracle drug or one that is normalizing, numbing and drugging active and creative children into a conformist stupor. Whatever conclusion you arrive at, bear in mind that the symptoms for ADHD are subjective, meaning that it depends on the values and views of the person doing the assessment and on your own values and views as a parent as well. If the assessor (and/or you) takes the view that children should, for example, be able to sit still in a classroom and listen for long periods of time, then the child is far more likely to be labelled ADHD. But if the assessor (and/or you) believes that children should be able to behave like children do – moving about a great deal and talking – then the diagnosis is less likely to be made. However, whether the child's behaviour meets some of the criteria for an ADHD diagnosis or not, if his behaviour interferes with life either at home or at school, then the child needs help of some sort and drug therapy may not necessarily be the solution.

To help you draw your own conclusions, the following information may prove useful.

ADHD (Attention Deficit Hyperactivity Disorder), is defined, by the

American Psychiatric Association and others, as a classifiable illness if an individual meets eight or more of the following criteria:

1. Cannot remain seated if required to do so.
2. Is easily distracted by external stimuli.
3. Experiences difficulty focusing on a single task or play activity.
4. Frequently begins another activity without completing the first (it is interesting to note that Leonardo da Vinci, normally regarded as the greatest genius of all time, and ranked number one in Buzan's Book of Genius, was consistently accused of this!).
5. Fidgets or squirms (or feels restless mentally).
6. Can't (or doesn't want to) wait for his turn during group activities.
7. Will often interrupt with an answer before a question is completed.
8. Has problems with chores or following through on a job.
9. Likes to make noises while playing.
10. Interrupts others inappropriately.
11. Talks impulsively or excessively.
12. Doesn't seem to listen when spoken to by a teacher.
13. Impulsively jumps into physically dangerous activities.
14. Regularly loses things (pencils, tools, papers) necessary to complete school work projects.

These forms of behaviour must have commenced before the age of seven, and must occur more frequently than in the average person of the same age.

This means that *at least half the population* will, by definition, exhibit these forms of behaviour more frequently than the average. Are they all therefore suffering from an illness?

Two classic cases are worth bearing in mind.

As a young girl in kindergarten, Mary-Lou Retton was so super-active that her parents were advised by the school teachers to put her on a course of drugs that would dramatically reduce her physical activity. Fortunately her parents were of a different opinion, and requested that the school find ways of using her extraordinary energy more appropriately.

Thirteen years late, Mary-Lou Retton, internationally renowned for her boundless energy and enthusiasm, easily won the gold medal in women's gymnastics at the Los Angeles Olympics.

A few years before Mary-Lou Retton experienced her difficulties in her early school years, a little boy by the name of Daley was experiencing the same problems in England. Similarly, his parents were encouraged to put him on a course of tranquillizing drugs. Like Mary-Lou's parents, Daley's insisted that he be given exercises and activities that would absorb his ebullience. Little Daley proved virtually indefatigable, wearing out every physical education teacher available.

It all paid off wonderfully well when Daley Thompson became the World and Olympic Decathlon Champion and stayed at the peak of his sport, shattering all previous world records consistently, for ten years.

Thom Hartman, in his excellent book *Attention Deficit Disorder: A Different Perception*, is firmly of the opinion that the labels are often wildly inappropriate. Hartman claims that schools are set up for what he terms 'the farmers' – those who will sit at a desk, watch and listen attentively to the teacher, and always do what they are told. This is the ultimate torture for those he labels the 'hunters', who are physically active; always scanning their environment; creative; impulsive; and always looking, like Leonardo da Vinci, for the next exciting event. Those 'hunters' are *not* ADDHDS: they are *energetic*!

All learning difficulties can be dealt with and the situation improved. In most cases the problems can be completely overcome.

brain child

JIM'S STORY

Jim's story shows the devastating effect that incorrect labelling can have on a young child.

From a very early age in his childhood, which had been spent in the southern United States, Jim had been diagnosed as 'severely learning disabled', had been publicly so labelled, and as a result had been ridiculed and ostracized. By the time he was 17, he had entered into what appeared to be a terminal depression, refusing to leave his bed for more than two or three hours a day, a behaviour which confirmed for many of those around him his label.

Jim was diagnosed by Vanda North as simply dyslexic and probably very bright. She and myself taught him basic information about the brain, and especially about how to memorize. Jim's imagination (as you might imagine!) from all those years of isolation was gigantic. He lapped up memory techniques, and was very soon easily able to remember 100 random items, in perfect order, in less than an hour.

Inspired by his sudden accomplishments and the self-realization of his quite extraordinary abilities, Jim 'came to life', became almost hyperactive, extremely physically fit, and reversed his behaviour, sometimes having to be forced to go to bed!

In a meeting one day, when Jim was publicly talking about his 'disability' and his transformation, he suddenly exclaimed, exultantly: 'I WASN'T LEARNING DISABLED! I WAS LEARNING DEPRIVED!!'

He was right.

Brain Damage

'Brain damage' – one of the most chilling phrases in the English language, and one that strikes terror into the heart of anyone who hears it spoken in relation to their children, themselves, their relations or friends. The phrase brings with it images of distortion, malfunction, disability, pain, and an utter hopelessness about providing any remedy or hope.

Indeed, up to the second half of the twentieth century, no one, in the words of Dr Glenn Doman, 'had ever seen, or heard of, a single brain-injured child who had been cured'.

With the dazzling advance of neurological, psychological and brain sciences, the picture has become changed, the outlook far more hopeful, and the phrase 'brain damaged' far less threatening.

The most dramatic evidence of our advances is in cases where one entire hemisphere of the cerebral cortex (upper brain) has been irreparably damaged either pre-natally, during birth, or post-natally. In such instances the damaged side of the brain will act very much like a multiply fused electric circuit, and will be constantly erupting with static and noise that can completely drown out the functioning of the remaining healthy hemisphere.

Led by pioneers such as the great Russian psychologist Alexander Luria, and medical explorers including Dr Doman, the first explorations of damaged brains were carried out, and the first hemispherectomies – the surgical removal of half of the cerebral cortex – were performed.

The results were, and have continued to be, staggering. One recent case involves 13-year-old Brandi Binder, who as a very young child developed such severe epilepsy that surgeons at the University of California and Los Angeles decided that they had no option but to remove the *entire* right side of her cerebral cortex at the tender age of six. Immediately after the operation Brandi had lost almost total control of the muscles on the left side of her body, the side 'controlled' by the right side of the brain.

After seven years of therapy, including mathematical and music drills, and physical exercises including leg-lifts, Brandi became a top student at the Holmes Middle School in Colorado Springs, Colorado. Her hobbies and skills now include music and art, skills that are usually associated with the side of the brain that in her is completely absent. Neurologist Dr Donald Shields, one of the UCLA paediatric team involved with Brandi's case, summed it up in a way that encapsulates our new thoughts about the human brain: 'If there's a way to compensate, a developing brain will find it.'

As long as there is focused and dedicated retraining of both the brain and the body, complete recoveries have been increasingly recorded. This is because modern science has now realized that the brain is not a static organ, but one of scintillating flexibility and adaptability. It is so 'plastic' that the remaining half of the cortex, when nurtured, stimulated and encouraged in the right way, will rewire its connections with the entire body, and in a surprisingly short time will take over all the functions of the missing hemisphere, while maintaining its own original functions.

It now appears that almost whatever the state of a baby's damaged brain, there is hope.

THINGS FOR YOU TO DO

 In his first few weeks of life, your baby will be given a routine examination to confirm that he is healthy and developing normally. However, if you become at all worried about anything, ask your health visitor or general practitioner (who will also be one of your child's Mastermind Group) to thoroughly check his brain and neurological systems.

If your child is suffering from learning difficulties or brain damage, always bear in mind that amazing flexibility and plasticity of the brain to adapt. There is so much that you and the health professionals can do.

chapter 15

pets

YES!

Animals and pets play an important role in a child's development

Recent research has confirmed that all animals, from the insect, through fish, amphibians, reptiles, birds and mammals have, as the basic 'computer chip' in their brains, a brain cell identical in structure and function to those that your baby and you possess.

It is perhaps for this reason that so many people feel what they describe as a 'strange kinship' with other living things. When they tell us this, they are relating to their pets on the basis of the same fundamental unit of intelligence and perception, the only real difference being the number and organization of those cells. You will recall the astounding intelligence manifested by the honey bee (see Part I, Chapter 1, Brain Cell, page 6).

Pets may be considered the ultimate 'toy', and they possess a number of life-enhancing qualities that no other toy can begin to match:

1. They are wonderful companions, and in the case of pets such as dogs will provide the child with an ongoing example and demonstration of unconditional love. All pets act as confessors. The stories are legion of children who confide to their pets their deepest secrets, concerns, and loves, knowing that on some deep level they will be listened to and understood. A pet will display total commitment to and faith in the child, qualities that are extremely important for her emotional development and her self-confidence. Very few cases are recorded of children behaving similarly with videos and computers!

2. Pets provide the child with early and invaluable training in the nature of responsibility for other living things, including their feeding, cleaning, environment and health.

3. In conjunction with item 2, pets also teach the child the valuable lesson of Patience.

4. Because of their relatively short life-spans, pets provide the child with an early opportunity to observe, understand and come to terms with Life and Death.

5. Early introduction to pets reduces the probability of hyperactive fear reactions from the young child when she sees dogs and other animals on the streets or in the parks.

6. Animals, like children, are masters, and therefore good exemplars, of Persistence. Think of the dog or cat (would one dare, in this instance, to call it 'purrrrrsistence'?!) when they want food. Their brains, which are vastly superior to that with which we normally credit them, work out all the different emotional and intellectual mechanics of their big inattentive ape-masters, and, like Olivia (see page 117), virtually always succeed in the battle of wits.

7. Many pets provide ideal stimulation for the tactile senses, and the opportunity to stroke, caress, cuddle and hug. This allows the child to develop those very important skills, while at the same time teaching her that a certain amount of discretion, care and tenderness is essential for the continuation of relationships, if not life!

8. In the case of dogs, such a pet can provide the added dimension of child protection.

9. Likewise, the lessons of discretion, care and tenderness will inhibit the child's inappropriate use of her curiosity. 'Scientific investigation' of nature, which often leads city-bred and petless children, who are unfamiliar with other life forms, to form the most ghastly 'objective' experiments on them, little realizing the impact they are having on another living being.

10. As you will increasingly realize, pets afford the opportunity for stimulation and development of the full range of cortical skills, as well as most of the senses and all of the multiple intelligences.

Animals are an intrinsic and necessary part of nature's garden: of Paradise. We have already established that your child should live in Paradise. We now conclude that pets must be part of it.

In my own childhood my Mum and Dad nurtured my love of nature, and encouraged and supported me in the acquisition of every imaginable kind of pet. Caterpillars, tadpoles, newts, sticklebacks, beetles, rabbits, cats, dogs, canaries, budgerigars and butterflies were just *some* of the inhabitants of my Garden of Eden. With them I played, confided, learnt the arts of patience, concentration, understanding and love, and forged bonds with the natural world which grow stronger with every passing day.

THINGS FOR YOU TO DO

 Have pets in your home from the moment your baby is born. As soon as your baby is old enough, involve her in little caring tasks associated with the pet such as putting out the dog's food bowls or cleaning out the hamster cage.

Select the best natural history videos (the BBC nature series and the Discovery Channel features are superb) as part of your IT training course (see page 275).

Read your child animal stories. Use them as bedtime and reward-time reading.

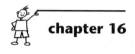

chapter 16

discipline — mental

—————————————☆—————————————

Mental discipline is one of the most important factors in your Brain Child's development. This refers to 'discipline' when it refers to behavioural guidelines and parameters established by the parents for the benefit of the child, and when also it refers to discipline in the sense of the channelling of curiosity in learning and concentration. Discipline in the first sense has already been covered in considerable depth in its twin chapter Truth Seeking (see page 134) and the extended story of Austin and its analysis.

—————————————☆—————————————

This chapter will therefore concentrate on the overwhelming importance of establishing firm guidelines and boundaries for your Brain Child's behaviour. Discipline of this sort has come into disrepute because of its association with punishment, restriction and inhibition. Such disrepute is appropriate only when mental discipline is misapplied. When it is appropriately applied it can be likened to the hand of a Michelangelo sculpting a David. It is utterly appropriate and most strongly to be desired.

The innate need (even *thirst*) of the brain for positive guidelines that help itself sculpt itself most magnificently, is evident in the list of words children use to describe the qualities of their favourite teachers, and the identical list that adults use when remembering their best teachers: 'Kind'; 'Strong'; 'Knowledgeable'; 'Positive'; 'Enthusiastic'; 'Energetic'; 'Supportive'; 'Strict'; 'Fair'. I have emphasized the last two intentionally, because they summarize perfectly, as children are wont to do, the essence of the matter.

Children love a teacher who is strict, as long as it is combined with the other mentioned qualities, because they then know that the teacher knows his or her own boundaries and territory, and they then feed off the security and freedom that this provides. 'Fair' completes the formula, guaranteeing that the discipline is appropriate to the goal. Two stories illustrate the point:

TONY'S AND TONY'S MUM'S STORY

When I was two years old, my mother, Jean, became slightly concerned about my mental and physical ineptitude when involved in the ritual of dining.

For months I had been sitting in my highchair being fed with a spoon by Mum, my various baby formulae. Time and time again Mum had tried to teach me the nature, handling and function of the spoon, miming in order that I might mimic, playing 'aeroplane' games, showing me in detail how to hold and direct the spoon, and even sometimes eating the food in slow motion herself in order that I might learn.

I seemed dull, unresponsive and unco-operative, occasionally deigning to take the spoon, only to look at it non-plussed, wave it around a bit, and then holding it at full arm's length, dropping it unceremoniously on the floor.

In the same way that I had had my flash of realization with OJ and his 100 words, Mum had a similar shocking thought: was more going on here than met the eye?!

Deciding to experiment, she explained to me in very clear terms that she was going to show me three more times how to do it, and if I dropped the spoon again she would not feed me the remainder of the food and would take away my plate.

To her initial concern I dropped the spoon with identical nonchalance three times. Her hand was forced. She took away the food and I was left howling futilely for more.

With slight trepidation but more determination, Mum tried the experiment at lunch, my next meal, and watched with consternation as I repeated my dull-headed performance. Once again Mum took away the food, and once again, to her credit, she persisted with her intuition and deprived me of my baby victuals.

To her absolute delight, when dinner-time arrived and she handed me the spoon, I immediately tucked voraciously in! Her intuition had been correct.

My baby brain, as had many millions of baby brains before me, had worked out that it was far simpler and in many ways far more pleasant, to have a giant servant waiting upon me hand, foot and mouth! Why bother to learn a skill that would deprive me of my servant, involve me in considerable extra effort, and reduce my influence over her, when all I had to do was drop the spoon in order to have her conditioned Pavlovianly to continue to serve me? Obviously there was no reason at all for learning such a counter-productive skill!

It was only when the appropriate and irrevocable discipline was applied that I willingly learnt, in view of the alternative of starving, and with immediate application and reward.

DR JANE SIBLEY'S STORY

When she was a new mother, Dr Jane Sibley thought long and hard about physical punishment, and because of the disheartening spate of violence and abuse cases involving children, decided to bring up her new baby using only mental rather than physical discipline. She decided on a course which provided only positive verbal reinforcement in attempting to guide the young child, David's, behaviour.

A prime example and opportunity occurred when Jane was having conversations with her husband. David had begun to interfere constantly, insisting by behaviour, word and gesture that he be the centre of attention. Jane picked the three-year-old David up, gave him a cuddle, and said to him: 'David, we would love you to stay and be with us during our conversation, but we can't hold that conversation if you continually interrupt.' David apparently understood, but like me when I was two, thought he was on to a good thing, and repeated the behaviour within the next five minutes. Jane responded in the same way, and once again David continued to interrupt.

This time Jane picked him up, spoke to him in the same manner, and concluded: 'As you obviously want to be alone and have decided not to be with us, I'm going to take you to your room. When you are ready to come back and join us without interrupting your Daddy and me, just let us know. We love you.' And so saying, Jane took David to his bedroom.

She reported that it took only five such 'trials' for David to recognize that the rule was an absolute, and that if he wished to be with his parents, which he generally did, then he had to change his behaviour. He did.

In encouraging your child to behave appropriately, it is always important to bear in mind that you are dealing with a master tactician and strategist, who will gauge your reactions, stamina, and weaknesses with uncanny accuracy. The young mastermind will use persistence and emotional disguise as constant devices to get her own way. It is essential that in all matters of serious discipline you, the parent, remain constantly in charge.

PIGGY-BACK STORY

One day a friend of mine, Brian, was staying with a number of couples in a giant country house, when he became deeply involved in a conversation with a single mum. The mother had one daughter, Victoria, a perfect little eight-year-old princess, onto whom the mother had poured all her love. The little girl looked as if she had just popped out of a fairytale.

The three of them and Victoria's nine-year-old friend decided to go for a walk in the beautiful springtime countryside, and they spent a wonderful hour walking through the woods and fields, climbing over styles and up trees and making a deliriously happy foursome.

The mood changed slightly when Victoria demanded (not asked) that her mummy give her a piggy-back, which the mother, who was obviously deeply exhausted, agreed to give her. They were walking along a half-mile-long road that led to the country house, and as they progressed my friend Brian noticed that the mother was becoming visibly paler, was obviously under extreme strain, and desperately needed to put her child down.

When she explained this to Victoria there was an immediate and violent reaction, the little girl suddenly turning into a demon-rider, hitting her mother's shoulder with her hand, like a riding crop, and loudly insisting that she wanted to stay put up there and that her mummy must keep carrying her.

To Brian's astonishment, the mother agreed and staggered on a few more steps, Victoria driving her on like a demonic slave master.

When the mum began to stagger, Brian stepped in and against the mother's protests firmly and calmly removed Victoria from the mother's back, and explained to her why he had done it.

The princess's face transformed into that of an ugly and hate-filled mask, as she screamed her continuing orders to be put back on her mummy's shoulders simply because 'I want to, I want to, I want to!'

The mother again protested, saying that Brian should help the little girl back on her shoulders because that was what Victoria wanted. Brian took control and denied Victoria this unnecessary privilege, at which point the little girl ran up the road towards her friend and began to hit the older girl, screaming all the while that it was her fault that she had been taken off her mother's shoulders.

Victoria then ran the rest of the way towards the house and entered it screaming and wailing at the top of her voice. She went straight into the kitchen, where everybody else was gathered and put even more energy into her yelling and stomping. By the time her mother and Brian arrived, Victoria was in a frenzy of tears and all the adults were thinking that something terrible had happened. Victoria was so far successful in her manipulations!

Brian explained, over Victoria's rising ululations, what had happened. Ten minutes had now passed, and Victoria was standing in the middle of the kitchen, fists clenched, mouth wide open, veins distended, tears cascading from her closed eyes and feet still stomping. Her mother was becoming desperate and said that she had to give her a piggy-back or Victoria might die.

Brian, taking his life in his hands, said: 'No, let her continue.' He then occasionally talked to Victoria through her screaming, telling her that it was the best performance of crying and yelling that he had ever seen and told her that it was her mother who needed attention, caring and love.

Victoria, a totally committed and concentrated banshee, continued for two non-stop hours until she drifted into a truly angelic sleep brought on by total exhaustion after 'yelling a marathon'.

The wonderful result of this story, Brian reported, was that when Victoria awoke a couple of hours later, she was completely transformed. There was no mention of what had happened and no desire to, in any way, 'ride' her mother again. Instead, Victoria spontaneously became her mother's carer, and was like a little Florence Nightingale for the next two days.

THINGS FOR YOU TO DO

Always discipline your Brain Child with direction, affection, care, strength and love.

Constantly bear in mind that mental discipline is a moulding that allows your child

discipline – mental

greater freedom and creativity, not restriction and pain.

Set clear guidelines and then 'catch them being good'!

Find out the reason why your child adopts a behaviour — it is often amazing and logical.

Discipline for action, not for result of action.

you and your brain child

---☆---

AMAZING ...

What a miracle!

Born with a million million of the Universe's phenomenally complex bio-computers, an imagination that is infinite and an analytical capability that can focus beyond the atom. All this supplemented by multiple probing intelligences that are capable of transforming the physical Universe and which have a boundless capacity to do good, and a memory that has no limits.

---☆---

Already one in 70 thousand million human beings, a unique individual, unlike any other that has lived, is living, or ever will live.

Driven by deep-rooted principles that spur the constant endeavour to connect everything with everything else, that impels it towards success, and that are based on a foundation of truth.

Gifted with senses that allow it to see to the far extremes of the macro-cosmos and micro-cosmos, to hear, taste and feel from an infinite sensory smorgasbord, and which also has an ability to duplicate reality *perfectly*.

Housed in a body that is the ultimate masterpiece of engineering design, surrounded by waiting masterminds willing and eager to assist in its pilgrim's progress, armed with an endless supply of the grappling hooks of curiosity and a concentration far more powerful than any laser. Supported by an army of defenders that is greater in number and more ferocious and tenacious by far than the sum total of all the armies in the history of the world.

Flexible and resilient beyond all imagining.

Blessed with the capabilities and opportunities to explore and create in the Universes of art and music to have as a companion, playmate and guide the ever-expanding electronic cosmos, and with games and other life forms as soul mates in an infinite playground.

And that, dear parent, describes YOU! (*See the Mind Map called* What I Know as a Parent.)

With such amazing qualities and attributes YOU are ideally qualified and suited to be the carer, the guide, the *parent* of your equally amazing Brain Child.

appendices

Schools

Choosing a school for your child can seem like a protracted and daunting task, and many parents spend inordinant amounts of time worrying about the issue. Published league tables, brought in partly to assist the parent, only inform on the results of a series of 'academic' standard achievement tests (and whether they actually do is debatable) and give few clues about anything else the school may or may not be achieving in terms of the all-round development of the child.

How can you possibly tell, on the basis of a short visit, what day-to-day life in a particular school will be like and, more specifically, what it will be like for your child? If you live in a remote country area, you may not have a choice at all, but if you live in a big city, you may well be able to select from half a dozen schools that are all within reach.

WHAT TO LOOK FOR IN A SCHOOL

The most important consideration is the overall atmosphere that you notice when you are walking around the school. Does the school seem uplifting, positive, and happy to you? Do children and adults alike seem smiling and purposeful? Are people (whether children or staff) busily involved and engaged in whatever they are doing? Does the feel of the place inspire you and make you feel positive? Is there a 'buzz' of busy activity? Does this school excite you and can you visualize your child coming here with joy and enthusiasm? Do the children look happy, engaged and confident? Are they chatty and polite, helpful, open and friendly? Do they say good things about the school (without a teacher being present)? Will your child fit in and make friends with the children in this school?

Look around at the physical state of the school. Is it well maintained decoratively and is it clean and tidy? Is there a sense of order and 'everything in its place'? Do things seem well-looked-after, even if they receive heavy use? Is the school colourful, bright and cheery in its appearance? Does it have a 'sunny' feel to it? Are there big, clean windows that admit plenty of sunshine and light? Is the playground spacious, clean and safe? Are there suitable playthings, such as climbing frames, and are they well maintained and up to date? Is there any green space and what provision is there for outdoor sports and games? Is there a quiet garden area, where more relaxing activities can take place and where children can grow things?

Indoors, is there good, recent work displayed on the walls? Is storage space well-appointed and easy for children to use? Is there plenty of equipment available, ranging from up-to-date computers and a well-stocked, well-organized library, to coloured pens and paper? Is there a 'hum' of activity rather than a deadly hush or out-and-out chaos? Are any of the teachers having to raise their voices in order to maintain control? Is there plenty of provision for play within the classroom as well as 'desk learning'? Is there creativity at work here? Are children arranged in groups with their tables facing each other or are the desks arranged to face the blackboard at the front? Is there group and pair work as well as individal work going on? Can you hear music, see art, see words and numbers being used, sense a variety of textures, colours, objects from other cultures, do you get a sense of freedom and open-mindedness? Do you sense an exchange of ideas and a celebration of difference? Are boys and girls treated equally? Are different races and cultures nurtured and treated equally? Is there vision in this school? Do you get the feeling that there is a global rather than a national perspective being fostered here?

When you talk to the teachers, are they positive and upbeat? Do they seem to love children and teaching? Are they enthusiastic and caring? Do they seem to be good role models for your child? Are they interested in the idea of 'learning how to learn'? Do they believe in nurturing 'the whole child'? Do they believe in the vast potential of all children – not just the so-called 'bright' ones? Do they foster goals for each and every child?

The more you answer 'yes!' to the above questions, the more 'right' the school will be for your brain child.

COMMON PARENTAL CONCERNS

One of the most commonly asked questions that parents ask when they are visiting a school is 'Is there much bullying in this school?' It is the one thing that parents seem to worry about a great deal and they usually, rightly or wrongly, assume that their child is likely to be the victim rather than the perpetrator. Whether the school is 'good' or 'bad', the answer should always be: 'Yes'. Because there is always going to be some bullying in a school, whether a lot or a little. The real issue is: How does the school deal with it? The alarm bells should sound if the school denies that there is any bullying at all in their establishment. They are lying. At one school a cup was presented annually called the Kindness Cup, awarded to any child who had been seen to have a particularly caring attitude towards others. All schools should foster good morals and good ethical behaviour between all individuals in their community and they should have a strong anti-bullying policy that is used and which works. Children become moral beings through believing in themselves and this comes through being in a caring community which is acting to promote truth and good morals. Bullying will die out in such a place. Is the school you are visiting fostering this approach?

GO WITH YOUR GUT FEELINGS

If you experience a positive 'gut reaction' to the school after you have thought about these questions, then you can feel reassured that it is certainly a good school and that your child will very likely be happy and do well there. In addition to attending parents' open days, which may not necessarily give you the whole picture, try to go to other events arranged by the school, such as plays, fairs, fund-raising events and special events such as sports days and socials. This will give you a real feel for the school. Ask the head for a copy of the latest inspectors' report and if you are given a school prospectus, look beyond the glossy pictures taken on sunny days.

These guidelines apply to any school you look at, but if you are interested in special styles of education you might want to investigate Steiner or Montessori schools, which have slightly different approaches. Bear in mind, however, that many of the revolutionary ideas of Steiner and Montessori are gradually being absorbed into mainstream education.

brain child

STEINER EDUCATION

Steiner emphasizes the whole development of the child – covering spiritual, physical, and moral well-being as well as academic development. Formal learning starts later than in mainstream schools and generally has a more creative and artistic emphasis. Steiner education respects the essential nature of childhood and enables each child to develop ability and confidence. Pre-school and primary education emphasizes emotional maturity, good judgement, creativity and initiative, along with the cultivation of a strong moral sense of responsibility.

Contact: Steiner Waldorf Schools Fellowship
Kidbrooke Park, Forest Row, East Sussex
England, RH18 5JB

Tel: 01342-822115
Fax: 01342-826004
Email: mail@swsf.org.uk

MONTESSORI EDUCATION

Montessori methods are based on the idea that children learn from self-motivated activity within a highly structured environment. Pre-prepared materials are used in a planned sequence that enables children to work with a high level of independence. The belief that 'play is child's work' prevails. According to the Montessori Society, Montessori is an attitude, not just a teaching system or a technique. Each child is individually loved and understood. Montessori is a spiritual attitude towards mankind, which begins with childhood.

Maria Montessori established an education system that relies heavily on children's reponses. Her work with mentally handicapped children led her to appreciate how the young human brain is stimulated by colours, shapes, textures and the relative size and weight of objects, and how all the senses must be appreciated. She soon realized that her programme could successfully be applied to all children, not just those with special needs, and she put her ideas into practice in schools which still bear her name internationally. She completely abandoned the traditional, rigid formulae for teaching reading, writing and arithmetic to young children aged three to six, and she encouraged instead free expression and self-discipline.

Montessori Foundation
17808 October Ct.
Rockville, MD 20855
USA

Tel: 1800 655 5843
Fax: 301 840 0021
Email: timseldin@montessori.org

Diet, Food and Nutrition

Eat as balanced and as natural a diet as possible, and this applies both to you and your Brain Child. Humankind's ability to digest and absorb foods has changed little in millions of years. We have been living on natural foods for the bulk of our evolution. We dug up roots, plucked fruits from the trees and bushes, fished and hunted. Only recently have we resorted to processed foods. Some are very good for us, while others are very bad. Study intensively the diet that is best for you and your child and eat accordingly. *Foresight Magazine*, the magazine representing the organization that is concerned with fertility and pregnancy care, emphasized it in the following way:

'A well nourished brain means a bright, curious, conversational little child who finds life a rewarding experience, and sees grown-ups as quite friendly and reasonable. There will be disagreements and disputes, of course, because small people lack experience; and there will be escapades! However, relationships and learning hold great potential when the developing brain is free from bio-chemical aberration (poisons like lead from car exhausts, artificial fertilizers in vegetables, tar from cigarette smoke and so on.)'

A VARIED DIET

Food is a fraught area when you are bringing up children. After the milk-only months are over, weaning takes place and often the young toddler can turn into a surprisingly fussy eater – refusing to eat certain foods or even to try a little taste. This is when parental patience can crack, and parents sometimes resort to feeding the child from a limited choice of acceptable foods. This is dangerous from two perspectives. First, the child realizes that he can be unreasonably fussy. This fussiness can continue throughout childhood and then into adult life. Second, a restricted diet could be preventing him from getting all the nutrients that he should have in order to grow and develop healthily.

The best diet is one that is varied, balanced between the different nutrients, locally grown, in season, and home-cooked. If you do let your child eat sweets and have fizzy drinks, then allow him or her occasionally rather than every day. Let them be treats. Encourage your child to drink plain water as much as possible. Apart from having no nutritional value, fizzy drinks are loaded with sugar and stick to the teeth long after the drink has been consumed, causing tooth decay. Don't give your child a 'taste' for junk food by encouraging it and keeping it in the house. Don't ban it either; just let him consume it occasionally when other children are having it, for example.

As soon as it is practical, include your baby in family mealtimes and have him sit with you at the table. Try to stick to regular mealtimes. He will soon want to experiment with what you are eating and participate in exciting family conversations. Meals will become an important focus to the day and food will come to be recognized as enjoyable life-enhancing fuel. If you travel to foreign parts, let your child try out new foods so that his range of enjoyable foods constantly expands.

FOOD TIPS

1. Buy fresh foods, when they are in season and if possible, locally grown. Avoid buying foods that have been grown using pesticides.

2. Combine the widest possible variety of foods so that any imbalance in nutrition is minimized.

3. Cook the food yourself, from scratch. Spend time preparing meals and enjoy the process of feeding the family. Cooking can be extremely relaxing, even after a hectic working day. Teach the children to cook too. Time is at a premium for many families, but the effort and creativity involved in home-cooking will be repaid in healthy children and meals consumed enthusiastically. Pre-prepared meals tend to be expensive, full of preservatives and over-salted.

4. Get your child used to regular mealtimes with good intervals in between. Take the time to all sit down together to eat. Any snacks should be healthy and nutritious without removing the child's appetite for the next meal. Avoid sweets, crisps, fizzy drinks and other 'empty calorie' foods.

brain child

GUIDELINES FOR NUTRITIONAL NEEDS AT DIFFERENT AGES

For babies from birth to six months breast milk contains all the nutritional requirements for the first few months of life. If you do not breast feed, for whatever reason, baby powdered milk formula is the only substitute. Do not give cows' milk before six months. Between four and six months the baby will be ready to have other foods as well as milk (breast or formula). Eventually the baby takes more and more food and less and less milk. This process is called 'weaning'. Iron requirements increase during this time, so it is important to make sure that he is receiving enough iron.

As the baby starts crawling and then toddling; energy requirements increase and there is a need for increased vitamins, particularly during growth spurts. Between one and two, the child needs more energy foods. He does not need a bulky, fibre-filled diet, otherwise he may fill up on these foods and miss out on valuable energy foods.

The young child (between four and six years) needs increasing amounts of energy foods and more protein, plus all the vitamins. (Good sources of energy are vegetables, fruit and nuts, meat and meat products, eggs and fish).

From seven onwards the child needs even more energy and protein.

GOOD FOODS SUMMARY

Group: Protein (high)
Foods: Lamb, beef, chicken, pork, eggs, cheese, legumes, nuts
Nutrient content: Protein, fat, iron, vits A, D, B
Group: Green/yellow vegetables
Foods: Cabbage, spinach, kale, sprouts, green beans, lettuce, squash, celery, courgettes

Nutrient contents: Calcium, chlorine, chromium, cobalt, copper, manganese, potassium, sodium

Group: Citrus fruits
Foods: Tomatoes, oranges, melon
Nutrient content: Vit C

Group: Other fruit and vegetables
Foods: Potatoes, corn, beets, carrots, cauliflower, apricots, pineapples
Nutrient contents: Carbohydrates, vits A, B, C

Group: Fats
Foods: Butter, margarine, vegetable oils
Nutrient contents: Vits A, D

TO SUM UP:

Your Brain Child's brain and body are, to a large extent, a product of the food he eats. And it is true to say that if you provide a good, healthy, good-quality diet (preferably of hearty, home-made food, cooked with love), your child will thrive and flourish, both mentally and physically. Food is fuel and if you put in low-quality, inappropriate fuel, your Brain Child's performance will be correspondingly inferior. Think back to the Formula One racing car mentioned earlier in this book. To perform well this car must be given the highest-quality petrol available. The same is true for your Brain Child, and, of course, for you – his loving pit-stop mechanic.

Reading List

Use these specially selected books to help you help your child develop to his or her fullest possible potential.

PART 1 THE BRAIN
Chapter 2 Brain Development

Russell, Peter, *The Brain Book: Know Your Own Mind and How to Use It*, Routledge, 1980
An excellent introduction to the brain, its development and learning, by an author who studied psychology and physics at Cambridge University, as well as studying, independently and in depth, learning-how-to-learn techniques, and the nature of meditation practices and their effect on the brain.

Ornstein, Robert, *The Amazing Brain*, Chatto and Windus, 1985
An amazing book by an amazing author on an amazing organ!

Greenfield, Susan, *The Human Brain – A Guided Tour*, Phoenix, 1998
An exhilarating and state-of-the-art update on the latest brain research and its implications for education and the future of the species.

Chapter 3 Left and Right Brain

Ornstein, Robert, *Psychology of Consciousness*, Arkana, 1996
An entertaining and eminently readable history of Professor Roger Sperry's original left-right brain research and its impact, both actual and theoretical, on education, psychology and the earth at large.

Gelb, Michael J, *How to Think Like Leonardo da Vinci*, Thorsons, 1998
Read this excellent book and apply, to the development of your child, the lessons it recommends.

Chapter 4 The Multiple Intelligences

Buzan, Tony, *The Power of Verbal Intelligence*, Thorsons, 2002
This book shows you how to harness the power of verbal intelligence and become brilliant with words – reading, speaking, remembering and understanding them. Pass on your own brilliance to your developing child.

Wilson, Glenn, *Improve Your IQ*, Warner Books, 1981
Contains an excellent introduction to the 'workings' of IQ with a step-by-step programme for improving yours. You can develop simple and personal examples to exercise your child's IQ.

Gardner, Howard, *Multiple Intelligences*, Basic Books, 1993
This is the book that formally introduced the concept of multiple intelligences, and gives an in-depth understanding of their nature, and of their implications for the education and personal and social development of your child.

Buzan, Tony, *The Power of Physical Intelligence*, Thorsons, 2003
Make the most of your physical potential by developing your mental power in tandem with your physical fitness. A must for every parent and child!

Buzan, Tony, *The Power of Social Intelligence*, Thorsons, 2002
Make friends easily and forge lasting relationships by developing your social intelligence. This book is the key to a more active social life.

Buzan, Tony, *Head First*, Thorsons, 2000
This book takes you through the ten amazing intelligences, showing you how to be brilliant with words, physically fit and more sensual. With practical exercises and simple techniques, you will learn how to be more in control of your time and in tune with your environment. Use what you

learn from this book to help your child develop the ten intelligences.

Chapter 6 Memory

Buzan, Tony, *Use Your Memory,* BBC publications, 2000
A memory 'operations manual', which introduces the history of memory systems, covers in depth the memory principles, and outlines all the major memory systems for facts, numbers, dates and poetry, etc. Apply your discoveries from this book to your child.

O'Brien, Dominic, *Learn to Remember: Transform Your Memory Skills*, Duncan Baird, 2000
The author is eight-times World Memory Champion and in this book he clearly outlines the methods he developed to make him one of the greatest memorizers the world has ever known. Again, apply your findings from Dominic's book to your child's own memory development.

Chapter 7 Creativity

Buzan, Tony, *The Power of Creative Intelligence*, Thorsons, 2001
This book is full of new fun facts, games and tools to help you make the most of creativity. Use what you learn from this book to encourage your child's creativity.

De Saint Exupery, Antoine, *The Little Prince*, Puffin Books, 1970
This is one of the classic works on imagination, creative thinking and education. It is, in the guise of a children's fairytale, a psychological/philosophical treatise on thinking, in all its manifestations, and written for children – of all ages!

Watterson, Bill, *Calvin and Hobbs Sunday Pages: 1985–1995*, Andrews McMeel, 2003 and *The Essential Calvin and Hobbs*, Time Warner Books, 2003
Read the entire Calvin and Hobbs collection. These exquisite cartoons, which in just a few years acquired a global following in the hundreds of millions, trace on a daily basis the confrontations between the untrammelled imagination of its hero Calvin, his furry-toy companion, the tiger Hobbs, and the relatively mundane, rigid and boring adult world. Riotously funny, deliciously provocative and educational.

Edward De Bono, *Children Solve Problems*, Penguin, 1972

Chapter 10 Mind Mapping

Buzan, Tony, *How to Mind Map*, Thorsons, 2002
Mind Mapping is a revolutionary system of planning and note-taking that has changed the lives of millions of people across the world. How to Mind Map is the basic guide to Mind Maps, brought to you by its inventor. Use it for yourself and to help your child.

Buzan, Tony and Barry, *The Mind Map Book*, BBC, 1993
A BBC 'book of the year', which outlines in depth, the theory behind and the practice of Mind Mapping, and which gives multiple practical examples from the fields of education, the family, business and the professions.

Buzan, Tony, *Mind Maps for Kids*, Thorsons, 2003
The amazing system of Mind Mapping is explained specially for children, using step-by-step examples in every subject across the curriculum. This book will help your child remember things, make clearer and better notes, revise, come up with ideas, unlock the imagination, save time, concentrate and do well in exams.

brain child

PART 3 BRAIN PRINCIPLES
Chapter 4 Success

Shaw, George Bernard, *Pygmalion*, Penguin Books

Read the book, see the play or the musical *My Fair Lady*. Analyse it in detail as an educational and learning metaphor for yourself and your child.

Chapter 6 Radiant Thinking

Van Vogt, AE, *The World of Null-A*, St Martins Press, 2003 and *The Pawns of Null-A*, Sphere, 1972

A simple but charming science fiction exploration of a world in which the realization of and practice of the principles of the multi-ordinate nature of words and reality and Radiant Thinking, summarized under the general heading 'General Semantics' are explored, especially by the main character Gosseyn, a phonic play on Go Sane!

PART 5 DEVELOPMENT/ENVIRONMENT
Chapter 6 Handedness

Edwards, Betty, *The New Drawing on the Right Side of the Brain*, HarperCollins, 2001

Contains wonderful exercises for experimentation with drawing and painting with the non-dominant hand, for you and your child.

PART 6 THE SENSES
Chapter 4 Nose – Smell

Suskind, Patrick, *Perfume*, Penguin Books, 1989

Try this book for a novel exploration on the theme of the development of the sense of smell.

PART 7 LEARNING
Chapter 1 Curiosity

Carroll, Lewis, *Alice's Adventures in Wonderland* and *Through the Looking Glass*

Ultimate explorations and adumbrations on the themes of curiosity, imagination, knowledge and perception.

Chapter 3 Logic

Buzan, Tony, *Head Strong*, Thorsons, 2001
Simple, effective ways to develop the astounding and untapped potential of your body and mind and the relationship between the two. Packed with exercises and colourful Mind Maps, this book offers a total brain and body fitness plan. Explore it for yourself and on behalf of your child.

Chapter 4 Mathematics

Doman, Glenn, *Teach Your Baby Math*, Gentle Revolution Press, 2001
A book of simple and fun methods for introducing babies and very young children to the wonders of mathematics. Based on the same research that inspired *Teach Your Baby to Read*.

Chapter 5 Art

Edwards, Betty, *The New Drawing on the Right Side of the Brain*, HarperCollins, 2001
Contains wonderful exercises for experimentation with drawing and painting with the non-dominant hand, for you and your child.

Rather than read about Conni Gordon's art method, you can contact her and her teachers at:

Conni Gordon Convention Presentations

427 22nd Street

FL 33139, USA

Tel: +1 (305) 532 1001

Fax: +1 (305) 532 5811

Email: connigordon@aol.com

Chapter 7 Reading

Doman, Glenn, *Teach Your Baby to Read*, Gentle Revolution Press, 2002

The original work that started the baby-reading revolution. In this seminal work Dr Doman, with his extended medical and psychological background, tells wonderful stories, gives detailed instructions on launching your own baby-reading programme, and dispels many of the irrational objections and commonly held inaccurate beliefs about the assumed disadvantages (there are no disadvantages) of allowing children to learn to read at the earliest stages of their life.

Dahl, Roald, *The BFG*, *The Giraffe, the Pelly and Me*, *Charlie and the Chocolate Factory*, *The Twits* and many others, Puffin Books

Read the books of Roald Dahl with your child for their richness, humour and delightful language.

Buzan, Tony, *The Power of Verbal Intelligence*, Thorsons, 2002

This book shows you how to harness the power of verbal intelligence and become brilliant with words – reading, speaking, remembering and under-standing them. Pass on your own brilliance to your developing child.

Chapter 9 Hot Housing

Walmsley, Jane and Margolis, Jonathan, *Hot House People: Can We Create Super Human Beings*, Pan, 1987

Chapter 10 Information Technology

Keene, Raymond, Buzan, Tony and Levy, David, *Man Versus Machine*, available through the Buzan Centre
A history of the battle, in various mind sports, between the carbon brain and the electronic brain.

Chapter 11 Mind Sports

Keene, Raymond, *Kingfisher Pocket Book: Chess*, Kingfisher Books, 1998
A beautifully illustrated introduction to the Royal Game.

Buzan, Tony with Keene, Raymond, *Buzan's Book of Mental World Records*, available through the Buzan Centre
The equivalent, in the realm of the brain and mind, of the Guinness Book of World Records. Contains basic introductions to the major games, their histories, a compilation of all known mental world records and explanations of the ratings and grading systems.

Chapter 14 Learning Difficulties

Brown, Christie, *My Left Foot*, Minerva, 2003
A glorious and almost unbelievable autobiography. When he was born, Christie Brown was pronounced by doctors to be so completely spastic and 'vegetable-like' that he should be immediately placed in an institution. Christie's mother sensed that a far greater intelligence than the doctors were giving credit for was trapped inside that convulsing body. This book tells the story of how the one controllable part of his body, his left foot, became

his communication tool with the Universe. The story, touching, humorous, enthralling, and ultimately encouraging, reveals that the 'vegetable' was, in fact, a genius.

Luria, Alexander R, *The Man with a Shattered World*, Harvard University Press, 1987
The seminal work, in which Luria explores the brain of a brilliant young soldier who was nearly killed in the Second World War when a bullet passed through his brain. The story relates the incredible conversations between Luria and the 'damaged brain' and their mutual exploration of ways to enhance the process of rehabilitation.

Hartmann, Thom, *Attention Deficit Disorder: A Different Perception*, Newleaf, 1999
Hartmann's 'different perception' is that the 'learning difficulties' labels are often wildly inappropriate. An enlightening and encouraging perspective on the whole area.

Appendices

Buzan, Tony, *Head Strong*, Thorsons, 2001
Contains a vitally important chapter on the brain and food.

Buzan, Tony, *The Power of Physical Intelligence*, Thorsons, 2003
Contains a fascinating chapter on the importance of diet and nutrition.

Acknowledgements

I would like to thank the following, all of whom have maintained the spirit of the child, and each of whom has been an inspiration to me in the conception of and writing of *Brain Child*: Sheikh bin Ebrahim Al-Khalifa, his beloved and inspirational daughter, Noora, and our mutual friend Sheikh Talib, for insightful, playful, creative and exemplary friendship, feedback and support; my dear neighbour, the 100-year-old eternal child Tom Benning, who still looks upon me as a baby and treats me in the way a baby loves to be treated; my dear friend and personal assistant, Lesley Bias, without whose continued dedication, affection and support *Brain Child* itself would not have passed the embryonic stage; my friend Teri Bias and my friend and godson, Richard Bias, for their unmitigated support of, and inspiration to, both Lesley and me; Donna and Superintendent Douglas Brand for their consistent fight for the rights of children to be taught to 'learn how to learn'; Nick and Chris Brock, captains of both the sea and thinking, for their support, ideas and stories; my friend, Lord Charles Brocket; my uncle and aunt, Mary and Peter Burn; my beloved brother and sister-in-law, Barry and Deborah Buzan, fighters for the development of intelligence, who decided to give birth to the Brain Children of their brains rather than of their loins; my father and mother, Gordon and Jean Buzan, who did, for my baby brain, well before modern research had confirmed its accuracy, precisely what a baby's brain would dream of in a Utopian world; my BLIs (Buzan Licensed Instructors) for their ongoing creative dedication and commitment to the concepts of Mental Literacy and to the children of the future; Craig Collins, my friend and colleague, who has been instrumental in 'opening up the East' to my work, and to his children, Alexis and Sophie, for their invaluable 'family feedback'; Lynn Collins and my dear godson, Michael Collins, for their living of the principles expounded in Brain Child, and for their many contributions to the book itself; John Christiansen for his ongoing support of my work and for his intense and valuable feedback on *Brain Child*; Professor Michael Crawford, Director of the Institute for Brain Research and Human Nutrition, for his invaluable work, knowledge and contribution to major areas of *Brain Child*; Borje and Paqui Denter whose life-long quest for children eventually resulted in the birth of their twins, Marcus and Camilla, and for their help with my research; Jo and Ian Docherty, parents of two magical children and Web Masters of the Brain Club website, which encourages and allows brains to talk about brains; Nathalie Fitzgerald; the entire Folley family, who for 20 years have provided me with the Utopian environment in which to think, create and write books such as and including *Brain Child*; Lorraine Gill, the artist, who fights for the artistic genius in every child; Dr Lana Israel, Rhodes Scholar, Brain of the Year, author, teacher, artist, and athlete, who is a living example of *Brain Child*-in-action; Swami and Desiree Israel for helping to create her!; Ray, Annette and Alexander (the great-godson!) Keene for upholding the torch of genius and for helping to provoke the planet to think; the extraordinary Jae Young Kim, who has helped ignite the fires of intelligence in Korea and Asia; Rolf and Lena Lindholm for their understanding and providing for me the glorious environment in Sweden, where part of *Brain Child* was written; Professor Stephen Lundin, professor of psychology and author of FISH!, for his imaginative and inspired comments; Vanda North, former President of the International Society for Accelerated Learning and Teaching, companion, friend, editor of all my works, including *Brain Child*, inspirational presence, who has supported all the others in these acknowledgements in their own efforts to support, defend and fight for the brain, and who throughout her life has maintained every positive quality of the 'Baby Brain'; Nicki, Strilli and Poon Oppenheimer for their 20 years' support of my vision, for their provocation of my thinking, and for their special contributions and information on Maria Montessori and her invaluable work; Graham and Maggie Payne for their support and especially for their providing me with my Brain Child god daughter, Emma; the genius artist Pecub, eternal child and incessant battler for the 'Rights of the Brain'; Robyn Pontynen for providing both detailed feedback and the paradise of Lizard Island, Australia, and its wonderful staff, where I completed the first draft of *Brain Child*; Kathryn Redgwell, herself the mother of a miraculous Brain Child, for her extensive research support, and for her hunting down of the Happy Homunculus; the management and staff of the Shangri-La Hotel in Singapore for providing me with the nutrition, environment, support and understanding that enabled me to finish in an atmosphere of complete creative beauty and calm, a number of chapters of *Brain Child*; Dr Joan Sibley, counsellor and poet, who added elements of both disciplines to *Brain Child*; Dr Andrew E. Strigner, MB, BSc, my mentor, whose work on the development of thinking strategies, nutrition, and the nurturing of the developing brain have made him one of the world's leading practitioners in the field; David Taylor; Sir Brian Tovey (ex-head GCHQ) and his dear wife Lady Mary Tovey for their constant battle to support the releasing of the multiple forms of intelligence, and for their unstinting support of me and my work; Dr Sue Whiting, five times Women's World Memory Champion, and John Whiting and their children, Carolyn, Helen and Fiona, for their passionate dedication to the principles delineated in *Brain Child* and to their role-modelling example for families of the Century of the Brain and the Millennium of the Mind.

I would like once again to thank my extraordinary Thorsons team for their previous successes with my work and for the effort and love they have all put into helping me give birth to *Brain Child*: Wanda Whiteley who was first inspired to commission *Brain Child* and who has overseen its development like the best of mums; Susanna Abbott, fellow Aikidoka, who as *Brain Child*'s Team Leader has guided the entire *Brain Child* project like an Aikido Master;

Carole Tonkinson, an Archangel who is a new mum herself and who has helped *Brain Child* immensely with her new-found knowledge from her relationship with baby Noah; Belinda Budge, who both manages and directs with care, compassion and professionalism; Laura Scaramella, who has spread my works around the world like wildfire; Liz Dawson, whose efforts handling publicity, I know, will make *Brain Child* a national and international star; Jacqui Caulton whose wonderful design work you hold in your hands; special thanks also to Stephanie Strickland, *Brain Child*'s illustrator, for capturing the childlike spirit of the book with her charming and delightful artwork.

As always, a special thanks to my 'Home Team' who have supported me so dedicatedly throughout the conception, writing, production and editing of *Brain Child*: my Personal Assistant, Lesley Bias, who has typed every one of the 250 thousand letters in this book!; Vanda North, founder and head of my international Buzan Centres, who has helped millions of mums and dads help millions of Brain Children; my Mum, Jean Buzan, for her superb editing and suggestions, and for raising me as a *Brain Child* would wish to be raised; and to my Literary Manager, Caroline Shott, who in a mere three years has made so many of this author's dreams come true.

index

Buzan Centres

Email: Buzan@BuzanCentres.com
Website: www.Mind-Map.com

Or:

Buzan Centres Ltd (Rest of World)
54 Parkstone Road
Poole, Dorset BH15 2PG
Tel: +44 (0) 1202 674676
Fax: +44 (0) 1202 674776

Buzan Centres Inc. (Americas)
PO Box 4, Palm Beach
Florida
FL33480, USA
Tel: +1 561 881 0188
Fax: +1 561 434 1682

MAKE THE MOST OF YOUR MIND TODAY